STUDIES IN ROMANCE LANGUAGES: 35

John E. Keller, Editor

CROSSFIRE

Philosophy and the Novel in Spain, 1900-1934

ROBERTA JOHNSON

THE UNIVERSITY PRESS OF KENTUCKY

Publication of this book was made possible by a grant from
The Program for Cultural Cooperation between Spain's
Ministry of Culture and the United States Universities.

Library of Congress Cataloging-in-Publication Data

Johnson, Roberta, 1942–
    Crossfire : philosophy and the novel in Spain, 1900–1934 / Roberta
Johnson.
        p.   cm. — (Studies in Romance languages ; 35)
    Includes bibliographical references and index.
    ISBN 0–8131–1824–7
    1. Spanish fiction—20th century—History and criticism.
    2. Philosophy in literature.   3. Spain—Intellectual life—20th
century.   I. Title.   II. Series: Studies in Romance languages
(Lexington, Ky.) ; 35.
PQ6144.J58   1993
863'.6209384—dc20   92–38875

In memory of my father

LAWRENCE R. FOX

CONTENTS

PREFACE

> So much of philosophy is fiction. Drama,
> doubts, fears, ambitions, ecstasies . . . if
> philosophy were a stream they would stock it
> with fishes. Although fiction, in the manner of
> its making, is pure philosophy, no novelist has
> created a more dashing hero than the handsome
> Absolute, or conceived more dramatic extrica-
> tions—the soul's escape from the body for in-
> stance, or the will's from cause.
>
> William Gass

Although, as William Gass indicates, all fiction is undergirded by a philosophical position, philosophy encroached more overtly on the territory of
the novel in Spanish fiction written in the first third of the twentieth century. In fact, the philosophical concerns of this body of literature at times
threaten to overwhelm the fictional elements; its characters represent
identifiable philosophical positions, its dialogue is consumed with philosophical discussions, and its plots are constructed to foreground specific
philosophical issues. There has not been such a widespread rapprochement between fiction and philosophy within one national boundary until
post-World War II France. The purpose of the present study is to explore
the philosophical, sociological and biographical background of this unusual phenomenon and to offer contextual analyses of some of the key
novels it produced: Miguel de Unamuno's *Amor y pedagogía* and *Niebla*,
Pío Baroja's *Camino de perfección* and *El árbol de la ciencia*, José Martínez
Ruiz's *La voluntad*, Ramón Pérez de Ayala's tetralogy and *Belarmino y
Apolonio*, Juan Ramón Jiménez's *Platero y yo* and Gabriel Miró's *El humo
dormido*, Pedro Salinas's *Víspera del gozo*, Rosa Chacel's *Estación. Ida y
vuelta* and Benjamín Jarnés's *El profesor inútil*.

Typically critics of these novels approach them from either a philosophical or a literary perspective with little attempt to see the relationship
between the two. The metaphysical and/or epistemological themes of
these works inspire their forms, which stretch the traditional epidermis of
the novel in unaccustomed ways. To cast philosophical issues in novelistic
terms, the authors drew on the vast storehouse of novelistic devices offered by the genre from its inception in romance and the picaresque to its
culmination in nineteenth-century realism. In order adequately to map

this innovative wedding of philosophy and fiction, some detours into Spanish cultural history are in order. In making these detours, I challenge some of the commonplaces of Spanish literary history of the early twentieth century, especially the notion of fixed generations with enumerable and unchanging characteristics and the assumption that fiction and philosophy, despite their radically different purposes and discourses, can be used interchangeably in the reconstruction of literary biography and history.

While I preserve the notion of generations, I interpret them as dynamic categories that overlap and interact, constantly defining and redefining one another. The writers within a generation changed over time, often due to contact with members of older and younger generations, and most of these philosophical novelists simultaneously or successively entertained conflicting philosophies. The often uneasy coexistence of generations (here specifically an older generation consisting of Unamuno, Baroja and Martínez Ruiz ["Azorín"] and a younger one encompassing José Ortega y Gasset, Ramón Pérez de Ayala, Juan Ramón Jiménez, Gabriel Miró, Rosa Chacel, Benjamín Jarnés and Pedro Salinas) with differing philosophical orientations produced a complex ideological configuration in early twentieth-century Spain. The novel, with its inherent dialogism, emerged as the ideal medium for expressing this philosophical confusion and for giving vent to the intergenerational hostilities that accompanied it.

In selecting specific novelists and novels for inclusion in the study, I have been limited by my philosophical approach. Thus, most regrettably, one major novelist—Ramón del Valle-Inclán—is absent, except for a few remarks on his quasi-aesthetic treatise *La lámpara maravillosa*. Since my definition of the "philosophical novel" focuses on novels that foreground philosophy in a discursive manner, Valle-Inclán's works do not fit the scope of this book. Not only do all other "canonical" novelists of the period fit, but their novelistic production is dominated by the philosophical narrative. The few narrative works of Juan Ramón Jiménez and Pedro Salinas, known more as poets than as narrators, also center on philosophical issues. Approximately two-thirds of the book is devoted to setting the background for and analyzing the major philosophical novels of the Generation of '98 written during the period from 1900 to 1914. These are works that engage with the Western philosophical tradition that made its entrance into Spanish intellectual life during their authors' formative years. The final third of my study takes up the second-wave philosophical novel, which in many ways was a reaction to the themes and practices of the first generation.

I am deeply grateful to the Graves Foundation for a grant that allowed me to begin this project, to the Comité Conjunto para la Cooperación Educativa Española y Norteamericana for a summer travel grant and a research grant to carry out the necessary archival research in Spain, to Scripps College for a sabbatical supplement and for summer stipends to continue research and writing, and to the University of Kansas Hall Center for the Humanities and General Research Fund for grants that permitted me to complete the book. Robert Spires, Jan Kozma, and Thomas Franz graciously read the completed manuscript and made many helpful suggestions, as did the anonymous reviewers for the University Press of Kentucky. During the years I was working on this project, Biruté Ciplijauskaité, Andrew Debicki, Inman Fox, Paul Ilie, Nelson Orringer, Robert Spires and Howard Young gave invaluable advice and encouragement. My husband, Bill Grant, deserves a special mention for his understanding and forbearance.

I also wish to thank the editors who permitted me to incorporate previously published material in a modified form. Portions of chapter 5 appeared as "Hunger and Desire: The Origins of Knowledge in *Niebla*" in *Selected Proceedings of the Singularidad y Trascendencia Conference*, ed. Nora de Marval-McNair (Boulder, Col: SSSAS, 1990), 93-105; part of chapter 6 as "La vida como problema en 'Adán en el Paraíso' de Ortega y *El árbol de la ciencia* de Baroja," in *Actas del Octavo Congreso Internacional de Hispanistas* (Brown University, 1986), 43-51; several pages of chapter 8 as "*Belarmino y Apolonio* a la luz de la novela filosófica de la Generación del 98" in *Actas del X Congreso de la Asociación Internacional de Hispanistas* (Barcelona: PPU, 1992), 19–24; and the last third of chapter 10 as "*El profesor inútil:* Benjamín Jarnés's Intertextual Dialogue with Unamuno" in *Siglo Veinte/20th Century* 6 (1988-89): 14-20.

The following sets of *Obras completas* are cited directly in the text of the study, where volume and page numbers are indicated after the quotation: Azorín, *Obras completas,* ed. Angel Cruz Rueda (Madrid: M. Aguilar, 1947-1954); Pío Baroja, *Obras completas* (Madrid: Biblioteca Nueva, 1946); José Ortega y Gasset, *Obras completas* (Madrid: Revista de Occidente, 1966-1969); Ramón Pérez de Ayala, *Obras completas,* ed. José García Mercadal (Madrid: Aguilar, 1963); and Miguel de Unamuno, *Obras completas,* ed. Manuel García Blanco (Madrid: Escelicer, 1966-1971). Other frequently quoted works are footnoted the first time they are cited; thereafter page numbers are indicated in the text.

INTRODUCTION

A friend of Miguel de Unamuno once expressed surprise that he was employing his time and intelligence in writing a novel when he could be working on a serious book. Unamuno momentarily rose to the bait, defensively replying that he was soon to begin a work of philosophy. His sense of his own mission quickly returned, however, when the friend wished to know his definition of philosophy—did he divide it into Ontology, Cosmology and Theodicy?[1] Unamuno held such categorical divisions in contempt, and he likewise rejected the artificial barriers set up between literature and philosophy: "El filósofo sólo nos da algo de esto en cuanto tenga de poeta, pues fuera de ello no discurre él, sino que discurren sus razones, o mejor, sus palabras. Un sistema filosófico, si se le quita lo que tiene de poema, no es más que un desarrollo puramente verbal; lo más de la metafísica no es sino metalógica, tomando lógica en el sentido que se deriva de *logos*, palabra. Suele ser un concierto de etimologías."[2] Taking this line of thinking even further, the Rector of Salamanca stated in the prologue of *Amor y pedagogía* that philosophy is a novel or a legend (*OC* 2: 431).[3] In that early novel Unamuno began practicing the flagrant disregard for the boundaries that have traditionally separated philosophy and literature, and he continued to do so in the remainder of his long writing career.

Unamuno suggested an altruistic reason for writing philosophy into fictional constructs when he claimed that philosophers like his university professor José Ortí y Lara and his friend Urbano González Serrano had thoroughly alienated the Spanish people from philosophy: "han hecho cobrar asco a esas cosas."[4] He believed the Spaniards to be philosophical barbarians, attracted only to "filosofía amena," and he defended his tragicomic approach to philosophy in *Amor y pedagogía* by calling the Castilians "bicho esencialmente cómico-trágico y *formal*, especie de beduíno a medio civilizar . . . [for whom traditional philosophy is a waste of time because he is] nutrido de Teología y de palabras, un discurrir libre y suelto, un estilo más sugestivo que instructivo y una serie de ejercicios espirituales para la razón no merecen el nombre de filosofía."[5] (José Ortega y Gasset echoed similar sentiments some fifteen years after Unamuno had abandoned the mission of instilling enthusiasm for philosophical thinking in the Spanish people.)

Since Unamuno was not the only Spanish writer of his day to seek out fiction as a medium for exploring philosophical ideas, one suspects other reasons for the preponderance of philosophical novels in early twentieth-century Spain. Clues to a fuller understanding of the phenomenon surface in Spanish intellectual history and in the sociology of literary production of the period. The first generation of philosophical novelists, traditionally called the Generation of '98, was the immediate heir to Spain's precarious entry into the world of modern philosophy some two hundred years after Descartes had meditated it into existence. Compared with the rest of Europe, the history of ideas in Spain has followed a singular path. When, in the sixteenth and seventeenth centuries, Bacon redirected Reformation Europe toward a secular, inductive, scientific approach to knowledge, and Descartes was launching his revolutionary projection of the rational ego as the fundamental proof of his own existence and that of God, Counter-reformation Spain retrenched firmly in its Catholic scholasticism, remaining effectively cut off from the major European intellectual tradition for about two centuries. Northern Europe embarked on a course that separated philosophical inquiry from the dogma of the Church, but in inquisitorial and reactionary Spain neither the secular inductive mode nor the deductive-rational mode could find fertile ground in which to flourish until the mid-nineteenth century. The Spanish Enlightenment was a superficial grafting of French ideals on what remained essentially traditional Spanish cultural forms. As Ortega said, "España es el país europeo que saltó un siglo esencial."[6]

Nor was early nineteenth-century Spain able to keep pace with the revolutionary fervor of the rest of Europe, occupied as it was with a very complex political situation. Not until about the 1860s, shortly before the birthdates of members of the Generation of '98, did a genuine modernization of Spanish intellectual life begin to take place. At this time Spain experienced the peculiar anomaly of the arrival of the German rationalist tradition (in the guise of Krausism) only a decade or so before the appearance (thanks to the 1868 liberal revolution) of the several manifestations of materialism and positivism represented by socialism, anarchism, Marxism and evolutionary theory. On the surface these two very different philosophical orientations might seem to have much in common—a very pragmatic side with specific aims of reforming modern society in a utopian mode—but their philosophical underpinnings could not be more different. The thorough assimilation of rationalism's various phases from Descartes to Kant and Hegel that prepared the rest of Europe for a truly philosophical debate on the merits of the social theories had not taken place in Spain. The two orientations simply clashed head-on during a period of twenty years or so, producing several generations of frustrated would-be philosophers.

Compounding this confusion was Nietzsche's arrival in Spain in the 1890s when Unamuno, Pío Baroja and José Martínez Ruiz began publishing under the stimulus of the several idealisms and socialist philosophies. Suddenly the German iconoclast was proclaiming the end of the metaphysical tradition that had only just taken root in Spanish soil in the 1860s. Spain had telescoped two and a half centuries of European thought into fewer than thirty years, provoking an ideological malaise and growing skepticism about the efficacy of any kind of philosophical thinking. What writers could salvage from this indigestible philosophical recipe was a vigorous affirmation of their individualism: "Soplaban sobre nosotros," wrote Unamuno, "vientos de anarquismo, de individualismo desenfrenado; apacentábamos los unos de la fórmula spenceriana del individuo contra el Estado; otros se nutrían en Nietzsche" (*OC* 5: 421). The brazen originality of the philosophical novels engendered by this individualism is one of the best manifestations of it.

The philosophical crossfire that took refuge in the novel at about the turn of the century was accompanied by a crossfire of a more personal order. The philosophical debates were often embedded in personal hostilities and rivalries that were particularly endemic to Spanish intellectual life of the 1890s. Unamuno, Baroja and Martínez Ruiz achieved literary maturity at a difficult moment in Spain when the expectations about writing for a living inspired by such models as Carlyle, Dickens, Balzac, Flaubert and Zola in the more industrialized areas of Europe were as yet unrealizable in a less developed country with a much smaller reading public. A professional middle class was growing—the families of Unamuno, Baroja and Martínez Ruiz belonged to it—but it was not ready to sustain very many writers of serious works. Unamuno's correspondence contains endless laments about the trials of his early professional life; Martínez Ruiz complained of the difficulties of initiating a literary career in his early tracts *Charivari* and *Literatura;* and in his inaugural address to the Real Academia Española, Baroja still vividly recalled the incredible obstacles placed in the way of the serious writer in Spain at the turn of the century.

While remuneration was nominal, the periodical press offered a means to stay afloat and to make a name for oneself, particularly if one were prolific enough. Unamuno, even after winning his chair at the University of Salamanca, wrote to Juan Arzadun that he had to suspend work on a longer, serious piece of writing because "las necesidades de la vida se imponen y necesito ganar suplemento a mi sueldo, hago algunos artículos" (57). But even this route to a modest income and a small share of the public eye was fraught with difficulties. Maeztu complained in a *Revista Nueva* article about the impossibility of getting new forms of writing accepted in *Madrid Cómico*, one of the most widely circulated and prosperous outlets for literarily oriented journalists: "*decadentes, regeneradores, esteticistas, jóvenes párvulos de las letras azules.* . . esos no cobrarán en *Madrid Cómico.* . . más que los arañazos que propinen *Clarín*, Taboada, *Sentimientos* o, como en este número los tres a coro."[7] Unamuno wrote to Juan Arzadun in 1898, some ten years into his career as an essayist: "No sabes lo largo y duro que es hacerse mercado. Yo empiezo ahora a recoger producto pecuniario de mis escritos" (59). These gains were as much the fruit of his insistent personal pressure on those holding the keys to the publishing establishment as they were public recognition of his merits as a thinker and writer. In referring to José Ortega y Munilla, gatekeeper of the prestigious literary medium *Los Lunes del Imparcial*, he remarked that one could only break down the barriers by "insistencia de presencia personal. Así se han convertido *Los Lunes del Imparcial* en coto cerrado o poco menos" (60).

At the turn of the century the writer who made a living by producing occasional and interpretive pieces for journals and newspapers was immersed in a tense, hostile world of interpersonal rivalry.[8] Writing was very much an establishment activity, and younger writers were almost entirely dependent upon the good opinion of successful older authors for an entrée into this inhospitable profession. Some of the clubiness continued into the new century; for example, in the first issue of *Prometeo* (1 [1908]: 64) Federico García Sanchíz mentioned that many editors still followed the custom of taking new authors to see Juan Valera for approval. The supreme arbiter of literary taste, however, was Leopoldo Alas ("Clarín"), whose articles of literary criticism, particularly his "Paliques," appearing in nearly every issue of the widely circulated *Madrid Cómico*, could, according to Manuel García Blanco, "asegura[r] la fama o [envolver] en el ridículo a un escritor que empieza."[9] So infamous was Clarín's hegemony over the Spanish literary scene that an anonymous *Revista Nueva* article entitled "Clarindustrial" ironically puffed "¿Funda un periódico y no enviarle a *Clarín* siquiera ocho duros al mes? ¡Qué locura!" (October 25, 1899: 121). Since obtaining recognition from the earlier generations of established writers was the "Open Sesame" to a writing career, and Clarín was the chief guardian, writers approached the task of paying him homage with the astuteness of a modern literary agent, sending him their books and writing him obsequious letters.

Unamuno, for example, anxious to know if Clarín had read his essays *En torno al casticismo*, seized upon some etymological error the Asturian writer had made in one of his articles to initiate a correspondence. He did not even attempt to disguise his intentions: "He puesto en los artículos 'En torno al casticismo' mucha alma y gran suma de trabajo; aunque llevo escribiendo algún tiempo en mi país (Bilbao), en la prensa *nacional* soy enteramente nuevo, tengo deseos de trabajar, de hacer lo que pueda por la cultura de mi país y de crearme una posición en las letras y algo que se añada a mi cátedra. Los principios son duros y aquí se lee tan poco lo que sale con firma nueva que sin recomendación es muy difícil salir adelante."[10] Several members of the first generation of writers to seek their literary fortunes in this century had ideological, personal and professional conflicts with the acerbic and ubiquitous Asturian critic (Alas, whose own philosophical orientation suffered several metamorphoses, had strong ties to the Krausist movement). Their flattering messages to Clarín in personal letters to him are contradicted in letters to other correspondents and in the hidden messages I tease out of the novels studied in later chapters.

The feisty philosophical and personal polemics that marked the beginning of the '98 attitude in the 1890s and that characterized its journals (*Almanaque de la Vida Literaria, Electra, Vida Nueva, Juventud,* all of short duration) suddenly submerged between 1900 and 1902, reappearing in the latter year in the deflected form of the novel. The novel admirably suited Unamuno's, Baroja's and Martínez Ruiz's ideological and artistic requirements at this point in their careers. Finding themselves in a genuine stalemate over the conflicting philosophies to which they had been exposed, tired of the fruitless interpersonal bickering in letters and journals (though these activities did not cease by any means), and ready for more sustained professional work, they buried their frustrations in the dialogics of the novel. The novelistic form served as a distancing mechanism for the authors—both from the ideas that obsessed and confused them and from the public that was always poised to seize upon their latest efforts for a new round of criticism and polemic.

Fiction is self-conscious about its philosophical mission, while the philosophical treatise or essay is generally blind to itself. The Spanish writers I concentrate on here invented a novelistic mode that is much more self-conscious about its philosophical purpose than are most novels. In their version of the philosophical novel, ideas are evident to the reader in an immediate rather than a latent way. The characters, rather than living immersed in the problems of love (like Emma Bovary) or the struggle for survival (like Lazarillo de Tormes), think and talk about life in the abstract as much as or more than they live it. Often these novels contain just as much story potential as other works on the same theme, but the more philosophically transparent novel refuses to flesh out its story, choosing instead to remain a minimal skeleton for discourse unrelated to character and plot. Compare, for example, Henry James's *Portrait of a Lady* and Unamuno's *Amor y pedagogía,* both of which focus on the problem of conceptual knowledge as it relates to daily living. In narrative terminology, a novel like *Portrait of a Lady* maintains its representational quality throughout, while in the more philosophical *Amor y pedagogía,* the representational dimension—the hermetically sealed, fictional world Ortega admired—often gives way to a discursive quality more akin to the essay. This discursive quality, what Todorov defines as "speech act[s] supposing a speaker and a listener, and in the speaker an intention to influence the listener in some way,"[11] overshadows the *sujet* or "presentation of phenomena which occurred at a certain moment of time without any intervention on the part of the speaker" (25). Of course, embedding this discourse in a novel gives it qualities that normal philosophical discourse does not have.

The journal article, the essay, and the philosophical treatise are all identified with the author's own personal voice, while in the novel none of the voices—whether the first or third person narrative voice or the voices of the characters in dialogue or interior monologue—is directly attributable to the author. Robert L. Brown, Jr., and Martin Steinmann, Jr., affirm that "Simply stated, situated discourse is always spoken *in propria persona;* fictional discourse never is."[12] Kenneth Seeskin puts it this way: "The writer of a treatise is, in effect, delivering a long speech to the reader,"[13] and Dabney W. Townsend, Jr., makes the following distinction between fiction and philosophy: "Philosophical works . . . are considered to possess a single correct interpretation of their 'meaning.' We have been taught that they say only one thing. Novels have different 'correct' readings."[14] Todorov calls literary narrative "mediatized," or "not immediate language"; the "I" of fiction is not the "I" of discourse (27). Mikhail Bakhtin borrowed an analogy from physics to illuminate the dialogic nature of the novel, saying the author's voice is refracted through the multiple voices of the narrative discourse; the author of a novel is a ventriloquist.[15]

Thus, like Martínez Ruiz's character Antonio Azorín, the author of a novel may be at the same time "místico, anarquista, irónico, dogmático, admirador de Schopenhauer, partidario de Nietzsche,"[16] finding tempting, suggestive gestures or negative effects in each position without subscribing to any. The novel offered early twentieth-century Spanish writers an opportunity to explore a variety of ideas without making the kind of commitment to one philosophical position required by journalistic or philosophical prose. Fiction afforded them the freedom unavailable to nonfictional discourse to distance themselves from a particular ideological position as well as from their predecessors or contemporaries who subscribed to it. The novelistic format allowed them to consider the validity of different positions without appearing incoherent or absurd. The normal procedure of the traditional philosophical treatise (and most of the writers in this study attempted the treatise or essay format) is to refute or correct existing positions, forcing an either/or judgment of the alternatives. Two or more philosophical positions may coexist within a single novel, and novels with different philosophical positions can exist side by side without canceling each other out. The dialogic nature of the novel elucidated by Bakhtin not only permits but encourages such multiplicity.

Of course, one of the novel's most important dialogic features is dialogue in which the voices of different characters with differing points of view clash and contradict one another. The early philosophical novels by Unamuno, Baroja and Martínez Ruiz employ a great deal of dialogue; they are very "talky" novels, and much of the talk centers on philosophical issues. Unamuno even employed the dialogue form in "Sobre la filosofía española. Diálogo," his impassioned plea for a Spanish philosophy that added sentiment to European philosophy.[17] The usefulness of dialogue for certain kinds of philosophical enterprises is not new; after all, Plato initiated philosophical dialogue as a genre with a purpose similar to that of our Spanish authors—namely, to achieve an inconclusive and open-ended philosophical position not available in the essay or treatise. In some ways the novelist-thinkers of both the Generation of '98 and the Generation of '14 returned to Plato's attitude toward philosophy, seeing it as quest and questioning rather than as the rhetoric and persuasion that have dominated philosophical discourse since the Middle Ages. Also in common with Plato, their fictional dialogues often take place between two people who relate to each other as master and pupil. As in some of the Platonic dialogues, the master in these novels is not always indisputably the winner of the argument; indeed, in neither the Platonic dialogues nor the Spanish novels does one philosophical position clearly prevail.

There is, however, a significant difference between the Platonic dialogue and the novelistic dialogues invented by Unamuno, Baroja, Martínez Ruiz, Ramón Pérez de Ayala, Juan Ramón Jiménez, Gabriel Miró, Pedro Salinas, Rosa Chacel and Benjamín Jarnés. A dialogue embedded in a novelistic context is colored by that context, especially by the implied author's and the narrator's view of the character who speaks the lines. This essential difference is crucial to understanding the way philosophy is present in the novels studied here. Often a character who espouses a particular philosophical position is thoroughly undermined by the narrator's attitude toward him or her, and thus the philosophical position is likewise cast in an unfavorable light. Narrative refraction through the narrator's attitude or dialogue between characters is frequently overlooked by those who write on Spanish intellectual history, and there are numerous cases of a character's being cited as the author's mouthpiece for his own philosophical position with no consideration of the novelistic context. By emphasizing dialogue over narration, the authors escape the dilemma of the narrator's veracity, allowing the truth to rest on what characters say. As Unamuno wrote to Jiménez Ilundain on May 24, 1899: "La forma de diálogo me permite mezclar con inducciones científicas fantasías poéticas."[18]

The profound interpenetration of literature (particularly the narrative) and philosophy that occurred in Spain at the turn of the century harbors a certain scorn for the traditional forms of each enterprise, but probably favors literature over philosophy, at least in principle. Unamuno's character Don Catalino believes in the superiority of poetry over philosophy, "sin habérsele ocurrido la duda—don Catalino no duda sino profesionalmente, por método—de si la filosofía no será más que poesía echada a perder,"[19] and Unamuno himself wrote in "Ideocracia" (1900): "De la ciencia de su tiempo, falsa según nuestra nomenclatura, las tomaron Platón y Hegel, y con ellas tejieron los más grandes poemas, los más verdaderos, del más puro mundo del espíritu" (*OC* 1: 958). For Unamuno, Spain's talent was literature, not philosophy; he believed Spanish writers were destined to write literarily rather than philosophically: "Es inútil darle vueltas. Nuestro don es ante todo un don literario, y todo aquí, incluso la filosofía, se convierte en literatura."[20]

In radically reforming nineteenth-century realism, which conceals its underlying philosophical biases in character, plot, description, and story, the first wave of Spanish philosophical novelists (or the Generation of '98) rejected the positivism with which it was allied, but their alternate narrative forms are not wholly successful as fiction. All three writers—Unamuno, Baroja and Martínez Ruiz—had recourse to characters whose philosophies stand for a large philosophical category. Rationalist philosophers from Descartes to Krause and Hegel are often collectively represented in one character, and the materialists or positivists receive similar treatment; the subtle distinctions between varieties of rationalism or materialism are sacrificed to novelistic expediency. This procedure frequently results in an oversimplified caricature which serves neither the purposes of philosophy nor those of fiction. Unamuno's goal was to address the lives of *hombres de carne y hueso*, but, as Carmen Martin Gaite points out, "es lo que precisamente nunca supo crear Unamuno,"[21] and Salvador de Madariaga asserts that some critics describe Unamuno's characters as "mere arguments on legs, personified ideas."[22] T. S. Eliot said that Goethe "dabbled in both philosophy and poetry and made no success at either."[23] However mistaken that statement may have been in the case of the German writer, it might be applied with some justification to the first generation of Spanish philosopher novelists. While these tendencies may have precluded the emergence of novels of the stature of *À la Recherche du temps perdu*, *To the Lighthouse* or *Ulysses*, whose philosophical overtones are kept in check by narrative considerations, it did help catapult Spanish fiction into the experimental mode a good ten years before the rest of Europe broke with realistic fiction. Even while pointing to the literary failure inherent in the philosophy-novel hybrid, I would hasten to add that these graftings inspire an intellectual interest through their sheer inventiveness that in some way offsets their problems as novels.

Scarcely had Unamuno, Baroja, and Martínez Ruiz made their 1902 debuts into the arena of the philosophical novel, thus marking a mature consciousness of their historical and philosophical circumstances, when a new generation announced its arrival in 1903 with the initiation of the journal *Helios*. This incipient generation, proclaiming its desire to "cortarse únicamente a medida y gusto de la belleza" (*Helios* 1 [April 1903, 1]: 1) began to gain ascendency over the '98 group by the end of the first decade. History repeating itself, the second generation maintained an ambivalent relationship to its elders—now Unamuno, Martínez Ruiz (soon to become "Azorín"), Baroja and Ramiro de Maeztu—very like the one between these writers and the generation of Clarín, Valera, Benito Pérez Galdós, and Emilia Pardo Bazán. While the new generation returned to specific interest in political solutions to Spain's problems (which the '98 abandoned in the first decade, at least as a concerted program),[24] their literary work is decidedly philosophical. Ramón Pérez de Ayala, Juan Ramón Jiménez, Gabriel Miró, Pedro Salinas, Rosa Chacel and Benjamín Jarnés continued the tradition of writing literary works with philosophical overtones, but their novels have a different flavor, one in which philosophy finds a more comfortable home. The more felicitous accommodation of philosophy to literature can in part be attributed to the emphasis on aesthetics (evident in *Helios*'s statement of purpose) and to the new philosophical issues that their novels addressed.

The Generation of 1914 (named for José Ortega y Gasset's seminal speech on "Vieja y nueva política" or for the onset of World War I) was the first Spanish generation to be fully international in its scope. Juan Ramón

spent a crucial year of his formative period in Paris and later became interested in Indian and English literatures;[25] Ortega studied in Germany
for almost three years; Pérez de Ayala had several long sojourns in England, and Gómez de la Serna made a second home in Paris. The Residencia de Estudiantes, founded in 1910 as a continuation of the Institución
Libre de Enseñanza, provided until the mid-1930s a focal point for
Madrid's intellectual activity and gave a more central locale for the exchange of ideas than the Generation of '98 had ever enjoyed. In 1913 Juan
Ramón Jiménez took charge of its publications, and Ortega's *Meditaciones
del Quijote*, arguably the first Spanish philosophical treatise fully within
the modern European secular tradition, was one of its early productions.

    Under Ortega's leadership, new European philosophical currents—
most notably phenomenology—replaced the false starts that Krausism,
latent Hegelianism, and the cult of Nietzsche represented. The philosophical issues the second generation novelists addressed were closely allied to Ortega's phenomenological approach to knowledge, capsulized in
the epigrammatic phrases "yo soy yo y mi circunstancia" and "perspectivismo." In the second generation, the '98 concern with the nature of the
Spanish soul and the problem of will and reason (among others) ceded to
an interest in perception and its expression in language as well as the relationship of language to existence, perhaps more natural topics for exploration through literature. As Jacques Derrida points out in *Speech and
Phenomena*, the role of fiction in phenomenology is privileged. In the first
issue of *Helios* some of the European thinkers who had captured the imagination of the Generation of '98 (especially in its formative years) were
now seen as passé. The reviewer of Fouillée's *Nietzsche et l'immoralisme*
announced the demise of the German thinker's influence, and a review of
Max Nordau's *Vers du Dehors* did not take him seriously as a philosopher.

    By 1914 when Ortega published his seminal *Meditaciones del Quijote*,
Spanish philosophy could stand on its own without the mediation of the
novelistic form, but significantly Ortega's first and in many ways most important work is ostensibly a meditation on the first modern novel (in its
original form a meditation on Baroja), and literary metaphor plays a large
role in Ortega's philosophical method throughout his career. Occasionally
he portrayed himself as a cross between a poet and a philosopher, a form
of centaur, and he claimed to have written several novels in his youth,
which he magnanimously set aside in favor of a career in philosophy.
Spain, he opined, needed a philosopher more than it needed another novelist. No doubt Ortega was thinking of the philosophical talent of the preceding generation that became subverted in the novelistic genre. Ortega,
with a more solid and less confusing philosophical formation, no longer

needed the novel to mask his ideas in 1914, although in his earlier career he did use characters and dialogue as a subterfuge.

The philosophical dialogue and discursiveness of the Generation of '98 novels were replaced by visual imagery and linguistic virtuosity— sometimes referred to as "poetic qualities"—that attest to the Generation of '14's acceptance of language as an ontological category. This faith in the power of language to produce reality linked this generation to the many vanguardist movements in Europe and Latin America, whose aesthetics rested on the same faith. The coincident generations mingled with one another at *tertulias* and in journals. For example, the ubiquitous Krausist-cum-positivist Urbano González Serrano appeared in *Helios* with a reprint of "Silencio," an article originally published in *Revista de España* in the early 1890s (that it is a reprint is not mentioned). Even though *Helios*'s expressed intention was to reorient Spanish letters toward a more aesthetic demeanor, it included Unamuno's "Vida y arte," which reaffirms his commitment to an art that concerns itself with real life. A series of Ganivet's letters appeared over several issues alongside poems by Ramón Pérez de Ayala dedicated to José Martínez Ruiz, a central member of the previous generation. The map of Spanish intellectual history becomes even more complex than it had been in the 1890s. Krausism, for example, which had been viewed with suspicion by the '98, lived on, at least in spirit, through the Institución Libre de Enseñanza, and critics have found more than subtle traces of it in many aspects of the work of Ramón Pérez de Ayala and Juan Ramón Jiménez.[26]

New underground (and not-so-underground) dialogues between members of the Generation of '98 and the Generation of 1914 formed new bases for novelistic crossfires (and even dialogues between philosophical treatises) from 1907 forward. The best documented of these dialogues (or disputes) is the one that was initiated between Unamuno and Ortega around 1909. Ironically, it centered on the issue of Europeanization that had distanced Unamuno from his predecessors, Clarín and Menéndez y Pelayo, but the roles are now reversed. The distance the Generation of '14 took from the two previous generations is evident from the first issue of *Prometeo* in which Federico García Sanchíz wrote of Madrid's literary landscape in geographical-generational terms. He described a series of mountains and foothills in three, four or even five gradations. The group in the background, including Benito Pérez Galdós, Marcelino Menéndez Pelayo, Armando Palacio Valdés, José Ortega Munilla (José Ortega y Gasset's father), Emilia Pardo Bazán, Joaquín Dicenta, Mariano de Cavia, Vicente Blasco Ibáñez, Eugenio Sellés and Octavio Picón, "el ya azulado y que llega a confundirse con las nubes" was the most "recio" (1 [November

1909]: 63). The late nineteenth-century generation that so vexed Unamuno, Azorín and Baroja had been defanged, and the Generation of '98 itself was well on its way to being relegated to *las nubes*.

In a period of eight years, the sharp cutting edge of the Generation of '98 had been blunted, and Ortega's group had begun to dominate the intellectual landscape. In 1906-1907 Unamuno wrote to Azorín indicating a weariness with the fame he had so avidly sought ten years earlier and a bleakness about a future generation to take up the cudgel his generation was laying down: "Cuando se encuentre aislado de todo, cuando le vayan dejando los papagayos lisonjeadores, cuando le vuelvan la espalda los jovencitos que azorinearon, cuando se venguen de usted porque les dominó mansamente, si entonces necesita desahogo, si le hace falta un corazón, aquí está el mío. . . . ¿Qué hay ahí? Por Dios, ¿qué jóvenes hay? Dígame lo que hay. ¡Todos dispersados! Maeztu en Londres, Baroja no sé donde, usted en su Azorín, yo en Salamanca, otros en sendos rincones. ¿Y la joven España? ¡Cuánto intento fracasado!"[27] In 1914 he had his answer; José Ortega y Gasset came to the aid of his sometime enemy when Unamuno was relieved of his rectorship.

By the time the second generation of writers was maturing in the latter part of the first decade, writing novels had become a viable livelihood (as indeed it did for Baroja at about this time). When Ramón Pérez de Ayala's father committed suicide in 1908 over financial difficulties, the heretofore dilettante writer set seriously to work, producing his tetralogy. He apparently believed publishing to be a more secure living than the business world that had sunk his father. Azorín wrote, not without a hint of envy, in 1910 (the year *A. M. D. G.* appeared) that "En 1896, el publicar un libro representaba un cúmulo casi invencible, penoso, de dificultades; llegar a ver impreso un artículo en un gran periódico era todo un triunfo. Hoy, cualquier muchacho que sienta ambiciones literarias puede desde luego publicar, con toda clase de facilidades, un volumen; los grandes periódicos están para todos abiertos."[28] In 1923 Ortega could write to Unamuno for permission to publish his article on Pascal in *Revista de Occidente* and confidently assert that "La organización económica de la Revista permite pagar muy decorosamente a sus colaboradores."[29]

Perhaps the generally freer publishing milieu from the second decade forward may partially explain another distinguishing feature of the second generation: women are much more in evidence in literary and intellectual circles. At least two of them—María Zambrano, a philosopher, and Rosa Chacel, a novelist (and a philosophical novelist, especially in her first work)—fall within the purview of my concerns here. The '98 Generation stands out as a desert for women writers of any kind, and the reasons for their disappearance from the Castilian literary scene for a period of some thirty years have yet to be sorted out. The focus of this study—the philosophical orientation of fiction from the 1890s well into the 1930s—may contain a clue to women's absence from the Spanish circles in the first years of the century. The intellectual preparation of the philosophical novelists took place in the universities, *tertulias* and public fora where new foreign ideas were being discussed, fora from which women were effectively shut out. Marking the important shift to include women in the second wave is the fact that behind its first journal was the guiding hand of a woman—María Martínez Sierra (it is said that she even chose its name). Each issue of *Helios* carried a section "Fémina," written by a woman and directed specifically to women.

An additional mark of the new generation is a tendency to theorize about aesthetic matters, which are often seen as an adjunct to the problem of perception and language. Ortega initiated the concern with aesthetic theory as early as 1910 in his essay "Adán en el Paraíso," in which he proclaimed art more appropriate than science for capturing particular human reality. Gómez de la Serna promoted new theories of art through his journal and *tertulia*, and Pérez de Ayala wrote numerous essays on different theoretical aspects of the novel and drama. Miró expressed his aesthetic ideas indirectly in his narratives and was goaded into an overt but unpublished declaration of his position in "Sigüenza y el mirador azul," an answer to Ortega's hostile criticism of his novel *El obispo leproso*.[30] The polemic between Baroja and Ortega on the nature of the novel, which had been brewing since about 1915, erupted into open warfare in 1925. Ortega's *La deshumanización del arte e Ideas sobre la novela*, published in that year, was an indirect critique of Baroja's open-ended, porous novels that wove elements of recognizable everyday Spanish political and social life into the fictional characters' story. Baroja immediately came to the defense of his eclectic version of the novel in the introduction to his *La nave de los locos* (1925). For Ortega there should be a complete divorce between art and life (a strong reaction against Ruskin's and Morris's utilitarian ideas on art), and the novel should create a tightly sealed, purely imaginative world that encapsulates readers, preventing their thinking about a world beyond the fiction. Ortega's essay in a way marked the end of the Generation of 1914 and the coming of age of the next generation, whose interests were predominately if not exclusively aesthetic in nature. The second generation's moderation of its political activity in the third decade paralleled that of the first generation in the first decade and was assisted in the former case by the dictatorship of Primo de Rivera, which made political action not only ineffective but dangerous.

Coincident with the aesthetic impulse of the second generation was a distinct sense of distance from the philosophical issues and their novelistic expression in the Generation of '98. The philosophical fictions of the '98 were violent reactions against late nineteenth-century thinkers and writers, while the philosophical novel of the '14 often parodied that of the '98. The second generation transformed the Generation of '98's deepest concerns—the power of the will and the nature of existence—into a great joke. So the crossfire continued, now more through intertextual reference than by the '98 technique of textual reproduction or parody of "real life" figures and conversations. Relations between writers were, however, more cordial on the surface; there was less rebellious hostility and less stridency than at the beginning of the century. Azorín, the first definer of the Generation of '98, described the difference between his generation and the new one in 1914, a key year for Ortega's generation: "¿Dónde está, en la gente novísima, querido Dicenta, el grito de rebelión de aquellos mozos de antaño? ¿Dónde están aquel ímpetu, aquel ardor, aquel gesto de independencia y fiereza? Ahora ¿qué es lo que hacéis, jóvenes del día? ¿Tenéis la rebelión de 1898, el desdén hacia lo caduco que tenían aquellos mozos, la indignación hacia lo oficial que aquellos muchachos sentían?"[31] Juan Ramón Jiménez wrote to Unamuno from Moguer sometime in the early twenties that he was an "idealista" who did not engage in polemics. As Azorín observed, it was a more methodical generation; it had "más método, más sistema, una mayor preocupación científica. Son los que *Nuevo Mundo* este núcleo forman críticos, historiadores, filólogos, eruditos, profesores. Saben más que nosotros,"[32] but it did not enjoy the spontaneity of the earlier writers. Azorín himself, having lost his earlier contentious anger, had turned bourgeois journalist behind the reserved and studied mask of his pseudonym. If Clarín in his day lamented the distinction between *viejos* and *jóvenes*, Azorín accepted it: "Dejémosle paso. Digamos de ellos, nosotros, ya un poco viejos lo que Montaigne decía de los mozos de su tiempo: *Ils ont la force et la raison pour eulx [sic]; faison leur place.*"[33]

The Generations of 1898 and 1914 overlapped and coexisted, in an uneasy peace, a tension that had more than a little to do with stimulating new ideas and new literary and philosophical forms on both sides. In fact, the term Generation of '98 was originally coined by Ortega in February of 1913 to refer to his own generation, but Azorín quickly coopted it and applied it to himself, Unamuno, Baroja and Maeztu along with a rationale for such a designation.[34] This appropriation, suggesting jealousy on the one hand and a genuine intellectual stimulation on the other, was characteristic of Spanish intellectual life from the 1890s into the third decade.

Without the philosophical and personal crossfires, it is hard to imagine that we would have the same literary and philosophical monuments—*La voluntad, Camino de perfección, El árbol de la ciencia, Del sentimiento trágico de la vida, Niebla* or *Meditaciones del Quijote.* The new generation cannot be understood without a consideration of its apprenticeship and continuing relationship with the older generation, and Unamuno, Baroja and Azorín's modified novelistic interests and style about 1912 are best viewed in the context of the new aesthetics.

Azorín's philosophical explorations through fictional constructs in *La voluntad, Antonio Azorín* and *Confesiones de un pequeño filósofo* metamorphosed into the static thematizing of time in works like *Castilla* (1912) and *Doña Inés* (1925), and both Unamuno and Baroja stopped writing philosophical novels of the discursive type early in the second decade. Baroja's *El árbol de la ciencia* (1911) and Unamuno's *Niebla* (1914) were their last efforts in the genre. Baroja turned increasingly to the adventure narrative, which he cultivated prolifically for the remainder of his long life and career. Unamuno developed a new version of the philosophical novel in which a single character plays out his/her existential angst in an antagonistic and uncomprehending world, a precursor to French existential novels of the 1940s and 1950s. I strongly suspect that Ortega's rising star on the Spanish philosophical horizon, bringing the new issues of perception and phenomenological description to the Spanish philosophical repertoire, was influential in the '98's move to abandon its oblique method of philosophizing in the novel. Since that method became a major object of parody in the fiction of the Generation of '14, however, it can be seen as occupying the center of the history of the Spanish novel for nearly thirty years.

1

THE GENERATION OF '98: EARLY PHILOSOPHICAL AND PERSONAL WARS

Unamuno's, Baroja's and Martínez Ruiz's early interests in philosophy were formed in the late nineteenth-century debates over 1) the place of the will and the intellect in human life, deriving from Nietzsche and Schopenhauer; 2) the role of environment in shaping human destinies, inspired by Darwin, Taine and socialist theories; 3) the nature of time and history, fueled by Hegel, Nietzsche and Bergson; and 4) the relative importance of scientific inquiry and artistic endeavor, informed by Spencer, Ruskin, Carlyle and Nietzsche. Krausism laid the metaphysical and practical groundwork upon which these controversies could build. As a philosophical movement, Krausism lasted a relatively short time before its cultivators turned to the practical activities of renewing Spanish politics and education, the latter especially through the Institución Libre de Enseñanza founded by Francisco Giner de los Ríos in 1876. Krausism was, however, the gateway through which Spain entered the modern philosophical tradition, as Leopoldo Alas, "Clarín," that acute observer of the Spanish intellectual scene, observed: "la filosofía en España era en rigor planta exótica, puede decirse que la trajo consigo de Alemania el ilustre Sanz del Río."[1] Several decades later, and with greater historical perspective, José Ortega y Gasset gave it its definitive place in Spanish intellectual history, called the *krausistas* the "único esfuerzo medular que ha gozado España en el último siglo" (*OC* 1: 212).

Krausism opened up discussion of the place of reason in life, put the Spaniards on "two feet" as Antonio Machado wrote,[2] and introduced genuine philosophical discussion into the conversations at the Ateneo, Madrid's intellectual center: "Krause fue para ellos el más inspirador de los maestros de esto no hay duda, pero con la filosofía de Krause había venido a España todo el idealismo alemán. . . . En las discusiones del

Ateneo habría mucho krausismo ciertamente, pero también se dieron muchas otras formas de pensamiento."³ Karl Christian Friedrich Krause proposed a rational Christianity that placed God at the center of rationalist doctrine. According to Krause, the individual, as the living image of God, was capable of progressive perfection, and humanity was marching inexorably toward "su etapa final de harmonía y plenitud."⁴ This *racionalismo armónico* empowered reason to synthesize the most disparate opposites: "orgánico e inorgánico, alma y cuerpo, naturaleza y espíritu, fondo y forma, individuo y estado, persona y sociedad, nación y región, estado nacional y sociedad humana, hombre y Dios."⁵

Borrowing from the subjective idealisms of Kant and Fichte, as well as the absolute idealisms of Schelling and Hegel, Krause's system had little to sustain it as a viable philosophy in the Western tradition, but what gave it its tenacity in the Spanish milieu, despite its obvious philosophical flaws and in the face of fierce opposition from orthodox Catholicism, was its practical side. This practical dimension was facilitated by Julián Sanz del Río's maneuverings with Krause's concepts of idea, ideal and humanity. The idea is purely spiritual and does not depend on the senses, but the idea contains a practical application—the ideal—which can be converted into an effective reality: "por ello la *idea de la humanidad*, imbuida de un carácter armónico superador de todas las oposiciones, conduce irremediablemente al *ideal de la humanidad*."⁶

Krausism's unrealistic emphasis on the perfectability of humankind dovetailed with the progressive spirit of nineteenth-century Europe and paved the way for the socialist philosophies that began to take root in Spain in the 1870s and 1880s. However compatible Krausism might be with the socialist ideologies in terms of their near-utopian call for social reform and the belief that reform is possible, these two positions are opposed on the relationship of the individual to the state and on what shapes human experience. The Krausists (as well as many non-Krausist Spaniards) could not accept Hegelian statism, the absolute subordination of the individual to the state inherent in socialist collectivism. Krausist liberals wanted the state to coexist on a parity with other social units—the family, the town, the province, and so forth. For Krausism, the free individual can create and change the world, while for socialism and anarchism, the social environment predominates.

Carlos Blanco Aguinaga has outlined for the years 1883-1885 the philosophical roots of the antipathy between Krausism and socialism, which he locates in Krausism's belief in the autonomy of the individual,⁷ a problem that became the focus of the early novels of the members of the

Generation of '98.[8] The efforts of critics to demonstrate the persistence of Krausist thought in the Generation of '98 have not taken into consideration the heterogeneous philosophical currents vying for these writers' attention during their formative years, or the writers' special interests at particular moments in their early careers (e.g., Unamuno's in Hegel and later in Kierkegaard, Baroja's in Schopenhauer and later in Nietzsche, and Martínez Ruiz's in Kropotkin and other socialist thinkers).[9]

The university careers of the '98 writers during the 1880s brought them into contact with Krausist ideas through professors of Krausist leanings and interaction with intellectuals at the Institución Libre and the Ateneo. They read Krausist ideologues such as Urbano González Serrano, who wrote prolifically in the most widely circulating intellectual journals. Both Unamuno and Martínez Ruiz maintained a friendly relationship with González Serrano, while rejecting most of his philosophical program. In many of these same centers of intellectual activity, the Generation of '98 writers, despite, or perhaps because of, their bourgeois backgrounds, also became aware of and sympathized with the socialist philosophies.

It is hardly surprising that philosophical confusion and skepticism ensued. The principal philosophical conflicts—the individual spirit or will against the determining factors of environment—had already begun to be aired in the controversy over Zolaesque naturalism. Emilia Pardo Bazán's famous "La cuestión palpitante" had complained that naturalists were forced always to select the external and tangible motives for human behavior to the exclusion of private and moral aspects, a situation she found artificial and unnatural. These conflicts were exacerbated for the Generation of '98 authors when they read and partially assimilated Schopenhauer's negative view of the will in the 1880s and 1890s, followed by exposure around 1900 to Nietzsche's exaltation of the will. Nietzsche seemed to offer to the individualist an escape (via the will) from the fatalism of environmental determinism, while social Darwinism tendered the possibility of achieving the superman precisely through the determining forces of the environment. Anarchism occasioned similar ambivalences. Nietzschean ideas left no room for the weakest members of the species, whom the anarchists wished to protect, but anarchist thought coincided with Nietzsche in its desire to improve the race by progressing toward the creation of a superior person.

The attraction of environmental determinism was shored up by Darwin's extremely powerful evolutionary theory, available in Spanish translation in the 1870s. *Transformismo*, as it was often called in Spanish, soon became the rage of *tertulia* conversation. As Diego Núñez points out, Spain, lacking a developed scientific community which could discuss

Darwin's ideas at the appropriate professional level, turned the subject into a matter for oversimplified public debate.[10] Herbert Spencer (who applied evolutionary theory to philosophy) and the social Darwinists such as Hippolyte Taine, Claude Bernard and Émile Zola received a great deal of attention in the intellectual journals, which throughout the later 1870s and the 1880s revealed tensions between the idealistic, spiritual Krausists and the scientific, fact-seeking materialists or positivists. If the reception of positivism in its various forms signaled a recognition in Spain of the importance of European scientific methodology, this very latent discovery was confounded by the simultaneous arrival of the writings of Carlyle and Ruskin and other preachers of the evils of technology from countries where the industrial revolution had been befouling the landscape for more than a hundred years. The result for a certain number of Spanish intellectuals caught in this crossfire between spirit and matter, idea and fact, science and anti-industrialism was to attempt to reconcile the demands of idea and fact in "krauso-positivism" (a hybrid about as odd as a mule and just as incapable of producing offspring, but which was, unfortunately, much less able to carry burdens). Unamuno lampooned this untenable solution in *Amor y pedagogía* by creating two characters, one the arch-positivist Avito Carrascal, who plans to raise a child in a completely scientific manner, and the other Don Fulgencio Entrambosmares—a German idealist—who is Avito's consultant on the project.

Unamuno, Baroja and Martínez Ruiz varied significantly in their understanding and assimilation of the philosophical currents that surged into Spain during their formative years. Unamuno, the member of his generation most academically and intellectually prepared to undertake the serious study of philosophy, translated Schopenhauer, but other philosophers, especially Spencer and Hegel, were more important to him in his early work. The extent to which Unamuno read and was influenced by Nietzsche is debatable, while Baroja seems to have diluted his early adherence to Schopenhauer, whose trace is detectable in his doctoral dissertation, with an interest in Nietzsche at the turn of the century. (Azorín's claim that Baroja was an uncritically ardent admirer of Nietzsche is belied in his equivocal novelistic treatment of him.) Of the three, Martínez Ruiz was the most superficial reader of philosophical works, preferring political and social theory to metaphysics. *Tertulia* conversation and journal reviews, rather than original works, were frequently the sources of Martínez Ruiz's knowledge of philosophy, as they were for the other writers. As Dr. Areilza wrote to Jiménez Ilundain: "Aquí conocemos algo de Nietzsche por 'La España Moderna' y por una colección de sus aforismos y sentencias, publicada por Lichtenberger, en francés, que la traje yo hace algún tiempo. Como aquí no existe 'La Mercure de France', le agradeceré me remita esos números que tratan de la filosofía de Kant a Nietzsche."[11] Baroja admitted that he was finally able to understand Kant (whom Unamuno believed could only be comprehended by Lutherans in any case) by reading Schopenhauer.

Two very important journals, *Revista de España* (1868-1895) and *Revista Contemporánea* (1875-1907), representing the two major new philosophical currents—idealism and positivism, respectively—competed for the attention of Spanish intellectuals during the formative years of the Spanish philosophical novelists. The journals of the Generation of '98— *Germinal* (1897-1899), *Revista de Literatura* (1898-1904), *Vida Nueva* (1898-1899), *Madrid Cómico* (which revamped its format in 1898), *Revista Nueva* (1899), *Nuestro Tiempo* (1901-1926), *Electra* (1901), *Alma Española* (1903)— inherited the tendency to philosophical controversy introduced by their predecesors, if not their longevity. *Revista de España* had a distinctly Krausist flavor and regularly included articles by leading Krausist writers such as Francisco Giner de los Ríos, Gumersindo de Azcárate and Urbano González Serrano, although the spirit of the journal was open to other orientations.

The optimism of Krausist ideas in numerous articles that reject the pessimism of philosophers like Schopenhauer and the consequences of Darwinism, particularly its apparent denial of the possibility of individual human action that transcends environmental determinants to behavior, is tempered by a certain number of articles that cast Zola or evolutionary theory in a favorable light. Julio Burell considered Leopardi and Schopenahuer to be links between high metaphysics and the theories of Darwin, Haeckel and Vogt ("La filosofía del dolor," no. 355 [1882]: 403-418), while in another issue Conrado Solsana wrote that Schopenhauer is a coward and that Schopenhauerism is a cholera-like plague (no. 350 [1882]: 243-252). Pedro Estasen asserted that Darwin had stolen the great secret from Nature, uncovering the fundamental stuggle of life—that to live is to fight ("La teoría de la evolución y la ciencia social," no. 334 [1882]: 253). In an earlier article, Benedicto Antequera affirmed that the diseases of society cannot become chronic as can disease in individuals, clearly distinguishing individual from collective life, often inseparable in social Darwinism ("La antropología transformista y sus errores," no. 292 [1880]: 526).

The assessment of the dilemma offered by Urbano González Serrano, a personal friend and mentor of Unamuno and Martínez Ruiz and one of the most assiduous contributors to *Revista de España*, summed up the general tenor of the journal. He saw no definitive solution for the debate between spiritualists and naturalists, although he personally preferred the spiritual orientation, arguing that modern sociology committed the unpardonable error of equating the social organism with natural ones. The approach prescribed the deductive method, recurring to induction only when formulating analogies between natural and social entities. He termed it reverse idealism; the inductions were formulated precipitously in abstract hypotheses that it took for realities ("La sociología científica," no. 369 [1883]: 25-35).

In continuations of this article González Serrano took on Spencer, an early favorite of Unamuno. According to González Serrano, Spencer produced violent analogies between physiological and social organisms and erroneously identified intelligence or reason with imagination (no. 375 [1883]: 346-347; no. 377 [1883]: 48). In the same forum a year later, González Serrano pursued his critique of Darwinism with a defense of reason and the accusation that the evolutionists overlooked the notions of salvation and redemption. He could, however, accept many of these same premises in Zola's naturalism because it "agita violentamente las dormidas energías del espíritu colectivo" (no. 423 [1885]: 39). In fact, by 1883 Valera (among others) believed that González Serrano had betrayed Krausist ideals and had been seduced by the positivists.

Revista Contemporánea, like *Revista de España,* attempted to assume an open ideological stance, embracing all that was new, but in the 1870s it was a much more receptive forum for Darwinism and in the 1880s its general political orientation was toward socialism and anarchism rooted in positivism. Its response to Krausism was correspondingly less enthusiastic. Despite the favorable turn that González Urbano's views took toward positivism after 1888, he was the target of negative reviews in *Revista Contemporánea.* "A," for example, indicated that, although he could not agree with González Serrano, he must be accorded the title of philosopher, who by "caminos más o menos extraviados, busca la verdad" (35 [1892]: 22). Alluding to his frequent recourse to quotations, another contributor suggested that González Serrano was less than original.

All the new philosophical ideas entering Spain from the 1860s forward were confronted with uniform hostility and vigorous objection from the conservative and Catholic orthodoxy. One of the most famous monuments commemorating this reactionary stance was *La historia de los heterodoxos españoles* (1880-1882) by Unamuno's professor Marcelino Menéndez y Pelayo. Of *Historia de los heterodoxos,* which defends traditional Spanish ideals against the foreign invasions, it has been said that "al tiempo que *fundaba* la historia de la filosofía española con su poderoso bagaje de erudición, la *castraba* profundamente con su sectarismo [y la convertía] en un campo de cardos agresivos y serviles."[12] As was typical of Spanish intellectual life in the late nineteenth century, philosophy became a political football in these debates. Positivism, Darwinism and Krausism were swept along with Marxism and socialism (assisted by socialism's having adopted evolutionary theory to show that revolution was natural and inescapable) in becoming anathema to the Church and to political conservatives. With the conservative turn of politics in 1875, Julián Sanz del Río and other Krausist professors were relieved of their university posts, and in their forced leisure they founded the Institución Libre de Enseñanza. The '98 novelists enlisted a host of narrative devices to mock and undermine the ideological conservatism and closed mindedness represented by such books as Menéndez y Pelayo's *Historia de los heterodoxos* and other reactionary manifestations, but their representations were complicated by equal ambivalence toward Krausism or idealism and the socialist theories.

In fact, Krausism had already come in for its share of sardonic satire from other quarters by the time the '98 writers were beginning to sign their names to journal articles (Unamuno, born in 1864, began publishing in local Basque periodicals in the 1880s; Martínez Ruiz, born in 1873, was first seen in print in Valencia and Monóvar in the early 1890s; and Baroja, born in 1872, offered opinions on sociopolitical matters in journal articles in the mid-1890s). The philosophy of idealist harmony had ceased to be an inspiration for original philosophical thinking and had settled into its role as catalyst for certain reformist enterprises, especially the Institución Libre de Enseñanza. The '98's view of Krausism was ambiguous indeed. Azorín underlined a passage in a book published in 1929 (one suspects with a smile of recognition) that portrayed Krausism as the philosophical laughing-stock of Europe. Baroja on occasion depicted the Krausists as dour, unilluminated types.

Despite its more modern and pragmatic roots, socialist thought did not offer a viable alternative to Krausist idealism for the '98 writers, and the plethora of conflicting and unsatisfying philosophies created a vacuum. Ganivet, for example, lamented the dearth of *ideas madres* to guide the nation, and Clarín wrote in 1889 of the *paz de Varsovia* that reigned in philosophical matters. According to José Luis Abellán, philosophy had two chairs at the University of Madrid in the 1880s, one occupied by the scholastic Ortí y Lara and the other by the Krausist Salmerón: "expresión manifiesta del clima de división y enfrentamiento conque aquella polémica se vivió en el ambiente universitario de la época."[13]

Each of the authors included in the first part of this study, while sharing certain methods, particularly the narrative subterfuge to mask frustration (and perhaps despair) at finding a viable philosophical solution to the "Spanish problem," dealt with the confused and confusing philosophical milieu in a somewhat different way. The early writing on social issues by all three authors reveals a socialist, Marxist and/or anarchist perspective, but as Cecilio de la Flor Moya points out, their socialism was always *sui generis*, grafted onto what he calls the "myth" of the free individual.[14] That Unamuno was thoroughly aware of his heterodox ideology is evident in numerous statements in his correspondence. In 1897 Unamuno wrote to Clarín about his peculiar marriage of mysticism and socialism: "Yo también tengo mis tendencias místicas... Éstas van encarnadas en el ideal socialista, tal cual lo abrigo. Sueño con que el socialismo sea una verdadera reforma religiosa cuando se marchite el dogmatismo marxiano y se vea algo más que lo puramente económico."[15] He wrote to Juan Arzadun that he felt he was "más socialista que antes y en las misma manera en que antes lo era. El socialismo corriente, marxista, sólo peca en aquello de que se inhibe. Una cosa es el racionalismo, y otra el materialismo teórico que a el unen muchos. . . . Lo malo del socialismo corriente es que se da como doctrina única, y olvida que tras el problema de la vida, viene el de la muerte."[16] A letter to Jiménez Ilundain of 1898 stated that it was an incurable individualism that caused him to be a socialist, however paradoxical that might seem.[17]

The need to think in a more sustained way about the philosophical issues underlying Spain's problems coalesced for the three writers in the 1890s. Baroja wrote his doctoral thesis on pain in 1893 (published in 1896); Unamuno brought out his essays "En torno al casticismo" in *La España Moderna* in 1895, and Martínez Ruiz, who had precociously begun issuing stinging little books of iconoclastic literary criticism from 1893 to 1897, produced a treatise on criminal sociology in the latter year. The treatise format, which resists ambivalence and paradox, proved inadequate to the writers' expressive requirements, and their philosophical preoccupations soon found more suitable accommodation in the novel. As early as 1897 in *Paz en la guerra* (begun even ten years earlier, according to his own indications in letters), Unamuno turned to fiction to accommodate the dualism and ambiguity of his mystic socialism. Baroja and Martínez Ruiz followed his lead in about 1900. Each published his first discursive philosophical novel in 1902: Unamuno's *Amor y pedagogía*, Baroja's *Camino de perfección* and Martínez Ruiz's *La voluntad*.

The novel ultimately became for Unamuno (as well as for Baroja and Azorín) a means of expressing personal and ideological differences without the unpleasant consequences of open and direct statement. The authors' correspondence corroborates their tendency to conceal their personal and ideological hostilities in the more veiled or private written forms of fiction and letter. The novel's multiple voices offered a blind behind which they could mask their ambivalent feelings about members of the powerful previous generation or toward members of their own generation. More than once Clarín came under attack for the capriciousness of his critical opinions, and arbitrary indeed was his paternalistic defense of the beleaguered Martínez Ruiz, whose attempts to make a name for himself by felling sacred literary cows in *Buscapiés* and *Charivari* were arousing the wrath of the literary establishment. Clarín scolded the impudent young Alicantine writer for his nastiness but praised the quality of his prose, all the while remaining curiously silent about Unamuno's *Paz en la guerra* (surely a literary effort much more deserving of notice than Martínez Ruiz's hasty tracts). Unamuno's letters to Clarín document the extent to which this slight vexed him in his bid for recognition as a writer.

Envy may have had a role in Clarín's silence. García Lorenzo Luciano suggests that Clarín saw in Unamuno a powerful rival who might eclipse him in many of the areas he had carved out for himself: the novel and essay as well as university professing.[18] Clarín's son affirmed that Clarín had read *Paz en la guerra* with great interest and that he had even made marginal notations in his copy. It is not hard to imagine Clarín's having found it easier to approach José Martínez Ruiz, whose less overwhelming intelligence and personality allowed him to assume the paternalistic attitude Unamuno would never have brooked. In the last chapter of *En torno al casticismo*, Unamuno complained of the great barrier erected by older writers against the work of younger writers with new ideas, and in a letter to Clarín he admitted that he was referring to him in that passage. Unamuno feigned indifference to Clarín's slight: "A Clarín le remití ejemplar, pero ni aun de mi libro ha dicho nada, después de haberme acusado recibo. No me extraña."[19] In one of his last letters to Clarín he revealed his bitterness over the Asturian critic's unsympathetic reception of his work, especially Clarín's unfavorable review of *Tres ensayos*, which he dismissed as a reshuffling of foreign ideas: " 'No cita a nadie [Unamuno quotes Clarín's review]; todo lo dice como si aquellas novedades, que lo serán para muchos, se le hubieran ocurrido a él sólo, o como si no supiera él que ya han sostenido cosas parecidas otros. Pero no se crea que esto es por vanidad, por echarlas de inaudito, etc.' Con el corazón en la mano, amigo Alas, no es esto una estocada?"[20]

While it is difficult to sort out all of the factors that went into Clarín's ignoring Unamuno's novel and publishing an unfavorable review of *Tres ensayos*, I suspect that a fundamental difference in philosophical attitude underlay his reactions to Unamuno. *Krausismo* and *casticismo* were two areas in which the writers were at odds. Throughout most of his career

Clarín had been associated with the Krausist movement (his doctoral dissertation, titled *El derecho y la moralidad,* was about Krausism). Unamuno's early reading of Hegel, who saw the individual subordinated to larger historical forces, is evident in his unpublished treatise *Filosofía lógica* (1886) and in his first published long essay, *En torno al casticismo,* with which Alas took issue, and in his interest during the 1890s in a socialist society. However much Unamuno may have courted the favor of the very visible Clarín (as well as that of González Serrano, who even in his later Krauso-positivist stage maintained the essentially optimistic Krausist stance vis-à-vis the prospects of individual perfection through education), his writings for journals belie his adherence to their philosophical positions.

For all his acerbic wit and wish to be an independent thinker, Clarín represented the same traditionalism and orthodoxy that Unamuno found so abhorrent in Menéndez Pelayo. In his prologue to E. Gómez Carrillo's *Almas y cerebros,* Clarín expressed fear of " 'la disolución del espíritu nacional' " and condemned the new writers whose appetite for things modern took "casi siempre el camino que va por el peor abismo, el aniquilamiento de la savia española, de la enjundia castiza."[21] Martínez Ruiz in *Literatura* wrote that the thesis of Clarín's drama *Teresa* was archaic, "no es señal de estos tiempos la resignación cristiana" (34). Maeztu also pointed out Clarín's reactionary views in the pages of *Revista Nueva:* "No quiso ver *Clarín* ese espíritu nuevo—estudiado tan admirablemente por el genial Unamuno—que iba a deshacer los viejos moldes del idioma castellano... Era más cómodo y productivo mantener en su integridad el dogma del casticismo" (October 15, 1899: 52). The *anticasticismo* of the 1895 essays *En torno al casticismo* that informed *Paz en la guerra* could not have been amenable to Clarín, who was wary of any tendency to annihilate the purity of the Spanish soul. It is possible that Clarín preferred to ignore Unamuno's "offensive" novel "polluted with foreign ideas" rather than write an unkind review of a book by someone with whom he had struck up a friendly correspondence. (The chivalric mode that dominated Clarín's approach to reviewing was not imitated by the Generation of '98.)

Corroborating this interpretation of Clarín's silence are the at first subtle and later very pointed references Unamuno made to the archtraditionalist Marcelino Menéndez Pelayo in his letters to Clarín. Early in their correspondence (perhaps to ingratiate himself with Clarín, a fervent admirer of Don Marcelino) Unamuno reminded the Asturian writer that he was Menéndez Pelayo's student, deftly sidestepping the fact that his *En torno al casticismo* is a frontal attack on the *casticismo* defended in Menéndez Pelayo's *Historia de los heterodoxos.* A letter of October 2, 1895, to Clarín even indicated a conciliatory attitude toward Menéndez Pelayo's sectarianism: "A usted, como a don Marcelino, con los años se le va ensanchando y serenando el criterio, que nunca creo fue cerrado."[22] In one letter Unamuno attempted to defend himself from the accusation that he was opposed to historical traditions.

After Clarín's unflattering article on *Tres ensayos*, Unamuno dropped all pretense and wrote candidly that he did not consider himself a disciple of "don Marcelino" or of anyone else (May 9, 1900). He accused Clarín of cowardice in his own assessment of the *sagrados*, while admitting that he himself had not had the courage to speak directly in public against Menéndez Pelayo (he even initiated an obsequious correspondence with him, asking his assistance in a publishing project). Unamuno's early subterfuge, an article entitled "Joaquín Rodríguez Janssen" that parodied the detector of *heterodoxos*, was prevented from being published in *La Vida Literaria* by Clarín himself, but he did finally manage a public revelation of his opinion of Menéndez Pelayo after his former professor's death. He savagely parodied Menéndez Pelayo's old-fashioned scholarship in the figure of Antolín S. Paparrigópulos in the novel *Niebla*,[23] and in his 1928 edition of *Historia de los heterodoxos* he wrote the marginal notation "horrible" on pages 425-426.

In his last letter to Clarín, Unamuno was similarly candid about his true feelings toward Urbano González Serrano, the Krausist professor with whom he carried on a long and friendly correspondence. González Serrano had committed the unpardonable sin of not responding favorably to *Paz en la guerra*, the work Unamuno thought his best to date. Again, Unamuno refrained from direct public statement, but he commented privately to Clarín that he could not abide the writings of his friend, "whom he dearly loved," because they were a mere mishmash of the ideas of others. Writers of González Serrano's type were subjected to a more public (though highly indirect) parody in the character of Fulgencio Entrambosmares in *Amor y pedagogía*. This sort of hypocrisy (public praise and private vituperation) was endemic to the Spanish literary scene of the day. Unamuno, who maintained the most warm and friendly relations with Azorín, praising and encouraging his campaign against such hollowed monuments of Spanish letters as Echegaray, in 1906 wrote to a friend that Azorín "es un levantino que empieza a aburrir y hacer bostezar a media España de la que lee."[24] Around 1909, however, Unamuno himself came in for a public drubbing (spearheaded by his cogenerationist Ramiro de Maeztu) over his anti-Europeanism, a tip of the iceberg in terms of the covert caricatures circulating in Spain about Unamuno. (Some of the most amusing of these are the now published letters of Unamuno's sometime "friend" Dr. Areilza.)

José Martínez Ruiz was also engaged in these ideological and personal wars. Though not as serious a student of philosophy as Unamuno, he also professed a kind of socialism in the 1890s while simultaneously maintaining, at least in public, a favorable relationship with leading Krausist thinkers. He did venture a critique of González Serrano in an article for *Revista Nueva* on October 5, 1899: "A González Serrano, el ansia de la crítica llévale a la abstracción. Preferencias por la 'metafísica idealista' noto en sus primeros libros la *Revista Filosófica* de París: hoy figura entre los mantenedores del positivismo pero quédale el gusto por las ideas abstractas. Ideas abstractas, independientes de toda contingencia, son para él *deber, amor, altruismo, voluntad.* Por imborrable tiene el 'sentimiento del deber', independientemente de espacio y de tiempo, pretende hacer la 'psicología del amor' para nada considera en sus críticas literarias las circunstancias personales y de ambiente" (89). It is ironic that the very ambivalence of which he accused González Serrano at the beginning ("duda en decidirse por una u por otra idea") and ending ("la duda es para González Serrano la blanca cabecera del filósofo que 'el hastío y la amargura' del poeta") of the article are exactly the caverns into which José Martínez Ruiz (when he became Azorín) and his cogenerationists fell.

Martínez Ruiz's relationship with Clarín was perhaps more complex than Unamuno's, given the Alicantine writer's more pronounced tendency to mask his true feelings. Martínez Ruiz has been depicted as an unambiguous admirer and disciple of the Asturian critic.[25] Some of the circumstances of Martínez Ruiz's early career, however, suggest that he may have harbored feelings other than gratitude toward Clarín for having come publicly to his defense over the *Charivari* scandal and for his paternalistic advice to read philosophers whose pretentions were more serious than those of the anarchists. In many of its strategies (detailed in chapter 4 of this study), *La voluntad* is a subtle undermining of authority and authoritative voices, consonant with Martínez Ruiz's early aversion to paternalism. José Rico Verdú locates the origins of this aversion in Martínez Ruiz's uncomfortable relationship with his father, a man whose temperament was markedly different from his son's. Martínez Ruiz distanced himself from his politically conservative and authoritarian father by dressing in an outlandish fashion (with tails and monocle) and by joining the Federalist party. His move to Madrid in 1896 to pursue a career in journalism was very much against his family's wishes, and there are indications that his return to Monóvar without completing his university degree in Salamanca was manuevered by the stern hand of the father.

Martínez Ruiz, like Unamuno, tried to call Clarín's attention to himself by writing to the powerful critic on a pretext. At a very early date in his career as a journalist (February 7, 1892), he sent a letter to Clarín ostensibly to introduce the Austurian critic to the works of a relative, Don José Soriano García, a Catholic apologist. He mentioned Soriano's one published treatise, *El contestador a una carta que se quiere suponer escrita por el (ahora) Príncipe Tallyerand al Sumo Pontífice Pío III* (Alcoy: José Martí, 1838), and offered to send Clarín some unpublished manuscripts, among them a work entitled *La filosofía del símbolo*. Martínez Ruiz was doubtless aware of Clarín's religious crisis and perhaps thought the material would be of interest to him, but he also seemed to be using the manuscripts as an excuse to approach this gateway to the wider world of publishing in Spain. Apparently Clarín did not remember this early letter because in the often-cited 1897 "Palique," in which he praised Martínez Ruiz's writing, he began by saying "No sé quien es este Martínez Ruiz." It is in the second "Palique" of 1897 that Clarín chastised the young hothead for his brashness in *Charivari*, while defending him as a writer. And in private correspondence, Clarín recommended to the upstart Levantine journalist that he leave his anarchist associations behind, read serious philosophy and write about the world in a more universal way. The critics who have studied the relationship between Martínez Ruiz and Clarín have dwelt on these documents as proof of Martínez Ruiz's role as devoted disciple to Clarín.

It defies belief that the rebellious young Martínez Ruiz could have accepted Clarín's paternalistic admonishments without a certain rancor, especially when one considers his close relationship to Luis Bonafoux, one of Clarín's most ardent antagonists. Martínez Ruiz went to Madrid in 1896 with an introduction to the editor of *El País* from the Puerto Rican satirist, whom he had met in the publishing circles in Valencia. Many of Bonafoux's works are present in Martínez Ruiz's personal library, most notably his nasty tracts on Clarín's alleged plagiarism of *Madame Bovary*—*Yo y el plagiario Clarín* (1888) and *Coba* (1889), both containing pen marks by Martínez Ruiz.[26] In his own *Literatura (Fray Candil, Galdós, Clarín, Altamira, etc.)* of 1896, Martínez Ruiz wrote that *Yo y el plagiario Clarín* had no equal "de Larra acá" (27). In the same booklet his defense of Clarín was notably understated: "Espíritu el de Leopoldo Alas ampliamente asimilador, más que talento genial y creador, no ha podido menos de asimilarse las maneras y el tono de aquéllos que tienen altar en su alma" (32).

From his earliest sallies as a literary critic, Martínez Ruiz had harsh words for Clarín. In July of 1891, six months before he attempted to gain access to Clarín by bringing Soriano's manuscripts to his attention, he wrote in *El Activo* of "el mordaz Clarín, mezcla de abeja y avispa."[27] In the 1893 *La crítica literaria en España*, he averred that "Clarín no es ningún genio" (22-23), and he criticized Clarín for deserting progessive ideas and becoming religious. Nor was Clarín overlooked in the acerbic *Buscapiés* of 1894, where he was proclaimed to be "over the hill": "Leopoldo Alas, a quien, según confesión propia, la inconsecuencia le seduce, ha soñado tal vez, con ser ese poeta cuya ausencia él tan amargamente lamenta, ese poeta creyente en su tristeza, que nos cantase a su modo, al ver nuestros progresos pegadizos, la melancólica queja: ... *ma la gloria non vido;* la voz de nuestro genio nacional, no sé si agotado, no sé si falto de ambiente propio en la moderna vida.' No faltan quienes juzgan a Leopoldo Alas un tanto retrasado, y tengan por anticuada para los tiempos que atravesamos ... esa *crítica juicio*" (13) and that "Leopoldo Alas, que comenzó siendo el campeón de las novísimas tendencias y el intérprete de una gran parte de nuestro público, ha recogido velas, y trata en la acutalidad de representar el papel de dueña dolorida de nuestras sempiternas tradiciones" (20). That Martínez Ruiz found Clarín's latent mysticism untenable is substantiated in the vignette "El misticismo de Urbino," also included in *Buscapiés.* Don Leopoldo Alas (named as such) is seated in his study smoking a cigar. He feels like a poet, but "le falta el *metrífico.*" His glory is solely derived from literary criticism; his fame is based on the crude work of a "jornalero literario." Suddenly he recalls his eloquence as an exalted revolutionary in his youth, but it was soon tamed by practical concerns: "¡Se predica la paz a toda costa aunque destruya carácter, aunque favorezca la injusticia fortificando su reinado! . . . en nombre de un optimismo que es materialista al negar a la acción humana una influencia capaz de destruir los efectos del determinismo natural de la obra del espíritu, y que por otro lado es cándidamente providencialista y casi idólatra, al esperar de lo alto una misteriosa y salvadora fuerza invisible que ha de ir realizando el ideal de la justicia en cada momento, según su grado, por un proceso invariable pero seguro, ajeno a la voluntad del hombre" (197-204). The parody concludes with the ironic invocation "¡Copiemos a *Clarín!*" (204).

Martínez Ruiz's criticism of Clarín and others became more veiled and ambivalent with each passing year. In fact the dedication to *Soledades* openly flatters Clarín: "Para el maestro Leopoldo Alas, Recuerdo de un discípulo que sigue y agracede sus consejos. JMR 1898." The book itself is an imitation of *Solos de Clarín* (1881), a loose collection of criticism, aphorisms and stories. The mysterious article on *Electra,* entitled "Ciencia y fe," is likewise dedicated to Clarín, and Martínez Ruiz's desire to please the critic may account for his reversal of opinion about Galdós's famous anticlerical play.[28] The article could be seen as an obsequious attempt to vindicate the Asturian writer's old-fashioned Christian message in his late (and unsuccessful) plays in the face of Galdós's resounding success with the anticlerical message of *Electra*. Martínez Ruiz's true sentiments regarding the role of the Church in personal life are revealed in the anticlericalism of his novel *La voluntad*.

"Ciencia y fe" could also be a more subtle attempt to prove his earlier point (in the *El Progreso* articles on Clarín's Ateneo lectures of 1897) that Clarín failed to take a firm philosophical stand: "místico, científico, [o] filósofo . . . falta en Clarín decisión por una u otra idea; visión clara de un ideal; espíritu decidido en pro de una sola causa. Al fado o al puente; o ciencia o misticismo."[29] Finally, if he did follow Clarín's suggestion that he study more serious philosophical works, he did not take his advice to avoid Bonafoux, whom he saw shortly before writing an article in *Vida Nueva* which appeared January 7, 1900. The article refers to Bonafoux as his "buen amigo." For his part, Bonafoux wrote in *Madrid Cómico* on November 4, 1899, that Martínez Ruiz had come in for severe critcism for defending his (Bonafoux's) writing.

Martínez Ruiz's differences with Clarín were aesthetic, ideological and personal, and these differences, along with the distaste for bourgeois complacency (evident in the second *Electra* review) and his disillusionment at Pi y Margall's failure to make a significant impact on national politics, became the impetus for the 1902 novel *La voluntad*. Like Unamuno, Martínez Ruiz found the distancing qualities of the novel an appropriate way to express his frustration at the cruel publishing world he had depicted in *Charivari*. The novel also could simultaneously express indirectly his cynical views of critics like Clarín whose "heterodoxo espiritualismo" he found untenable in the Ateneo lectures of November 1897 only a few months after Clarín's defense of the *enfant terrible* in *Madrid Cómico*. The muted criticism evident in the *El Progreso* review of the Ateneo lectures and the more open irritation at the success of *Electra* found their way into *La voluntad* through parody and deflection.

Before the novels of 1902 absorbed and transformed the overt hostility of the '98 generation, a new set of short-lived journals gave the writers an outlet for their combativeness. Clarín recognized this new confrontational style in an article he published in the younger writers' journal *La Vida Literaria:*

Yo he atacado a mucha gente, pero no por vieja. No nos quejábamos nosotros de puestos escogidos por los de más edad, sino que procurábamos conseguir el ambiente de notoriedad necesaria, defendiendo lo que creíamos bueno, censurando lo malo, viejo o nuevo. No había tacto de codos entre los principiantes para protegerse, los aptos y los ineptos, y alabarse unos a otros por frescos y rozagantes. No se nos escapaba la fácil observación de que las nulidades presentaban su mocedad como título. Ahora, francamente, entre muchos jóvenes de mérito, pululan otros que son los más amigos de la bandería, para hacerse pasar colectivamente; y son los más feroces defensores de la paradoja de la despreocupación moral y religiosa.[30]

The division between *viejos* and *jóvenes* created an invisible but impenetrable wall that was seemingly on everyone's mind. The old defended tradition; the young sought new ideas imported from Europe. In a *Madrid Cómico* (18, no. 790, April 9, 1898) article entitled "Viejos y jóvenes," Emilio F. Vaamonde contradicted "Zeda," who in *La Época* had called the new generation "Lear's children." In Vaamonde's opinion, the young writers were too respectful of their elders. Unamuno leapt into the fray in the very next issue, typically agreeing with neither position. According to the professor of Greek at Salamanca, the young are "soberbios" and the old "tacaños":

La cuestión capital en todo esto es económica. No sirve declamar contra los viejos. Tienen derecho a la vida, y si han sido útiles, tienen también derecho a una recompensa lo más proporcionado a sus servicios. Y como quiera que el trabajo literario no está retribuido en España de manera que quepa hacer ahorros ni hay suficientes derechos pasivos, se resarcen los viejos explotando su antiguo prestigio. Nada más justo que el 'no hay que empujar'. Lo que todo viejo sensato debe procurar, es crearse una familia literaria, que ha de ser el báculo de la vejez de su prestigio. . . . ¡Si hubiese usted pasado como yo por siete oposiciones en cinco de opositor y en dos de juez de ellas, habría visto en extracto concentrado, y sin hipocresía, todo eso de los viejos y los jóvenes y de los catarros y cofradías! ¡Qué de lecciones aplicables a la brega literaria![31]

Clarín's collaboration in *Almanaque de la Vida Literaria* asserted that the *viejos/jóvenes* issue was fallacious, and worse, it was not *castizo*, since such distinctions came from France (!). He continued the theme in the same journal on July 6, 1899 (no. 26: 417); he was happy to contribute to the *Almanaque* because the "elemento joven" predominated, and he was "muy amigo de la juventud" (despite what those same "jóvenes" may have been saying in public and more often in private): "Amo a la juventud; pero no la adulo. Deben reconocer los jóvenes que, los que no lo somos ya, tenemos más motivos para juzgarlos a ellos que ellos a nosotros. Nosotros hemos pasado por lo que son ellos y ellos no han pasado por lo que nosotros somos. . . . Ellos piensan que no serán como nosotros; nosotros sabemos que hemos sido como ellos." He quoted Nietzsche to indicate that he was aware of the latest fads of the young, whose nature it was to be excessive in their venerations, as in their scorn. Clarín averred that he had been the object of both extremes at the hands of the younger writers: some called him *maestro* while others proclaimed him nothing more than a "gacetillero *retórico.*" What he apparently did not know was that some (such as Martínez Ruiz) were doing both.

The indefatigable Maeztu railed against the hegemony of Clarín in *Madrid Cómico,* basing his arguments on the *viejos/jóvenes* issue: "Hemos de perder todos esperanza... ¿de salir del infierno? ¡No! de colaborar en el *Madrid Cómico* cuántos seguimos siendo jóvenes. . . . De hoy en adelante, *Madrid Cómico* se robustecerá con sangre vieja" (he mentions Clarín, whose "pernicioso influjo" he does not lament). Joaquín Dicenta wrote in "Los jóvenes" that today's literary youth had been born into an infernal atmosphere:

¿Qué han encontrado los literatos jóvenes al venir a la *vida pública?* ¿En qué atmósfera nacieron? ¿Con qué literatura se han nutrido? ¿Qué camino habían abierto a sus ojos los escritores de la generación anterior? ¿Dónde estaba el Balzac viejo que sirviese de arranque a los Zolas futuros? ¿dónde el pezón que alimentase con raudales de genio a la juventud hambrienta de enseñanzas? . . . Declaro que los nuevos sólo hallaron biberones calcados en moldes extranjeros, o hechos con cristales viejos del derribo romántico. Una lactancia artificial en la que había poca leche de recibo: ése fue el tratamiento empleado con ellos; porque hay que confesarlo: a los literatos recién nacidos se les ha tratado y se les trata con muy mala leche.[32]

The ambivalence of the young toward the old is summed up in Martínez Ruiz's reaction to Galdós's *Electra* in February of 1901. Unamuno too eventually distanced himself from Galdós, although not in such a violent manner, employing instead the epistolary mode, his favorite medium for personal invective. In a letter congratulating Azorín on his outspoken criticism of the mediocrity of some of his elders, Unamuno evoked "nuestro mucilaginoso Galdós,"[33] and on another epistolary occasion: "Terminé mi diálogo sobre la filosofía española hablando de Galdós como pude terminarlo mentando al Moro Muza, pero no puedo continuarlo tratando de él, por dos poderosísimas razones; 1ª la que tengo hecho firme propósito de no escribir sobre autor alguno español vivo, y 2ª que no he leído nada de lo que ha escrito Galdós en estos últimos años. Ni siquiera 'Electra' conozco."[34]

The younger writers founded their own journals to gain easier access to publishing avenues and to more freely express their ideas, often informed by socialist and anarchist ideology. The tone of the '98 journals was more strident and personal than that of their predecesors such as *Revista de España* and *Revista Contemporánea,* which displayed a certain *noblesse oblige* toward rivaling ideologies. A series of historical events—the failed revolution of 1868, the attempt at a Republic in 1873, the corrupt constitutional monarchy of the Restoration installed in 1875, and the loss of the last colonies in 1898—now formed a wall that forever precluded the utopianism inherent in both Krausist and socialist/anarchist models. Nietzsche, Schopenhauer and Kierkegaard had intervened to make suspect any optimistic rationalism. These key philosophers introduced the Generation of '98 authors to the problematics of the will that preclude an ideal solution to the philosophical debates of the nineteenth century. Discovery of an ideological underpinning to solve Spain's problems—a solution that the protagonists of the debates (represented in the journals *Revista de España* and *Revista Contemporánea*) fully believed would be forthcoming with time—also began to seem remote.

The older writers were, however, still very much present. The younger generation was coming into its own, but it could not afford to turn its back on the powerful opinion of its mentor-antagonists. *Vida Nueva*, edited by Blasco Ibáñez, Mariano Cavia, Galdós, and Felipe Trigo (among others) and which published articles by as heterogeneous a collection of writers as Clarín, Emilio Castelar, Dicenta, Echegaray, Gómez Baquero, González Serrano, Menéndez Pelayo, Navarro Ledesma, Núñez de Arce, Ortega Munilla, Maeztu, Rusiñol, Unamuno, Federico Urales, Valera, Francisco Pi y Margall and Joan Maragall (among others), indicates the mingling of older and younger writers that is representative of all the '98 journals. The generation of '98 continued to present an obliging front to the earlier generation, but the confrontational nature of their relationship persisted.

Almanaque de la Vida Literaria (1898-1899), a spin-off from *Madrid Cómico*, incorporated some of the pungent, satirical humor of its parent magazine, adding another dimension to the stridency and combativeness of the younger generation. The jokes were often personal and pointed. The dramatist José Echegaray, who was criticized by the new writers for his banality, was the subject of such one-liners as "Don José Echegaray no escribe más de tres dramas en este mes" (*Almanaque* 1 [1899]). And the younger writers were spotlighted with favorable mentions and reviews. *La evolución de la crítica* by José Martínez Ruiz, who was received by the older generation with reserve and even hostility, was given a laudatory review in *Almanaque de la Vida Literaria*, which also sponsored sales of the same author's *Pecuchet demagogo*.[35]

The bristly commentary on both literary and social issues prevailed and was extended to rivalries between journals themselves. In the first issue of *Almanaque de la Vida Literaria*, an article by Tomás Carretero began in a typically hostile fashion: "Eugenio de los Montes pasó una vida digna de un príncipe ruso, hasta que un día tuvo la desgracia de leer *Revista Moderna* de Lázaro." And in the March 1899 issue, the editors lamented that the "simpática revista" (*Revista Nueva*, founded by Luis Ruiz

Contreras) attacked one of its dearest contributors (possibly Clarín, who was also the target of later articles such as "Clarindustrial"). In the journal *Electra* the generation jelled, and there one begins to see the submersion in fiction of the ideological and personal conflicts that had been occupying the young writers. In the first issue of March 16, 1901, Baroja published "Política experimental" and "Domingo en Toledo." With a change in narrative voice from first person to third, the latter article was incorporated into chapter 30 of *Camino de perfección*, which appeared the following year to herald the initiation of the generation's hegemony. In the April 13, 1901, issue, under the title "El amigo Ossorio," Baroja unveiled the first two chapters of that novel exactly as they were to appear later in book form. José Martínez Ruiz, in many ways the most combative member of the new generation, continued his pamphleteering diatribes with "Los jesuitas" in the April 6, 1901, issue, and in the March 30, 1901, number, Valle-Inclán reviewed Baroja's *La casa de Aizgorri*. The generation's members increasingly reviewed each other's work as the members of the older generation died or diminished in power and importance. (Recall that it was the contemporaneous Maeztu who took José Martínez Ruiz to task for his reversals on *Electra*.)

Juventud, a very short-lived journal founded in late 1901, contained pieces almost exclusively by the new writers (Baroja, Martínez Ruiz, Maeztu and Valle) with only a genuflection toward the ideas of their elders: one article by Giner, "La idea de la universidad," one by Rafael Altamira, "Psicología nacional," one by Joaquín Costa, "Buena nueva" (on the need for students to study abroad, a prescription that Ortega would follow), and two by the Krausist Adolfo Posada. In the March 15, 1902, issue (the last in the Madrid Hemeroteca collection), José Martínez Ruiz wrote in "Todos fuertes" on Baroja "el nietzscheano." Their two novels published that same year continued their personal and journalistic discussion of the place of the will in human destiny.

If the journals (however ephemeral) marked the consciousness of certain common social and cultural goals, 1902 saw a dawning of artistic maturity. In that year the philosophical and personal controversies that marked the formative years of Unamuno, Baroja and Martínez Ruiz were channeled into a novel by each author that reflected the philosophical crucible of the previous decades. I now turn to those contentious early philosophical novels, which served as a means for the authors to explore and emancipate themselves from the constraints of impossible logical solutions to the philosophical and personal dilemmas they had experienced.

2

UNAMUNO:
A BOLD NEW HYBRID

In 1902, after nearly a decade of journal writing, attempts at serious treatises (some aborted, some published) and several sallies into the novelistic arena, Unamuno, Baroja and Martínez Ruiz each produced a novel of clear philosophical overtones that made an indelible mark on the history of Spanish fiction in this century. These are Unamuno's *Amor y pedagogía*, Baroja's *Camino de perfección* and Martínez Ruiz's *La voluntad*.[1] The polemical generation now submerged its personal and philosophical conflicts in the camouflage afforded by characters, dialogue and plot. All three philosophical novels embody the '98 quandaries over will and determinism, idea and matter, shaded according to each individual author's experiences and philosophical reading. If Unamuno now regarded his earlier idols Spencer and Hegel in an ironic light, Baroja, whose youthful philosophical reading centered on Kantian rationalism, now wavered between Schopenhauer and Nietzsche, and Martínez Ruiz, more thoroughly involved than the other two in socialist thought and sociology, struggled with determinism and the liberating possibilities of reason or will. In each novel, education—the formation of the young—is at issue, and one can discern the goals and preoccupations, if not the substance, of Krausism flickering dimly in the background.

However different these three novels are, they share common ground in evoking a genuine malaise (what Inman Fox and others haved called "crisis fin de siglo") and an iconoclastic stance toward the cultural milestones of the nineteenth century. With an antirealistic, highly stylized narrative form, Unamuno shattered positivism and idealism, the two great abstract systems that underwrote nineteenth-century progress. Baroja invoked Nietzsche in an eclectic narrative mode that echoes Spanish Golden Age genres as well as nineteenth-century realism and decadent literature. Martínez Ruiz undermined other nineteenth-century shibboleths—the will and history—in a novel that reduces narrative qualities to a minimum, supplanting them with documents and philosophical disquisition.

Unamuno occupies a unique place in the history of philosophical fiction. Viewed in its chronological development, his novelistic canon bridges the gap between major eighteenth- and nineteenth-century philosophical novels (those of Voltaire, Carlyle and Kierkegaard) and the post–World War II existential version of the genre cultivated by Jean Paul Sartre and more recently by Milan Kundera. Unamuno's philosophical novels (and all his novels are philosophical to a greater degree than those of most of his contemporaries) fall into three general types: 1) *Paz en la guerra* provides the fictional flesh for a philosophical skeleton formed from the central ideas of *En torno al casticismo*. In fact, the novel was probably begun before the essays and finished afterward, and one could doubtless elaborate a dialectical process of creation between them. 2) *Amor y pedagogía* and *Niebla* are versions of the grotesque, parodic, satirical philosophical novel à la *Candide* with elements of the Romantic irony of *Sartor Resartus*. In these works Unamuno developed dialogue as the main vehicle for presenting and confounding philosophical ideas. 3) *Abel Sánchez, La tía Tula, San Manuel Bueno, mártir* and *Cómo se hace una novela* are novels in which an original philosophical position is presented, not only in the dialogue but in the characters' actions and fates. They are existential novels, allegories or fables of the anguish of existence without the certainty of God, religion or other absolute measures of personal identity and moral values. It is this last type that prefigures the philosophical-fictional procedures of *La Nausée* and *The Unbearable Lightness of Being*.

Amor y pedagogía was written at a crucial moment of intellectual transition for Unamuno, after more than a decade of intense study of German idealism and English positivism. Unamuno's interest in idealism began with Hegel, and his relationship to Hegel's thought was long and complex. In 1901 he wrote to Federico Urales that of all the philosophers he had read, Hegel had the most profound influence on him.[2] He said that after Hegel he fell in love with Spencer, but always interpreted him in a Hegelian way, since the English thinker was a very crude metaphysician. In the unpublished "Filosofía lógica" (written in 1886), his philosophical first effort (and probably his only attempt at a classical philosophical treatise), Unamuno grappled with the age-old split of idea and world that Hegel's idealism and Spencer's positivism represent. He clearly wanted to save parts of each approach, and with courageous innocence proposed to give "una explicación lógica de la nociones metafísicas, resolver el valor positivo de las nociones suprasensibles y desarrollar su función lógica."[3] Proceeding in the manner of traditional philosophical exposition, he began by refuting previous arguments with which he did not agree, most notably those of Descartes, Fichte, Krause, Hegel and Spencer. He did accept Hegel's notion of Idea ("todo lo ideal es real y todo lo real ideal. Aceptado" 38), but modified it to say that consciousness is not different from the sum of events and ideas, events related to ideas and these related to events, that is, the sum of everything known: "El punto de partida son los hechos, la representación que dice Schopenhauer. En los hechos nadie duda, podrían decir que son ilusión, pero la ilusión es algo, ¡es ilusión cuando menos!" (20).

Opposing pure rationalism and idealism, he asserted that physical sensations are our basis for knowledge; common sense tells us so: "sostengo y sostendré con el sentido común [here Spencer shows through] *la percepción directa de las cosas* por los sentidos" (28, Unamuno's emphasis). Again following Spencer, he posited a relative relationship between subjects and objects (he would mark Spencer's refutation of Kant's notion of time and space in his copy of the *Essays* [London: Williams and Norgate, 1891, 238]: "indissoluble cohesion between the consciousness of the *self* and an unknown *not-self*, as constituting dictum of consciousness which his is both compelled to accept"). The *hecho* is "subjetivo y objetivo, e interno y externo a la vez" (29), and occurs in the world. This early fragment reveals a very original thinker in the young Unamuno, one who might have had a career in philosophy if the Spanish situation had allowed.

Armando F. Zubizarreta, who first discovered the unfinished treatise and published a summary of it in *Tras las huellas de Unamuno*, treats it as a work deriving from Hegel, but in fact some of its ideas anticipate the phenomenology of Edmund Husserl (e.g., his emphasis on the primacy of the consciousness and his critique of psychologism) and even more strikingly that of Husserl's disciple Maurice Merleau-Ponty (especially his critique of Descartes and his positing the locus of knowledge in perception, or *hecho* in Unamuno's terminology). As did Merleau-Ponty some sixty years later, Unamuno posited a primitive consciousness and a reflexive consciousness (still part of his epistemological baggage in 1911 when he completed *Del sentimiento trágico de la vida*). Like Merleau-Ponty, Unamuno went right to the source of all rationalisms' impetus and confronted Descartes head-on. "El sentido nunca se engaña en su objeto propio," wrote Unamuno refuting Descartes's methodical doubt of sense perception. And he continued, "Es un axioma que delante mío hay un tintero, que lo veo, y que lo veo como lo veo, es decir, que la percepción es evidente por sí misma" (21). His critique of Descartes's idealism, however, does not lie entirely within accepted practices of philosophical argument: "Si llegara alguien que dijera que el tintero sólo estaba en su mente y no fuera, no sabría lo que decía" (22). (Unamuno continued his dialogue with Descartes in *Niebla,* begun in 1907.)

In chapter 10 of the "Filosofía lógica," entitled "El conocer," Unamuno suspended the essay with these tantalizing words: "Aunque esto parezca cuestión ociosa merece fijarse en ella, es clave para resolver más de una pretendida dificultad" (94). Nelson Orringer believes that Unamuno's treatise was thwarted by his attempt to see the mental images of God and the soul (also relativized subjects and objects) as " 'ideas' in Hegel's sense of form or proposition lying beyond common sense."[4] There may be extra-philosophical reasons as well for his abandoning the project. A number of blank pages remained in the notebook he had used to begin his logical philosophy, and, never one to waste money, Unamuno picked up the unused pages to begin a new essay "Sobre el casticismo" (unfortunately not dated). For the moment this essay remained abortive, as Unamuno managed to write only the title and a quotation from Carlyle in English before interrupting the project. Carlyle's words are revealing, and suggest that Unamuno may have abandoned his philosophical treatise as much for reasons of form and general purpose as for the logical impossibility of the philosophical task he had set himself: "The latest Gospel in this world is, Know thy work and do it. 'Know thyself?' long enough has that poor 'self' of thine tormented thee; thou wilt never get to 'know' it, I believe! Think it not thy business, this of knowing thyself; thou art an unknowable individual; know what thou canst work at; and work at it like a Hercules! That will be thy better plan. Th. Carlyle. Past and Present. book third, Chap. XI (III. 11.).".

As we know, the piece on *casticismo* appeared as a series of chapters in *La España Moderna* in 1895, now titled *En torno al casticismo.* Had Unamuno already decided in the late 1880s that his "work" was not that of an idealistic Hegelian system-builder but rather that of a practical thinker whose vocation was to apply his ideas to real human problems in the world around him? Such would seem to be the case, if we can judge by the remainder of his writing career. Never again did he attempt to produce a traditional philosophical treatise, although the temptation did not leave him entirely. In 1892 he declared his intention to write a "Nuevo discurso del método," and in 1913 or 1914 he projected a "Lógica," neither of which exists even in manuscript form. Unamuno's more practical turn first took the form of writing elaborate course outlines for *oposiciones* for chairs in metaphysics. These outlines reveal that he had acquired a broad knowledge of nineteenth-century philosophy, despite the poor preparation he must have received at the university. After finally winning his chair in Greek language and literature at the University of Salamanca in 1891, which gave him a measure of economic stability, Unamuno was able to carve out time from his other activities—teaching, journalistic writing and work for the Socialist party (particularly between the years 1894 and 1897)—to return to his earlier interest of fusing materialism and idealism. In the essays *En torno al casticismo*, he finally found "what he canst work at": not the rigidly prescibed linear form of the treatise but the flexible format of a series of articles that weave around a problem in serpentine-fashion, in this case Spanish *casticismo*.

The articles that form the book double back upon themselves to reveal the problem and its solution in a flowing, circular manner, rather than in orderly segments that build logically one upon the other. Like "Filosofía lógica," *En torno al casticismo* begins by outlining certain fundamental philosophical concepts, but it develops them in a metaphorical, literary fashion.[5] The next step, of course, is the philosophical novel. Within the essays themselves Unamuno defended the use of art as the most direct path to true knowledge. According to Unamuno, we arrive at a revelation of being through love, never through the mind alone: "de aquí brota el arte, arte que vive en todo, hasta en la ciencia, porque en el conocimiento mismo brota del *ser* de que es forma la mente. . . . he pensado en la mayor enseñanza que se saca de los libros de viajes que de las de historia, de la transformación de esta rama del conocimiento en sentido de vida y alma, de cuánto mejor nos revela un siglo sus obras de ficción que sus historias de la vanidad, de los papiros y ladrillos" (24, 33).

The five essays that comprise the work are ostensibly an analysis of the evils plaguing Spain, couched in the broader context of a theory of history that draws on both materialistic determinism and idealistic formulations of the basis of knowledge. The results are fascinating, even if untenable; the sources are too disparate and the methodologies too incompatible. As Herbert Ramsden has shown, the basic analytical methodology derives from Taine, a geographically deterministic approach in which the physical features of the land take precedence over other factors in determining national character.[6] The epistemological center of knowledge is "el nimbo" or "las grandes nebulosas":

En la sucesión de impresiones discretas hay un fondo de continuidad, un nimbo que envuelve a lo precedente con lo subsiguiente, la vida de la mente es como las olas, un eterno crepúsculo que envuelve días y noches, en que se funden las puestas y las auroras de las ideas. Hay verdadero tejido conjuntivo intelectual, un fondo intraconciente en fin. . . . Esa doctrina . . . es la que mejor aclara metafóricamente la constitución de la mente humana. Cada impresión, cada idea, lleva su nimbo, su atmósfera etérea, la impresión de todo lo que la rodea, la idea de las

representaciones concretas de que brotó. Aquellas figurillas de triángulos (figurillas de que hablaba Balmes) no son sino parte del nimbo, de la atmósfera de la
idea, parte del mar de lo intraconciente, raíces del concepto. [*OC* 1: 813-814]

The sources of the ideas in *En torno al casticismo* are diverse. The reference to Balmes (whose works were available to Unamuno in his father's
library and who first introduced him to Descartes and the European
philosophical tradition at age fourteen) and to the triangles remind one of
Descartes's geometrical proof for innate ideas and the existence of God.
In fact, Unamuno's entire description of the way mental life functions is
reminiscent of Descartes's famous wax example. (Recall that in 1892 Unamuno was beginning a "Nuevo discurso del método" while navigating in
"pleno idealismo."[7]) The notion of the interconnectedness of knowledge
echoes Hegel's privileging the social and eternal aspects of human life
over the individual in his/her particularity. Unamuno raised this interconnectedness to the level of history; history was "intrahistoria," a perennial
present that flows ceaselessly, invoking evolutionary principles to achieve
the compatibility of the two. He had seen similar attempts to graft evolutionary determinism and metaphysics in Spencer and evolution and
psychology in William James. On the one hand, Spain has a *tradición
eterna*, but that *tradición* can only survive if crossbred with other European
strains to infuse it with new vigor in the name of progress. The language
of *En torno al casticismo* is heavily interlarded with evolutionary (biological) metaphors and analogies, but continuity seems always to dominate
over change in Unamuno's scheme.

By 1907 when he began his second comic-burlesque philosophical
novel *Niebla*, Unamuno was ready to laugh at his notions of the cosmic
nublo. He was already mocking Hegel's absolute idealism in *En torno al
casticismo*, even though it informs the epistemology of those essays. His
gentle critique of the German thinker in *En torno al casticismo* foreshadows his more pungently ironic stance of *Amor y pedagogía:* "[Hegel] [c]om-
prendió que el mundo de la ciencia son formas enchufadas unas en otras,
formas de formas y formas de estas formas en proceso inacabable, y quiso
levantarnos al cénit del cielo de nuestra razón y desde la forma suprema
hacernos descender a la realidad, que iría purificándose y abriéndose a
nuestros ojos, racionalizándose. Este sueño del Quijote de la filosofía ha
dado alma a muchas almas, aunque le pasó lo que al baron de Munch-
hausen, que quería sacarse del pozo tirándose de las orejas."[8]

In 1900, five years after the publication of this heroic attempt to reconcile the irreconcilable readings in philosophy, biology and psychology
that had consumed him for almost twenty years,[9] and with a major spir-

itual crisis conquered, Unamuno felt the need to purge himself of his former preoccupations and put them in proper perspective in a comic-burlesque-tragic-ironic-satiric novel. His *Tres ensayos* (1900) announced the new Unamuno, who had given up on the notions of universal spirit and collective social action, but he rejected his earlier practice of exploring his ideas through fiction as he had in *Paz en la guerra* (that he did have ideas to explore is evident in the projected *Tratado del amor de Dios*). He indicated to Jiménez Ilundain that he wished to avoid using his most intimate thoughts for novel writing as Huysmans had done in *Au Rebours*.[10] His own new approach (as he wrote to Rodó) would include distance and iconoclasm, a *desahogo* couched in a humoristic genre little cultivated in Spain.[11] This unusual genre gave him the opportunity to satirize the contradictions and logical difficulties that the philosophical treatise, or even the looser format of the essays *En torno al casticismo*, could not adequately circumscribe.

Perhaps none of Unamuno's novels is more ambiguous and complex in its philosophcial content than *Amor y pedagogía*, coming as it does at a moment when Unamuno was shifting his allegiances from science and idealism to the antirationalism that marked the rest of his writing career. Manuel García Blanco traces the genesis and progress of the novel, composed in a shorter time than many of his works.[12] In fact, one senses a certain urgency about the composition of *Amor y pedagogía*. In a November 3, 1900, letter to Francisco Giner de los Ríos, Unamuno wrote that he had to suspend work on the "novela pedagógica-humorística," in which his goal was to "*fundir*, fundir y no mezclar, elementos grotescos y trágicos, y tal vez le ponga a modo de epílogo un ensayo sobre lo grotesco como cara de lo trágico."[13] But he was anxious to get back to it, and on December 12, 1900, he announced to Juan Arzadun that the novel was finished, although he would spend some time polishing it. The polishing may have been more than a few cosmetic touches, as Unamuno wrote to José Enrique Rodó on December 13 that being named rector that autumn was ill-timed because he was deeply involved in writing a novel.

One of the projects Unamuno set aside in order to devote all of his spare time from university duties to *Amor y pedagogía* was a series of *Diálogos filosóficos*, in which he planned to "dejar . . . mi alma, el impulso negador y nihilista de mi inteligencia ultra-lógica, post-kantiana, y el impulso afirmador de mi voluntad, que quiere forzar a mi mente a que crea."[14] Eight months earlier, he had confided to the same correspondent that he wanted to fuse science and art, thinking and feeling.[15] It appears that he found it easier to carry out these projects in the novel form, which allowed him to "verter una porción de cosas que se me cocían dentro" and

to express "ciertas crudezas."[16] Some of the things that were stewing inside him were anger over his treatment at the hands of critics like Clarín
(an acknowledged Krausist) and González Serrano (a Krausopositivist),
and he was increasingly discontent with both idealism and positivism that
did not meet his philosophical needs. *Amor y pedagogía* is a kind of exorcism of the Spencerian and Hegelian ghosts still haunting Unamuno's intellectual dwelling space.

The radical shift in approach suited several of Unamuno's other goals
as well. He was eager for wider acceptance of his work, and, while *Paz en
la guerra* had sold well, he was disappointed at its critical reception by
people he admired.[17] Likewise, in its journalistic form *En torno al casticismo* did not bring him the fame he desired; in fact, it garnered him the
label of "conservative" from critics such as Maeztu.[18] To perform the novelistic exorcism and to improve his novel's reception, Unamuno drew
upon the techniques of several earlier philosophical novels: Voltaire's
broad satire of Leibniz in *Candide*, Carlyle's subtle and complex irony in
Sartor Resartus, and Dickens's sentimental satire of utilitarianism in *Hard
Times*, all enormously popular efforts. In 1900 Unamuno was translating
Carlyle's *The French Revolution* for Lázaro Galdeano's *La España
Moderna*,[19] and he had decided to devote himself to reading Kierkegaard.
Both Carlyle and Kierkegaard had used fiction for a philosophical purpose; the success of their methods could not have been lost on Unamuno,
but what most attracted Unamuno at this point was probably Kierkegaard's critique of Hegel's system, which privileges the social over the individual (rather than the Dane's existential methodology, which has more
in common with parts of *Niebla* and the later novels). Carlyle's ambiguous
treatment of the Germanic-style clothes philosopher Teufelsdreuckh supplied a more immediate model for a fictional personification of Unamuno's critique of Hegel.[20]

Unamuno now couched the disassociation he had found endemic to
Spanish culture in *En torno al casticismo* (the division between science,
idea and sentiment) in terms of an extended allegory in which each character, living in a private sphere and unable to communicate effectively
with the others, represents one of the approaches to life. The central al-
legorical figure pits Avito Carrascal (Form) against his wife Marina (Matter). The philosophical references are wide-ranging and diverse. Paul
Olson is surprised that Unamuno mentions only Molière's *Les Femmes sa-
vantes* as his source for the Matter-Form allegory, as Artistotle had endowed man and woman with these philosophical categories in *Physics*, I,
9, as did Plato in *Timaeus*, 50 c.[21] Carlos Blanco Aguinaga's work on Unamuno suggested to Olson that Hegel could also have inspired Unamuno's

associating matter and form with a male-female dichtomy, as the German philosopher identified woman with nature and man with history. Other sources not mentioned by either Unamuno or his critics are John Stuart Mill and Thomas Carlyle, whom Unamuno was doubtless reading in the original English in the 1890s, when his English competency allowed him to dispense with a dictionary. Unamuno marked the following passage in his personal copy of Mill's *System of Logic. Raciocinative and Inductive:* "that *form* combined with other *matter* does convey more."[22] (Mill, the quintessence of logic, who had managed to reach the end of his life without losing his childhood faith in God, was a great mystery to Unamuno.) Additional evidence for Unamuno's having recalled the passage in Mill, who insisted on the deductive nature of science, is the arch-positivist Avito's decision to marry deductively. (In *Niebla*, Avito has returned to the church, out of despair over the suicide of his son, but does not necessarily recover his childhood faith.) In *Sartor Resartus*, Carlyle wrote that "Matter exists only spiritually, and to represent some Idea, and *body* it forth."[23] Marina is the spiritual "matter" to which Avito plans to give his idealistic form in the creation of the perfect child, a genius to be raised in an ideally preconceived, rational scientific manner.[24]

Like Voltaire's Dr. Pangloss, who represents the ridiculous extremes of Leibniz's philosophical optimism, Avito and Marina are respectively absurd embodiments of science and nature (tinged with religious faith). They are summaries, composites, representing the tragic dichotomy between reason and faith, the schism forged by Descartes, who initiated modern philosophy by severing mind and world, philosophy and theology. Avito is a metaphor for the branch of European thought spawned by the seventeeth-century mathematician that views all aspects life in terms of weights and measures. Rational idealism, the other branch equally attributable to Descartes, is embodied in Avito's friend, Fulgencio Entrambosmares. Spencer, Mill and all those who rely on materialistic, evolutionary or biological conceptions of the world (although Malthus is the only specific thinker mentioned, 320-323) are the targets of Unamuno's satire in Avito Carrascal, whose scientific child-raising project leads to the suicide of his progeny. The project is doomed from the beginning as Avito switches from his *a priori* plan to marry Leoncia, finding himself attracted to Marina instead. In direct oppostion to Avito's scientific plans for him, their child Apolodoro shows early signs of imagination and creativity. Biology has overcome pedagogy.[25]

Hegel and all grand system-building philosophers are the objects of parody in Don Fulgencio Entrambosmares, whose counsel Avito requests for his experiment in child-rearing.[26] It is ironic that the positivist Avito seeks support in Don Fulgencio, whose rational system-building is just as distant from real life as his own. Don Fulgencio is writing a treatise entitled *Ars Magna Combinatoria* (loudly echoing Leibniz) in which he demonstrates his conviction that philosophy is nothing more than a combinatory act carried to extremes. He takes what he considers the four fundamental ideas—life and death in the real order and rights and duty in the ideal order—and combines them in every possible way: "derecho a la vida, derecho a la muerte, el derecho al derecho mismo y el derecho al deber; el deber a la vida, el deber a la muerte, el deber al derecho, la muerte de la muerte misma y la muerte de la vida. ¡Qué fuente de reflexiones, el derecho al derecho, el deber al deber, la muerte de la muerte y la vida de la vida!" (*OC* 2: 337). (Echoes of the imaginative combinations assayed by the Krausists are evident here.) While every indication points to Unamuno's having added the treatise on origami by Don Fulgencio at the end of the novel in order to meet his editor's length requirements,[27] he was not one to sacrifice the integrity of his work. First, he had Carlyle's example of Teufelsdreukh's "Philosophy of Clothes" in *Sartor Resartus; Sartor* is quoted in the treatise on origami. The essay on Japanese paper folding gave Unamuno another opportunity to mock Darwinistic categories and to substantiate Avito's trust in Don Fulgencio as a positivist mentor of very dubious merits. Fulgencio (whose symbolic surname means "between the two seas") embodies (in ironic fashion) all the philosophical orientations Unamuno was trying to weld together in his *En torno al casticismo.*

If *Candide*'s broad satire in the form of Dr. Pangloss's metaphysico-theologo-cosmologo-logy (asserting that there is no effect without a cause) provided a model for the destructive aspects of Unamuno's treatment of Avito's and Don Fulgencio's philosophical positions, Carlyle's *Sartor Resartus* is much closer to the subtle and ironic vision of Don Fulgencio. Voltaire's purpose was to destroy the position of a known philosopher (Leibniz's optimistic "this is the best of all possible worlds") by placing an oversimplified and exaggerated statement of his ideas in the mouths of ridiculous characters, then contradicting the philosophy at every turn by the events that take place in the novel. Without such specific reference to identifiable philosophers, Unamuno used some of the same strategy, but he extended Voltaire's diversion of fiction to a philosophical purpose. Since the enlightenment thinker's mission was simply to ridicule one philosophy, he could allow himself the luxury of setting the characters in motion for a genuine adventure story that engages the reader on its own terms. The vicissitudes of Candide and Cunegunde's lives are proof of

Pangloss's mistaken notion of the world, and the reader can easily forget the philosophical message of the novel for long stretches and become immersed in the characters' fortunes, or rather misfortunes.

No such immersion is possible in *Amor y pedagogía*, partly because Unamuno complicated the philosophical situation. Avito is a positivist who thinks he is following in the footsteps of his mentor Fulgencio Entrambosmares, but Fulgencio's philosophical program is enigmatic. He may at one time have been the positivist Avito believes him to be, but he is also writing the *Ars magna* in the vein of German idealism, and he indulges constantly in aphorisms in the style of Nietzsche or Pascal. Fulgencio's character is just as ambiguous as his philosophical position and method. He takes himself seriously as a philosopher, but he does not take philosophy seriously in the same way that Avito does. He does not let his philosophical pursuits dictate the way he lives his life, and thus he escapes Avito's tragic end. Unamuno was ultimately parodying all abstract approaches to life, none of which is any more adequate than Avito's rigid and simplistic positivism.

The Carlylean model for Entrambosmares is not surprising. After all, Carlyle lived and worked in that locus between Romanticism and Victorianism that had so many parallels with Unamuno's turn-of-the-century space. Teetering between positivism and spiritualism, both are ambiguous and ambivalent places that fiction handles better than the essay, as both Carlyle and Unamuno recognized. And both writers strove to deride excessive materialism or positivism in favor of a position that included a trascendental element (Carlyle's "everlasting yea" and Marina's and Apolodoro's dreams of eternity); in doing so, they both made a distinction between form and spirit. In *Sartor* this dichotomy is represented in clothing, or the exterior, as opposed to interior imagination; in *Amor y pedagogía* it is couched in the two abstracts of the title and in the narrator's nicknames for Apolodoro's parents—*Forma* and *Materia*.

However serious the philosophical enterprise in these works (and I think Carlyle's is more serious, or at least more constructive than Unamuno's), Teufelsdreuckh and Fulgencio are treated with narrative distance and ambiguity; their natures are a combination of the solemn and the ridiculous, and their treatises (included at length in the novels), while on seemingly trivial subjects—clothes and origami—are simultaneously a parody of materialist philosophies and a sincere maneuver to lure the reader into a new way of viewing the world. However, in Carlyle's version of the philosophical fiction (it would be a mistake to call *Sartor Resartus* a true novel), the life of the character is a pretext to engage in discursive philosophizing. Consistent representation of the fictional world breaks down in numerous places to allow the editor to expound on Teufelsdreukh's philosophy of clothes. As Unamuno would in later novels, Carlyle used fiction in *Sartor* to bring forth a new—though not necessarily original—philosophical position rather than to ridicule an existing one as did Voltaire.

Unlike Carlyle, Unamuno managed to maintain intact the cocoon of the fictional world by embedding the philosophical discourse in the speech of his characters rather than in the narrative commentary. He never lost sight of the lives of the characters in order to engage in philosophical discourse as did Carlyle in *Sartor.* Dialogue differentiates Unamuno's version of the philosophical novel and maintains it within the parameters of the novelistic genre when Carlyle's and Kierkegaard's fictionalized philosphical works must be excluded from it. Dialogue attempts to bridge a gap between two people of different mindsets, but it rarely achieves its goal, leaving room for misunderstanding, misinterpretation or partial communication. Unamuno employed dialogue's asymmetry and indeterminacy to great advantage. In *Amor y pedagogía*, the dialogue creates an unsettling quality, a lack of certainty. Avito misunderstands Marina, Apolodoro and Fulgencio; Apolodoro fails to comprehend Avito, Fulgencio and Clarita, and Clarita misunderstands Apolodoro, ad infinitum. The first meeting of Avito and Fulgencio is an excellent example of the ongoing miscommunications that inform the novel's action:

> Don Avito queda confundido ante esta profundidad del hombre, y como al entrar en el despacho le salta a la vista de lo que 'el fin del hombre es la ciencia', vuélvese al maestro y decide preguntarle:
>   —¿Y el fin de la ciencia?
>   —¡Catalogar el Universo!
>   —¿Para qué?
>   —Para devolvérselo a Dios en orden, con un inventario razonado de lo existente...
>   —A Dios... a Dios... —murmura Carrascal.
>   —¡A Dios, sí, a Dios! —repite Fulgencio con enigmática sonrisa.
>   —¿Pero es que ahora cree usted en Dios? —pregunta con alarma el otro.
>   —Mientras Él crea en mí... —y levantando episcopalmente la mano derecha, añade—: Dispense un poco, Avito. [*OC* 2: 338-339]

If Avito had perceived the ironic tone with which his idol pronounced these sentences, he would have spared himself and his son a great deal of anguish.

Unamuno held, in common with Carlyle, the puppeteer's view of his characters, and it is here that the novel fails. In his essay "Maese Pedro

Carlyle," Unamuno likens the English writer to the puppeteer in *Don Quixote* who so infuriates the Don with his authorial intrusions. Unamuno did not reveal his hand so directly, but his characters are clearly born of the wooden stuff of ideas, designed to confront one another in a kind of philosophical Punch and Judy show. Unamuno even manipulated Carlyle himself, calling him a realist (contradicting Taine, whose designation of Carlyle as an idealist misled Unamuno for a time) in a clear attempt to justify his own tenuous claim to realism. He also used Carlylean language (clothes and tailors) in explaining his attitude toward ideas. Tailors, he wrote to Juan Arzadun, mask and hide our personalities. The necktie represents the greatest tyranny of all (one wonders if *Sartor* was the inspiration for Unamuno's eschewing the typical dress for men in favor of the clergyman's collar that became his trademark): "quiero que la prenda se ciña a la dimensión real. . . . Yo hago con las ideas lo que con los trajes; los uso mientras me sirven. Cuando los veo ajados por el tiempo, los doy vuelta o los regalo a un pobre."[28] If he did not give his former allegiances to materialism and idealism to the poor, he did turn them around and put them to another use in *Amor y pedagogía*.

The reception of his comic-burlesque novel could not have been any more pleasing to Unamuno than was the critical reaction to *Paz en la guerra*, and he did not complete another full-length narration until 1913. Zubizarreta (81) remarks on how profoundly Unamuno's friends' comments affected him, and Mario Valdés suggests that Unamuno interrupted work on *Niebla* in 1907 because he was overwhelmed by the vast number of changes suggested by friends. Unamuno wrote to Rodó on May 15 of 1902 (just as *Amor y pedagogía* was appearing in the bookstores) that he was very anxious to know how the novel would be received. He did not have to wait long. Jiménez Ilundain wrote on May 22 that *Amor y pedagogía* had affected him so adversely that he had had to lay it aside until morning. At first he thought he had gotten indigestion from dinner, but he discovered the next day that his distaste for the book was independent of his digestive process. In a number of letters to his friends while writing the novel, Unamuno emphasized its comic-burlesque aspects; Unamuno considered himself a humorist and complained bitterly to Camille Pitollet that he had destroyed one of his most cherished illusions in denying him the title.[29] Joan Maragall also published a piece on *Amor y pedagogía*, and he wrote to Unamuno privately, summarizing his impressions: "En general no me gusta la mezcla de lo artístico y lo filosófico; siempre resulta algo híbrido. Y, sin embargo, es tan de nuestro tiempo."[30]

One wonders if Unamuno would have pursued his early inclinations toward pure philosophy if he, like Santayana (who was born in Madrid in

1863 one year before Unamuno and who experienced many of the same philosophical influences), had escaped the confused and confusing ideological milieu of the Spain of his times. Of course, we will never know, but in some ways Unamuno's work, if more heterogeneous, eclectic and unclassifiable than Santayana's, is more interesting to us in our postmodern era as Santayana's begins to lose its impact. The philosophical ambivalence and generic hybridization that *Amor y pedagogía* represents continue to attract a substantial amount of critical attention.[31]

In chapter 5, I will return to Unamuno and *Niebla*, his last novelistic effort to confront idealism head-on, but in the following chapter, I continue with an account of the early philosophical novels of his cogenerationists Pío Baroja and José Martínez Ruiz.

3

BAROJA: A SOLUTION
TO THE PROBLEM OF WILL

While neither Baroja nor Martínez Ruiz was as penetrating a student of philosophy as was Unamuno, their novels of 1902—*Camino de perfección* and *La voluntad*—are fueled by the same triangle of religious faith, science and idealistic philosophy that undergirds *Amor y pedagogía*. Baroja's and Martínez Ruiz's first philosophical novels are interrelated, stimulated by their friendship, mutual experiences, philosophical reading and conversation (and perhaps envy, at least on Martínez Ruiz's part). Not coincidentally the protagonists of both novels are out-of-step with the Spanish bourgeois milieu; both try to find solace for their intellectual and artistic souls within a labyrinth of Spanish backwardness: bigotry, intellectual stagnation and unenlightened relations with women. In both novels mysticism is a metaphor for what is best and worst about traditional Spain. Fernando Ossorio's personal quest, his *camino de perfección*, encompasses a period of religious mysticism to end in secular marriage. Justina, although unsuited for the religious life, takes the veil at her uncle's urging and dies in her attempt to achieve spiritual perfection. In each book religious faith, mysticism and Catholic dogma confront secular philosophy, particularly the ideas of Schopenhauer and Nietzsche.

José Martínez Ruiz and Baroja both began writing for the periodical press at about the same time in the early to mid-1890s, but Baroja followed his medical career somewhat more seriously than Martínez Ruiz studied the law. The latter heard the call to professional writing much earlier, and although he was some nine years younger than Unamuno, his rise to national recognition (infamy in his case) was almost simultaneous with that of the Basque writer, whose *Paz en la guerra* of 1897 was his first widely read work. In that same year Martínez Ruiz also gained the notice (or more accurately the rancor) of the literary establishment when he published, under the title *Charivari*, the journal he had kept of his first experiences in the Madrid literary world, including notes on the scandalous rumors and gossip circulating about several of its members.

In 1900 Martínez Ruiz introduced himself to Baroja, who had just published his first book, *Vidas sombrías*, to resounding critical acclaim. Baroja and Martínez Ruiz immediately became friends, as they shared interests in the political and social problems of Spain and in making a name for themselves as writers. Doubtless they reminisced about their student days in Valencia, where they had each come in contact with anarchist ideology. (Although Baroja and Martínez Ruiz coincided at the University of Valencia, they apparently never met there; the letter from Baroja to Martínez Ruiz dated 1893 is clearly a mistake for 1903.[1]) They also endured similar struggles and failures in journalism during the 1890s—the hostile older generation, the difficulties with editors, and the arbitrariness of criticism. Both had experienced painful rejections and ousters from journals for which they wrote.

Important works of philosophy became available in Spanish translation shortly before or during the first year of their friendship—Henri Lichtenberger's book on Nietzsche's philosophy (in French, 1898), Schopenhauer's *El mundo como voluntad y como representación* (1898 or 1899), Unamuno's translation of Schopenhauer's *Sobre la voluntad de la naturaleza* (1900, copy in Martínez Ruiz's library) and Nietzsche's *Así habló Zarathustra* (1900) and *El origen de la tragedia* (the edition in Martínez Ruiz's library, translated by Luis J. García de Luna, has no date, but it was published by B. Rodríguez Serra before he died on December 21, 1902; Martínez Ruiz also owned a French version that probably predates the Spanish version). Unlike Unamuno, whose talent for languages was prodigious, Baroja and Martínez Ruiz were limited to French and Spanish.

Doubtless these two friends, who saw each other on nearly daily walks in Madrid and at *tertulias*, discussed the ideas of these works (the relative merits of the will and the intellect, the nature of reality, and others), ideas that became the center of their 1902 novels. Echoes of Lichtenberger's interpretations of Nietzsche turn up in both *Camino de perfección* and *La voluntad:* that the free spirit is an intellectual pessimist, that Christianity invented the "soul," "spirit" and "free will," that Kant's notion of the noumena and the categorical imperative are Christian dogma, and that Nietzsche is less original than supposed, having derived much from Stirner and Kierkegaard. Both men introduced an ironic (even satirical) perspective on philosophy into their fiction shortly after they became friends. In the background of the two works one can hear echoes of heated café discussions on the "world as image," "the strong conquering the weak" and "the eternal return," laced with the sardonic wit for which Baroja in particular was known. (The correspondence from Baroja to Martínez Ruiz during the early years of the century [available in the Casa-Museo Azorín in Monóvar] indicates that they read to each other from work in progress; writing and café talk intertwine). It has been asserted by critics that *Camino de perfección* and *La voluntad* exhibit an uncritical incorporation of the ideas of Nietzsche and Schopenhauer, but the novels are, in fact, a forum for an ironized and dialogized assessment of the contradictions in the philosophical positions of these and other philosophers.

Galdós's play *Electra*, which created a sensation at its opening in January 1901 by dramatizing the Church's power (in this case over the lives of young women), confirmed the Nietzschean call to slay dogma and provided a further stimulus to the incipient novelists Baroja and Martínez Ruiz. The play, based on the now famous case of Adelaida Ubao, who was persuaded by a priest to enter a convent against her parents' wishes and perhaps against her own inclinations, struck a particularly responsive chord in the minds of intellectuals critical of the Restoration government and its protective attitude toward the Church. Both Martínez Ruiz and Baroja were present at the opening of the play, participated in the intellectual celebrations of the play's message (including the founding of the journal *Electra*), and wrote reviews of it for newspapers (although Martínez Ruiz's reaction is more equivocal than Baroja's for reasons I speculated upon in chapter 1).

In 1900-1901, when Baroja and Martínez Ruiz began writing their first "philosophical" novels about young men who lack ideological and practical direction, all these undercurrents—resentment of the older generation and the bourgeois establishment, a critical attitude toward Chruch dogma and mysticism, and a sympathetic reading of Schopenhauer and Nietzsche—fused in a new and powerful way. Baroja's novel was an immediate success, first in serial form in *La Opinión* (April-October 1901) and then in book form in March 1902, hailed by numerous intellectuals who gathered at a banquet to honor the novel and its author.

Martínez Ruiz made three attempts to incorporate the same material into novels—*Diario de un enfermo, Antonio Azorín* and the third and most successful, *La voluntad*.[2] Dissatisfied with his own efforts to match his friend's success, Martinez Ruiz truncated his first two attempts; both *Diario de un enfermo* and *Antonio Azorín* have an unfinished quality about them. That Baroja was much on his mind as he composed the three narratives is evident in several respects. The Basque writer appears as the thinly disguised character Olaiz in *Diario de un enfermo* (1901) and again in *La voluntad*, both as Olaiz and as a character named Baroja, who recieves several letters from a character named Martínez Ruiz at the end of the novel. In the latter work Yuste quotes a passage from Baroja's *La casa de Aizgorri* to illustrate his idea of exemplary prose style. The banquet organized by Martínez Ruiz in March of 1902 to celebrate the appearance of *Camino de perfección* is reenacted in *La voluntad;* there are also echoes of

Silvestre Paradox in the inventor Daza's attempt to launch a torpedo and in the Pickwickian subtitle of *Confesiones de un pequeño filósofo:* "pequeño libro en que se habla de este peregrino Señor." Begun before *La voluntad* and completed in 1903, *Antonio Azorín* ends with the first-person, epistolary format with which Baroja concluded *Camino de perfección*. That Martínez Ruiz was driven by a desire for fame and perhaps saw in his friend a model for achieving it is corroborated by the first-person narrator in *Diario de un enfermo* (who is envious of a friend's successful play) and by Maeztu's commentary on Martínez Ruiz's grandstanding in his article on *Electra* in *Madrid Cómico*.[3]

The interpersonal references are not limited to Martínez Ruiz's works; in *Camino de perfección*, Ossorio was educated at the Piarist school in Yécora (Yecla), as was Martínez Ruiz, and he travels to Yécora in the penultimate stage of his *camino*. Baroja had spent several days with Martínez Ruiz in his native Alicante (especially Monóvar, Yecla and environs). *Camino de perfección*'s brief description of the school and Ossorio's education in Yécora probably reflect that trip and Martínez Ruiz's account of his youthful experiences. Martínez Ruiz developed similar material about the school and his own education there in *Confesiones de un pequeño filósofo*. Both Baroja and Martínez Ruiz included conversations with Piarists in their novels. Material from a trip the two authors took together to Toledo surfaces in articles for journals and in important sections of their 1902 novels (Martínez Ruiz also used it in *Diario de un enfermo*), but in each case they report the events as a solitary journey. *Camino de perfección* and *La voluntad* both contain descriptions of paintings to underscore certain philosophical and ideological positions, a practice doubtless inspired by the authors' reading of decadent literature (e.g., Huysmans's *Au Rebours*, a very popular novel with intellectuals in *fin-de-siècle* Spain, incorporates art work). They both include philosophical conversations between characters on the nature of matter and its eternal preservation or dissolution, perhaps inspired by Nietzsche's notion of the eternal return, as well as by Lucretius, Guyau and others.

An example of the "cross-pollenization" that occurred between the two authors is the similar resolutions of their protagonists' lives. In *Diario de un enfermo*, the character attempts to overcome his metaphysical malaise by marrying (there are certain Nietzschean anti-intellectual overtones in the narrator's vitalism). But the solution is not permanent; the wife dies, and he commits suicide. Baroja's Ossorio in *Camino de perfección* (also perhaps following a Nietzschean program, though arrived at much more circuitously) marries, has a child and seems to achieve a kind of happiness and stability. Completed after the publication of *Camino de perfec-*

ción, *La voluntad* has Antonio Azorín return to his village and marry, but as a consequence he loses his status as a thinker and writer. Baroja's Ossorio recognizes that village life can be disastrous for the will ("allí [in Yécora] su voluntad desmayada se rebelara y buscara una vida enérgica, o que concluyera de postrarse aceptando definitivamente una existencia monótona y vulgar"[4]), but he does not succumb. It is no accident that Martínez Ruiz writes to Baroja (as one fictional character to another) at the end of *La voluntad* describing Antonio Azorín's monotonous and vulgar existence. The intertextual dialogue between Baroja and Martínez Ruiz did not end there, as Baroja's *El árbol de la ciencia* resurrected the character with *fin-de-siècle* malaise, this time returning to Martínez Ruiz's solution of 1901, in which the character commits suicide after the death of his wife. (Ironically, Azorín suppressed this ending when the novel was reprinted for the first time in the 1946 edition of his *Obras completas*).

Azorín wrote indefatigably about Baroja, producing a review nearly every time the Basque writer published a book. The theme of many of these reviews is "¿Qué es la filosofía de Baroja?" and although he never solved the riddle (no one has), he did argue against Baroja's real or imagined negative view of the intellect: "no, no y no. La inteligencia no es enemiga de la vida."[5] When Baroja began the series *Memorias de un hombre de acción* based on his relative Aviraneta, Azorín recognized that the philosophy of the Nietzschean man of action was now losing prestige, and he astutely asked if Aviraneta is a "superhombre" or a "serpihombre." Again defending the thinking man, he affirmed that Goethe, Spinoza and Kant were also men of action.[6]

More than Unamuno or Martínez Ruiz, Baroja preferred nature to intellectual ruminations about it. Unamuno's Hegelian idealism was tempered first by Spencer and later by Kierkegaard, but he never really abandoned his search for the transcendental. Baroja, while attracted to metaphysics, had his feet firmly planted in materialistic ground; his metaphysics and positivism were mixed in inverse proportions to Unamuno's. While very different in their details, the resulting philosophical novels have some general similarities. Baroja, like Unamuno, borrowed widely from diverse genres to accommodate his heterogeneous and conflicting philosophical interests. Silvestre Paradox's *mixtificaciones* are no more bizarre than are Baroja's own novelistic inventions, and any attempt to derive a coherent philosophical position from his novels, as Azorín and others have done, is quite futile.

Baroja also wrote a few pieces on Martínez Ruiz, particularly in the early days of their friendship. Baroja waxed less enthusiastic about Martínez Ruiz than did the Levantine writer about him. He wrote in *El Globo* (no. 8, 959 [June 15, 1900]) that he was disappointed in *El alma castellana*, and his prologue to *La fuerza del amor* (1901) states that this theatrical piece does not reflect the best of Martínez Ruiz. The two men, of very different temperaments and philosophical orientation, played off against each other both in real life and in their early philosophical fictions. Rather than having plagiarized Baroja's *Camino de perfección* in *La voluntad* (as has been suggested[7]), the Alicantine writer's novel constitutes a formal answer to his Basque friend's narrative. Martínez Ruiz's formation in Taine and the social scientists tinted his vision with a much more deterministic hue. His character is overwhelmed by his circumstances, while Baroja, perhaps more readily accepting of Nietzsche's assurances of the power of the will, allowed his character to overcome the obstacles of his environment. In Baroja's 1902 novel, environment seems to shape character, but new environments supersede previous ones, and ultimately individual will defeats environmental factors. Both novels employ an array of narrative devices that confound any attempt to distill definitive philosophical positions.[8]

Baroja's library, though unfortunately not open to the public, has been reviewed in part by José Alberich, who gives statistics on the books it contains, grouping them by disciplines. Alberich's list reveals a wide and eclectic reading in metaphysics.[9] Without consulting publication dates and marginal notations, it is impossible to determine when Baroja read any particular philosophical work, but his early journal articles divulge some of the thinkers with whom he was familiar in the 1890s. For example, the pieces on Russian literature, written at age seventeen for *La Unión Liberal*, reveal a (probably second-hand) knowledge of Schopenhauer, whom he categorized as a pessimist, Büchner (identified as the author of *Fuerza y materia* and as a naturalist), Max Stirner (described as the author of *Único y propiedad*, on whose philosophical system the modern Russian nihilists based their passion for destruction), and Turgenev, Bakunin and others (classified as nihilists). By his own admission, he was a desultory medical student, preferring to devote his time to reading cheap editions of nineteenth-century fiction and philosophy. By the time he was well along in his medical studies at the universities of Madrid and Valencia, he had read at least Kant, Fichte and Schopenhauer in French and Spanish translations. In *Familia, infancia y juventud* Baroja declared that he read Schopenhauer in the third year of medical school (1889), and in *Juventud, egolatría* he wrote that "El leer el libro *Parerga y Paralipómena* (de Schopenhauer) me reconcilió con la filosofía. Después compré, en francés, *La crítica de la razón pura*, *El mundo como voluntad y como representación* y algunas otras obras" (*OC* 5: 185).

In Valencia, where he completed his medical degree between 1891 and 1893, Baroja, like Martínez Ruiz, came in contact with anarchist social and political theory, although he did not write political or social tracts in this period as did his friend. His interests tended more toward metaphysics than political or social theory. In *Juventud y egolatría* he could declare that "La metafísica es lo que más me atrae" (*OC* 5: 185). He considered *El mundo como voluntad y representación*, along with the *Summa Theologica* of Saint Thomas Aquinas, Descartes's *Discourse on Method* and Kant's *Critique of Pure Reason* as the great philosophical treatises of all time (*OC* 7: 484). Despite his admiration for some of the major idealist thinkers, he was thoroughly unimpressed with Krausism. Referring to a self-styled Krausist in Cestona, where he briefly practiced medicine, Baroja wrote "Supongo que cuando estudió en Madrid cogería ese sarampión germánico de ínfima clase,"[10] and he described the followers of the Krausist Salmerón as "hombres graves, barbas negras, miradas sobrias, aire profético" (*OC* 7: 572).

The two books that he read again and again and that influenced him profoundly were Schopenhauer's *El mundo como voluntad y como representación* and Claude Bernard's *Introducción al estudio de la medicina experimental:* "Para mí, Schopenhauer y Claudio Bernard eran los iniciadores de dos caminos teóricos que me hubiera gustado recorrer y para las cuales no tenía itinerario: el de la ciencia, para el que me faltaba protección, y el de la filosofía, para el que no estaba bien preparado" (*OC* 7: 988). He attempted to combine these two philosophically opposed interests in his doctoral dissertation on pain (*El dolor* [*estudio psico-físico*]), written in 1893 and published in 1896. Schopenhauer's notion that pain is the source of knowledge lies at the heart of his thesis, but he diverged in very important ways from Schopenhauer's premises, eschewing a metaphysical approach in favor of a physiological one: "el dolor se ha considerado más como idea transcendental que como fenómeno; por eso ha escapado su esencia de las investigaciones de los pensadores, que armados de razones metafísicas han querido buscarla. Si el dolor como *noumeno* o cosa en sí, no se descompone por los reactivos más sensibles de la célula nerviosa, ni se aísla al pasar por el filtro cerebral de más pequeños poros, en cambio como fenómeno permite el análisis" (*OC* 8: 357). Rather than knowledge promoting pain, as the German thinker would have it, pain, for Baroja, was the locus of knowledge; priority rests with the sensorial.

Baroja's scientific formation and his virtually unwavering Darwin-informed belief in the possibility of progress underlay his metaphysics and his ethics: "creo que hay una fuerza superior a mis instintos, y esta fuerza es la Evolución. . . . el resultado inconveniente de la masa humana

que quiere mejorar no sabemos para que. . . . todo precepto moral que
ayude la evolución, es bueno; todo precepto que la dificulte, es malo."[11]
Not even art can escape science; in a rather inelegant allegory of the modern relationship between art and science (published in *La Vida Literaria*
in March 1899), art is an aging bull and science a young cow, from which
art attempts unsuccessfully to hide: "Así el Arte trata de huir de su com-
pañera la Ciencia, la robusta vaca protectora, con las ubres henchidas de
jugo vital y la Ciencia le sigue y le sigue y le encuentra siempre."[12] José
Antonio Maravall calls Baroja's position "biologismo de carácter filosófico."[13] Neither a narrow positivism nor a pure abstract metaphysics
sufficiently explains Baroja's position, as Maravall has pointed out: "su
obra está anclada en las corrientes de vitalismo que había de trascender
ese positivismo un tanto estrecho—y que a Baroja en ocasiones no deja
de parecerle irrespirable: recuérdese su adversión hacia Taine—. Ob-
servemos una curiosa diferencia entre las fuentes de sus ideas de tipo
científico y sus lecturas filosóficas—Kant, Fichte, Nietzsche, Schopenhauer, Bergson—."[14]

By 1899, when he had become familiar with some of Nietzsche's
ideas, he expanded his basic notion of pain, now seeing it not only as the
origin of knowledge, but as the force behind human progress: "El dolor es
una fuerza impulsora del progreso. La Humanidad como un caballo fog-
oso, corre en busca del ideal. . . . 'El árbol de la sabiduría no es el árbol
de la vida', dijo Byron" (*OC* 6: 865-866). This shift in emphasis from
Schopenhauer's metaphysics to a materialist physiology and then back to
positivistic metaphysics in the years just prior to launching his literary career and producing his first philosophical novel, *Camino de perfección*, has
not been taken into consideration in studies of the philosophical content
of that novel, which see it as based almost exlusively on either Nordau,
Schopenhauer or Nietzsche.[15]

Baroja's first contacts with Nietzsche have been well-documented, so
I review them only briefly here. In a February 15, 1899, article, Baroja
lambasted Nietzsche's egoist ethics and cited his lack of originality in
coopting Darwin's notion that each life tends to build its force at the expense of other lives, but he approved Nietzsche's anti-Hegelian individualism. Baroja's rudimentary idea of Nietzsche's philosophical position at
this point is belied in his assertion that Nietzsche's view of the will is essentially that of Schopenhauer. His first negative assessment of Nietzsche's contribution was greatly modified in two articles written in 1901.
The shift is due principally to his conversations with the Swiss writer Paul
Schmitz, who introduced him to Nietzsche's correspondence. He now understood that Nietzsche's ethics were derived from a desire to break with

all dogma, a position with which Baroja could sympathize. Baroja praised the German philosopher for a love of truth that drove him constantly to revise his former positions, destroying not only long-established traditions but his own personal intellectual history as well.

These two articles entitled "Nietzsche íntimo," while certainly more benevolent than the earlier piece on the German philosopher, should not be taken as an unqualified endorsement of Nietzsche or as the beginning of a discipleship. Baroja rendered few of his own opinions in the articles, preferring to quote long passages from the letters. He set the scene for his encounter with the letters by describing El Paular, where he met and conversed with Paul Schmitz, who translated the letters to him orally. That Baroja did not instantly embrace an uncritical Nietzschean position is evident in the use of dialogue and in the closing words of the first article: "Y mientras mi amigo leía las cartas y comentaba entusiasmado el inmoralismo y el anticristianismo de Nietzsche, yo pensaba en la vida tranquila y exenta de preocupaciones de los viejos cartujos que yacían bajo las losas de granito, y mientras tanto seguía cantando la fuente invariable y monótona su eterna canción no comprendida."[16]

Baroja also employed dialogue and mildly ironic counterpoint in his novels to undermine any monolithic approach to a philosophical position. If Baroja was saturated with Nietzsche, as has been averred,[17] he was likewise saturated with Schopenhauer, Claude Bernard, evolutionism and the scientific method. Clearly a formula with multiple saturations is alien to the laws of chemistry; something had to cede, and what vanished was any singular philosophical viewpoint. Elements of all his favorite philosophers entered into his dialogic format (for example, his forthright grafting of Nietzsche onto Darwin in his 1902 explanation of his ethics). Quoted above is his assertion that he believed that evolution—humanity's blind striving toward betterment—is the guiding force of life (over and above individual instincts). He also evoked the Nietzschean notion that good and evil are not absolute: "la fuerza tiene más derecho que la debilidad desde el momento que el fuerte promete más a la evolución que el débil; el culto del yo es ventajoso, puesto que el hombre fuerte y egolatra trata de convertir su ley en ley general."[18] Such consciously absurd graftings often inform the "philosophical" dialogues embedded in his novels.

From early on, Baroja's approach to his philosophical sources was much more selective and critical than has been acknowledged to date. While rejecting the notion of the categorical imperative, he nevertheless admired Kant as the "gran enemigo de las teorías absolutistas" (*OC* 5: 882-883). He also indicated that he only came to understand Kant through reading Schopenhauer, but clearly, even in his early reading of

Schopenhauer, he did not wholly endorse Kant's disciple, as has some-times been suggested. The title of one of his earliest novelistic efforts, *El pesimista* or *Los pesimistas*, an aborted prototype of *Camino de perfección* be-gun during his years as a medical student, gives a hint of the ironic treat-ment he planned for Schopenhauer, the arch-pessimist. In an essay (*OC* 5: 882), he rejected Schopenhauer's notion of *ataraxia*, thought by many to be Baroja's ideal goal for life, based on evidence from the novels. *Ataraxia* is never presented in a novel as a viable alternative to the active life.

Very early Baroja found in the dialogics of dialogue a method of pre-senting several possible theoretical postions that cancel each other. In "El anarquista y el regicida," published in *La Justicia* on December 14, 1893, the two political attitudes—anarchy and monarchy—are ironically juxta-posed. That the conversations take place in "la barca de Caronte [que] se desliza por las turbulentas aguas de la laguna Estigia,"[19] contributes to their mutual destruction. In another article published in the same journal on January 4, 1894, a reactionary, a demagogue and philosopher each de-livers a monologue. The juxtaposed monologues have an effect similar to that of dialogue in their mutual annihilation. While less radical and hy-perbolic than the other two, the last philosopher to speak appears weak and irresolute: "A medida que el hombre avanza siente nuevas necesidades; antes sólo quería la satisfacción de las materiales, después pidió y obtuvo las morales; ahora pide más, quiere no sólo gozar de las consideraciones que merece en tanto que hombre; exige bienestar, enseñanza, trabajo seguro, educación para sus hijos. El problema es difícil y la solución se hará de esperar."[20] In "Los regeneradores" published in *El Globo* on December 23, 1898, Baroja elected the dialogue format to confront the idealistic attitude of a Krausist with the Schopenhauerian posture that proclaims that life is pain.

Although he published short fiction in journals beginning in about 1893, some of which has aspects of the ironic philosophical dialogues just mentioned, Baroja did not apply his story-telling talents to philosophical concerns until 1900-1901 in *Aventuras y mixtificaciones de Silvestre Paradox*, which attempts a Pickwickian tone to satirize Madrid intellectual life at the turn of the century. At about the same time, both Baroja and Una-muno eschewed the nineteenth-century Spanish realist-naturalist mode à la Galdós and Clarín and sought models in the English comic-ironic-satiric style in order to expose the inadequacies of science and German idealism (Baroja stated in his memoirs that he found the Spanish realists extremely disagreeable). Scientific experiment and philosophical theorizing in Baroja's novel occupy only two chapters in Paradox's varied, picaresque life among Madrid's bohemians and misfits, as compared to Unamuno's sustained effort against abstract thinking in *Amor y pedagogía*. Not until *Camino de perfección* does philosophy become a more integral part of the characterization and action of the novel, but Baroja's most interesting achievement in both novels, and one of the sustaining features of his entire opus, is an odd blend of genres that serves his philosophical purposes and gives his novels their modern flavor.

Silvestre draws upon the colorful types and places that captured Baroja's imagination during his days as a baker and sometime writer in Madrid. Like Mr. Pickwick, the protagonist is an educated eccentric with a moral side not found in the earlier *pícaro*. Baroja, however, inverted aspects of his Dickensian model, endowing Silvestre with the same poverty and the astuteness to overcome it that characterize the sixteenth- and seventeenth-century Spanish *pícaro*. But Silvestre's astuteness, reaches the level of criminality only at the end of the novel, when he abandons his boarding house without paying, because a true *pícaro* has robbed him of all his money. The robbery is yet another inversion of the Pickwickian model, as it is Silvestre's manservant (his "Sam Weller") who fleeces him and leaves him destitute. These inversions belie Baroja's post-Dickensian, modern ideal that traditional notions of good and poetic justice are illusory.

Having failed as an inventor, Silvestre takes up philosophy, which he finds has the advantages of being absolutely useless and, contrary to his former pursuit of science, does not require costly experiments. He concentrates on the German idealists—Kant, Hegel and Schopenhauer—quickly learning to dismiss Krause, whose philosophy he compares to "cualquier tienda de muebles usados de la calle de Tudescos." He also finds most of the other German philosophers and the French thinkers "saldos procedentes del desvalijamiento" (*OC* 2: 68). Reading Kant, Hegel and Schopenhauer teaches him that philosophy is an abyss and that his former reflections "no habían pasado jamás de lo fenomenal, transitorio, y, por tanto, sujeto a las leyes de una mezquina causalidad. Vio claramente que no había llegado hasta entonces al *Noumeno*" (*OC* 2: 68). His general conclusion at the end of three months of reading is that "Kant era Kant y Schopenhauer su profeta" (*OC* 2: 68).

With such an apprenticeship, he is now ready to write his own treatise in which he groups together all the truths enunciated by his favorite philosophers to form a system or body of doctrine in harmony with the facts and discoveries of modern science. Typical of his eccentricity, Paradox believes it commonplace and old-fashioned to write his ideas out in treatise form, so he invents a system of exposition by diagrams. Following Kant's impulse to categories, he is able to group all his diagrams into two parts: 1) "todo lo correspondiente al origen del yo" and 2) "lo relativo a la voluntad y al reflejo" (*OC* 2: 69). As a scientist, Paradox is a determinist, confirming that all human acts have a cause outside the person, but he also attempts to incorporate into his first treatise the individual-centered idealistic philosophies he has absorbed. Thus he explains the ego-centered nature of humanity by a series of circles, all of which contain the letters "N-Y" (*no-yo*) in the center, excepting one which encircles "Y" (*yo*): "El hombre procedía del cosmos. Pero como el hombre lo primero que afirmaba era su personalidad, de ahí que el nombre filosófico del cosmos era lo que no es yo" (*OC* 2: 69). He combines science and metaphysics again in the third diagram, in which he reduces all matter (both physical and mental) to one; gold is identical to oxygen, heat identical to thought: "la fuerza vital, forma nada más de la fuerza única, tenía, según Silvestre, dos aspectos: el de Voluntad-nouménica, que él llamaba en griego *Dynamis*, por encontrarlo más pintoresco, y el Reflejo nouménico" (*OC* 2: 69). Baroja subjected his own doctoral thesis to ironic treatment when Silvestre posits synesthesia (Baroja's term for primary sensorial knowledge in his thesis) as the basis of the noumena rather than of phenomena (as in the thesis). Silvestre may have disdained Krause, yet his conclusion has a decidedly Krausian cast: "Llegado a este período de perfección, la Humanidad superior, irá desapareciendo de la Tierra, y su espíritu, formaría parte de la conciencia del universo, que ascendiendo y ascendiendo llegaría a tener Voluntad, a individualizarse y a ser Dios" (*OC* 2: 70).

Combining elements from as many as four or five philosophical positions in impossible arrangements, this parodic melange does not inform Silvestre's life (as do philosophical precepts in *Camino de perfección*), except that, like Fernando Ossorio, his past determines his future (he escaped an unhappy family life by apprenticing himself to a traveling carnival), while he simultaneously acts as a free agent whose fortunes turn with a change of scene and friends. The segment in which Silvestre takes up philosophy leads to a series of scenes depicting the bohemian world of Madrid publishing. The few other instances in which philosophical notions are specifically mentioned are relatively disconnected from Silvestre's story. After the publishing debacle, Silvestre determines that his philosophy can be summed up by the concept of resignation, and toward the end of the novel a German watchmaker evokes Nietzsche's vitalism and will to power.

There is a mystifying duality in Baroja's works. He appeared to take seriously certain philosophical positions in essays, while simultaneously satirizing the same positions in his fiction. For example, in the 1899 ar-

ticle "Sufrir y pensar" he postulated an epistemology almost identical
to Schopenhauer's, while in *Aventuras y mixtificaciones* he parodied the
German thinker's notions.[21] This dualism (respect coupled with cynicism) is typical of the '98 attitude toward philosophy, especially toward
metaphysics.

The philosophic schizophrenia multiplies in *Camino de perfección*, a
rich concoction of serious philosophical concepts that are simultaneously
accepted and rejected. Its novelistic action integrates in a much more
fundamental way the philosophical problems that Silvestre parodied. The
origin of the novel is to be found in the visit that Martínez Ruiz, Baroja
and several others made to Toledo in November or December of 1900 to
explore this center of Spanish Catholicism and religious art (particularly
that of El Greco). Baroja published articles on the trip entitled "Tierra
castellana: Santo Tomé" in *Mercurio* on March 3, 1901, and "Domingo en
Toledo" in *Electra* 2 on March 27, 1901. "Domingo en Toledo" is almost
identical to chapter 30 of *Camino de perfección*, except that it is written in
first rather than third person, in which most of the rest of the novel was
originally cast. This coincidence may explain Baroja's having begun the
novel in first person, then shifting to third person in chapter 3, a transition that has long puzzled critics. At a crucial juncture, the first-person
perspective is no longer viable, and a heterodiegetic narrator takes over.
Perhaps by this time Baroja had already begun publishing *Camino de perfección* in *La Opinión* and the dye was cast; there was no going back to
invent a new beginning to the novel in order to keep the narrative voice
consistent. When Ossorio arrives in Toledo, Baroja inserted "Domingo en
Toledo," merely changing the first person to third.[22]

There are four other journal articles incorporated into *Camino de perfección*, a technique that Martínez Ruiz also used in his early novels. "El
amigo Ossorio," which appeared in the first issue of *Electra* on April 13,
1901 (five months before *Camino de perfección* began to be serialized in *La
Opinión*), formed the first two chapters of the novel and was the only portion to be left in the first person. The characterization was based on a
medical student whom Baroja knew indirectly at the University of Madrid
and on a character he invented in his early abortive novel *El pesimista*.
Fernando Ossorio is also an expansion on the homonymous character
briefly introduced into a chapter of *Aventuras y mixtificaciones*. It is difficult to determine whether in April of 1901 Baroja clearly saw the possibilities for a novel that would combine this character with his experiences
at El Paular and in Toledo. That his friend Martínez Ruiz was writing an
autobiographical novel about a young man who wavered between the intellectual life and vitalism (*Diario de un enfermo*) could certainly have been

a stimulus to him during the summer holidays of that year. The two articles outlining his encounters with Nietzsche through Paul Schmitz at El Paular, also written in the first person, were incorporated into chapters 13 and 14 of *Camino de perfección* in the third person. Thus two personal dialogues with friends were transfomed into key philosophical passages on Catholic theology and Nietzsche's anti-Christian message to form the underpinnings of the novel and provide important elements of its dialogics.

In addition to numerous brief conversations of a philosophical nature in *Camino de perfección*, two extended philosophical dialogues in chapters 14 and 63—the first on Nietzsche and the nature of matter, the other on Catholic theology—serve as structural pillars to the narrative. The first appears after thirteen chapters that chronicle Fernando's early debauchery, the second, after thirty-eight chapters on his attempts to find the right road and just before the final seventeen chapters, in which Fernando resolves his dilemma. Baroja buried his philosophical themes in the narrative tissue better than either Unamuno in *Amor y pedagogía* or Martínez Ruiz in *La voluntad,* better than even he himself did in his other major philosophical novel, *El árbol de la ciencia* of 1911. The characters, while representing one or another philosophical posture (for example, at least three characters are referred to as "volterianos"), are not so allegorically overdetermined as Unamuno's. Even though the two more specific and extended philosophical dialogues provide the philosophical motivation and structural support of the novel, theoretical talk does not make up a large portion of the novel's fabric as it does in Martínez Ruiz's *La voluntad.*

The action is well established before the first dialogue occurs; thus philosophical commentary affirms action rather than predisposing it. (Baroja may have learned the technique of integrating digressions on philosophical subjects from Dostoyevsky, whom he read as a very young man.) The protagonist Fernando Ossorio's *camino de perfección* is an inversion of the mystical journey that leads to union with God; it is a modern-day search for a meaningful and satisfying life path amidst the evils of urbanization and an increasing estrangement from nature. Nietzsche offers a "modern" solution centered on the exhaltation of life, while traditional Catholicism appears increasingly unable to meet the challenges of modernity. The composition of *Camino de perfección* (published in serial form from August to October of 1901) doubtless began on the heels of *Aventuras y mixtificaciones*, which was serialized from April 1900 to February 1901. It must have provided Baroja with his first real income from writing, for he claimed that his first two books, *Vidas sombrías* and *La casa de Aizgorri,* which he printed at his own expense, were not commercially successful. It is a matter of speculation whether *Camino de perfección*'s episodic, picaresque format can be attributed to its having been composed under the pressure of producing regular installments, but its design does suit its philosophical purposes. If the philosophical episodes in *Aventuras y mixtificaciones* were only a means of adding one or two more chapters to a serial novel, they form the thematic underpinnings *Camino de perfección*.

The artistic achievement of *Camino de perfección* lies in Baroja's borrowing from several genres—the decadent novel, mystic literature, the picaresque novel, the serial crime or adventure novel, Shakespearian tragedy and the nineteenth-century realist novel—to build his philosophical case. The novel is essentially the philosophical journey of a young man attempting to find a proper attitude toward the world. The genres are employed successively to highlight Ossorio's psychological and attendant philosophical position at any particular time. The frequently overlapping genres create a dissonance that underscores his psychological and philosophical confusion. A common approach to *Camino de perfección*, suggested by the novel's title, is to see its structure as an imitation and secular inversion of the stages of the mystical experience: *vía purgativa, vía iluminativa* and *unión*.[23] Juan Villegas, on the other hand, interprets Ossorio's journey in terms of the progress of a mythical hero—leaving home, encounters with counselors, descent into darkness and eventual triumph. Villegas assumes that Baroja hit upon this scheme subconsciously through the similar pattern found in the serial adventure novels of which he was so fond.[24]

Neither view of *Camino de perfección*, as mystic path or as hero's progress, can appreciate the rich cacophony of the novel. The picaresque and adventure novel elements, which parallel the mystic journey, provide a counterpoint to the mystical stages. If the mystic soars out of his or her body toward union with God, Fernando, like the *pícaro*, who is motivated by the basic requirements of physical survival, is constrained by his corporeal being throughout the novel. Rather than a unidimensional mystical path, it is a picaresque adventure road, punctuated by stopovers that foster Fernando's spiritual growth. Two of the pauses contain the most significant philosophical dialogues, the one on Nietzsche, the other on Catholic dogma. Baroja found in the two genres that responded to the extremes of the sixteenth-century Spanish soul—mysticism and the picaresque—a means of expressing the modern dilemma between determinism and will. Determinism or dogma emerges in science (Fernando begins as a medical student), art (he turns to painting for several years during his "decadent" period) and religion (the brush with mysticism in Toledo and his continued interest in attending chruch in Yécora), all of which Fernando leaves behind. Will is synonymous with nature, which eventually Fernando embraces. The adventure novel mingles with the picaresque mode further complicating the philosophical message. Unlike the *pícaro*, the adventure hero is not limited by his environment, and Fernando ultimately frees himself from his oppressive surroundings and upbringing. Further entangling the generic and philosophical composition are references to Shakespearian tragedy and to the realist-*costumbrista* novel. In tragedy neither heredity nor environment can doom or save the hero, whose fate is sealed by forces beyond earthly existence, while the realist novel portrays the character's life as determined by a combination of milieu and individual will.[25]

Fernando's understanding of himself begins in philosophical confusion. He is a determinist, but he wavers between environmental determinism and hereditary determinism. At the beginning of the novel, Fernando explains to the narrator that his dilemma stems from his education, which was carried out in a baffling duality. He was raised by his grandfather, a virulent Voltaiarian, but he was much of the time under the tutelage of his governess, a fanatical Catholic: "yo me encontraba combatido por la incredulidad del uno y la superstición de la otra" (7). Then he accuses heredity of occasioning his lack of direction; in his family there has been insanity, suicide, mental retardation and alcoholism. The genres of the first two segments of the novel—the scenes in Madrid and the adventures on the road prior to Fernando's stay in Toledo—foreground the dichotomy between social determinism, which allows for the possibility of change, and hereditary determinism, which is more absolute.

The first segment in Madrid draws primarily on the decadent novel, its suffocating unnatural interior settings, fetishes, perverted eroticism and eroticism infused with religious images, while the scenes on the road fuse elements of the picaresque and the serial adventure or crime novel. The first two chapters, narrated from an outsider's first-person perspective, end with the narrator and Fernando walking at sunset on one of the hills overlooking Madrid. The freedom and mobility that this walk in nature suggests is coopted when Fernando becomes involved in a perverse love affair with his aunt. As the elements of the decadent novel (based on the determinist premise that degeneracy is inherited and irreversible) assume narrative primacy, Fernando's world becomes limited and claustrophobic.

Rather than ending with the pessimistic, fatalistic closure typical of the decadent genre, Ossorio escapes to a picaresque-adventure scenario. A friend fortuitously suggests that he leave Madrid and take to the road, that he encounter pain and struggle for a while. The decadent genre recedes as the picaresque mode and the serial adventure crime novel take over. Baroja foreshadows the new orientation in one of the last scenes in Madrid, which takes place in a wretched bar: " 'Se encuentra aquí uno en plena novela de Fernández y González, ¿verdad?—dijo Ulloa—. Le voy a hablar de vos al posadero" (41). (Fernández y González was one of the authors of adventure serials that formed an important part of Baroja's reading.) Both the *pícaro* and the criminal are products of their social environment. The adventurer may escape the environment's limitations more readily than the *pícaro,* but the possibility that a change of venue may provoke a change in behavior and fortune always lurks in the background of both the picaresque novel and the adventure story. Although Fernando has a long road to travel before his search for "perfection" is complete, he never again falls into the degeneracy of the Madrid segment. His road includes stops in typical Spanish inns and taverns peopled with mean-spirited characters reminiscent of *Lazarillo de Tormes* or *El buscón.* At one point he lodges in a room with a bed that recalls that of the *hidalgo's* house in *Lazarillo:* "Era un cuarto ancho, negro, con una cama de tablas y un colchón muy delgado" (52). And he rents a horse whose hyperbolic description rivals those of many a picaresque author: "El caballo era un viejo rocín cansado de arrastrar diligencias, que tenía encima de los ojos agujeros en donde podrían entrar los puños" (56).

These segments, especially those tracing Fernando's time on the open road, are interlaced with references to the romantic adventure novel: "A Fernando le recordaba la noche y el lugar, noches y lugares de los cuentos en donde salen trasgos o ladrones" (45) or "—Ha creído que soy algún bandido, pensó Fernando . . . se encontró con un castillo que se levantaba sobre un loma" (50). The picaresque and adventure novel elements reappear whenever Ossorio is in transit from one locale to another, signaling the role of environment in change. At the end of these encounters with pseudo-*pícaros* and pseudo-adventures, Fernando enters into his first philosophical dialogue with the German Schulze at El Paular. The topic of the conversation became a favorite one in many Baroja novels— the northern European penchant for metaphysics and the Spanish dismissal of it. Schulze says the Spaniards have quite sensibly denied the existence of metaphysical problems. When Ossorio replies that he is nonetheless troubled by them, Schulze recommends Nietzsche, about whom Ossorio has a negative opinion for his doctrines that glorify the ego. To exemplify Nietzsche's philosophy of the will, Schulze takes Ossorio on a physically demanding overnight hike into the mountains.

Fernando's second long philosophical dialogue, in which he is a more authoritative participant, can only take place after he has experienced more of life's possibilities, especially a consideration of the religious option. The Toledo sequence, which occupies the central position in the novel and in which Fernando has a brush with mysticism, offers an alternative both to Schulze's advice to read Nietzsche and concentrate on the physical side of life and to the the Piarist's Scholasticism, which he confronts in Yécora. The encounter with the farmer Polentinos, a modern Spanish Lear, marks a shift from the picaresque adventure mode to the next stationary setting in Toledo. The elements of Shakespearian tragedy in Polentinos's story and the farmer's outlook on life ("Todas las vidas son malas," 80) reintroduce the spectre of determinacy and inevitabilty of the early chapters, only this time through rustic metaphysical argument rather than genetics or biology: "Si la vida no es más que una ilusión. Cada uno ve el mundo a su manera" (82). After his brief sojourn with Polentinos, Fernando falls ill and in his delirium accepts the *filosófico arriero*'s assessment of the nature of life. As Noma and Weston Flint have pointed out, Fernando tends to adopt the attitude or philosphical position of the people he meets.

Just as Fernando was saved from the grim end of a decadent hero, he is wrested from the jaws of the arbitrarily determined fate of a Shakespearian Hamlet. The Toledo chapters are a crucible of genres: decadence reappears briefly as Fernando attempts to seduce a nun; the comic-satiric surfaces in the scenes at the governor's house, and the adventure novel is represented in Fernando's swashbuckling friend, a military officer. Taking the fortuitous discovery of some pages from the *Ejercicios* of Saint Ignatius of Loyola as a sign of his calling, Fernando briefly considers following the contemplative religious life, but his sensual nature overcomes him. What he likes best about the Catholic religion are its sensual aspects—the art, the music, the incense: "¿por qué los sentidos habían de considerarse como algo bajo, siendo fuentes de la idea, medios de comunicación del alma del hombre con el alma del mundo?" (104). Ossorio's conclusion echoes Baroja's doctoral thesis about the source of human knowledge, but a major difference between the doctoral thesis and the philosophical content of *Camino de perfección* is that in the intervening several years Baroja encountered Nietzsche's ideas, which gave him a new way to understand the metaphysical notion of *noumena* as the life force or will. Fernando's personal interpretation of Saint Ignatius has Nietzschean overtones: "había en el libro, fuera del elemento intelectual, pobre y sin energía, un fondo de voluntad, de fuerza" (109).

Reflecting some of the burlesque tone of *Silvestre Paradox*, Baroja introduced a pedagogue who is going to write a book "en el cual plantearía, como única base de la sociedad, ésta: el fin del hombre es vivir" (115). This revelation occasions much mirth among those who witness the declaration, but Ossorio espouses the same conclusion at the end of the novel: "Y, al mismo tiempo de esta germinación eterna, ¡qué terrible mortandad! ¡Qué bárbara lucha por la vida! ¿Pero para qué pensar en ella? Si la muerte es depósito, fuente manantial de vida, ¿a qué lamentar la existencia de la muerte? No, no hay que lamentar nada. Vivir y vivir . . . ésa es la cuestión" (180). Ultimately, Fernando adopts the philosophical position that Schulze attributed to most Spaniards—that metaphysical speculation is unproductive and useless.

After a shorter interval of adventure novel material (a journey by train and coach full of mysterious and sinister notes, paralleling the adventure story material in the transition from Madrid to the countryside), Fernando enters the conventions of the romantic genre at Yécora, where he seeks forgiveness from a woman he seduced years ago. The Christian romance denouement of a reconciliation between sinner and victim is thwarted. The woman is deeply embittered and unforgiving, as her tarnished honor denied her the range of suitors she might otherwise have had, and she has married a brutish man who poisons her life. Cleansed of his religious leanings, Fernando enters into his second long philosophical dialogue, this time with a Piarist, in a location very unlike the beautiful El Paular where he conversed with Schulze about Nietzsche.

Like the conversation with Schulze, this interchange begins with a discussion on the nature and perdurability of matter. In this conversation, however, Fernando has come into his own as a thinker and his ideas are more fully developed. The Piarist tries to demonstrate that God sustains matter by means of His will. Fernando employs that premise to turn the Piarist's argument inside-out, declaring that the world then must have a cause outside of God. The Piarist counters with the well-worn cliché that God created the world from nothing. Fernando's rebuttal recalls Schulze's notion (probably derived from Nietzsche's idea of the eternal return) that matter is never lost: "no queda más que un aniquilamiento teológico, y a ese yo me sometería sin miedo" (165). The Piarist accuses Fernando of Pantheism, and Fernando counters with the assertion that the world is immutable, that substance, spirit or matter, whatever one calls it, is infinite, that life and death, good and evil are the same. The disconsolate Piarist concludes that Fernando does not believe in free will, but Fernando distinguishes between the physical world and the moral: "En el mundo físico todo es irrevocable; en el mundo moral, al contrario, todo es revocable" (168). Ultimately the scholasticism of the priest and Fernando's notions, based vaguely on several secular philosophies, provide no common ground on which to engage. The Piarist ends the conversation with an exasperated "—No se puede discutir con Ud." (168). Fernando's best argument against the priest, however, turns out to be the irony that his would-be religious converter is a skirt-chaser.

Most of the final segment of the novel, which takes place in the home of Fernando's relatives in Valencia, is drawn from several nineteenth-century realist or *costumbrista* novels, but the transition to Valencia once again summons the picaresque mode. A troup of actors Fernando met in Yécora travels at the young man's expense until he tires of their wiles and eludes them.[26] The scenes in his uncle's home are reminiscent of *Doña Perfecta*. The family, while pretending an awkward hospitality to the elegant young man from the city, scarcely conceals its hostility toward him. He is given a very nice room, as was Pepe Rey, and, like Pepe's room, it is described in careful detail. In imitation of *Pepita Jiménez*, the segment is narrated as a series of letters or part of a journal written by a young man who is slowly falling in love. In addition to the epistolary account of an awakening love interest, Fernando's having considered entering the religious life, country outings with his love object, and a duel in the casino with a rival also echo *Pepita Jiménez*. The details of Baroja's casino scene are uncannily similar to Valera's. Baroja's borrowing from the nineteenth-century novel, which he claimed to despise, could be attributed to his need to find a quick solution to his hero's cunundrum in order to meet a deadline for the serialized version, but it also suits his philosophical purposes. The protagonists of nineteenth-century novels grow and change through interaction with the social milieu. Although Baroja's character has changed, his transformation takes place more despite his milieu than because of it. He has sought out each locale for its potential benefits to his spiritual needs—rural Castile, Toledo and Yécora—but each fails utterly to inspire him.

The strange ending of *Camino de perfección*, in which nineteenth-century fictional formulae are invoked to settle this rootless hero into his new life as a married family man, lends an additional ironic touch to the conflicting generic modes that propel the novel. The realist ending clashes with the decadentist beginnning—the former informed by environmental determinism, the latter by hereditary determinism. Many critics find this "happy ending" inconclusive because Fernando's mother-in-law sews a page of the Bible into her grandchild's clothes, perhaps neutralizing Fernando's innocent plans to raise the child without the constraints of religion he believes occasioned his own tortured route to happiness. A more sustained and powerful operant in the novel's inconclusiveness is the manipulation of its genres. No intelligent reader can accept within one work the reversal of philosophical premise implied by a beginning in genetic decadence and an ending that emphasizes realism's dialetical process. In its foreshortened and elliptical form, the realist sequence at the end of *Camino de perfección* parodies the realist genre, which painstakingly builds characters' motivations through a wealth of psychological, social and physical detail. Contributing to the parodic effect is the combination of elements from *Doña Perfecta* at the beginning of the Valencia sequence and an ending from *Pepita Jiménez*. *Doña Perfecta* closes tragically with the death of the young man at the hands of the girl's family and the townspeople, while in *Pepita Jiménez* the protagonist gives up his religious vocation to marry the woman, all approved by family and town. (Vernon Chamberlin has convincingly argued that *Doña Perfecta* is Galdós's refutation of Valera's idealistic portrayal of Spanish village life.[27])

Baroja's novel is ultimately a denial of all theories and precepts, be they religious, metaphysical, political or otherwise, underscoring the message of Baroja's article "Mi moral": "La Humanidad se ha separado de la ley natural; hay que volver a ella; toda esa mal estrecha de leyes y preceptos sociales y religiosos; en vez de coadyuvar a los mandatos de la naturaleza, los dificultan" (1). Baroja did not say what he considered to be the *ley natural*, but one suspects that he had some vague notion of following one's instincts, which he naively assumed would lead us to the kind of moral solution that Fernando finally finds. Nor is the ending of *Camino de perfección* particularly Nietzschean, as has been asserted on occasion. Fernando's exaltation of life at the end of the novel is couched in Nietzschean terms but comes in the wake of the ridiculous pedagogue's dictum that the purpose of humankind is simply to live and Fernando's own pronouncement that his desire to seduce Adela in Toledo is "la vida . . . que quiere seguir su curso" (129). In addition, Fernando has chosen to marry and live within the confines of bourgeois morality rather than follow his libido with endless seductions. Contradicting Nietzsche, who extols art as a means to truth, Fernando increasingly shuns art, first going to the artless Yécora, and then falling back on an existing photograph when he fails to achieve a satisfactory likeness of Dolores with his paintbrush. If he begins in the Nietzschean phase of Dionysus and then seeks out the extreme opposite Apollonian mode, he ends outside the two—in a mindless natural state.

The heterogeneous and conflicting genres in which Baroja couched Fernando's journey from spiritualism to vitalism preclude assigning it one particular philosophical orientation, but vitalism does seem to prevail, if precariously. In the next chapter, I explore Martínez Ruiz's *La voluntad* as a formal response to Baroja's novelistic excursus into the will and determinism. While equally irreverent toward the nineteenth-century realist tradition, the Alicantine writer's 1902 novel is much less sanguine about the possibilities of salvation through will and nature, especially if these take the form of matrimony.

4

MARTÍNEZ RUIZ:
AN ANSWER TO
BAROJA'S SOLUTION

Compared to Baroja or Unamuno, the early Martínez Ruiz was more interested in social and political theory than in metaphysics, and he was a
more strident and open critic of the previous generation in the 1890s. The
themes of the nature of time, reality and the will versus the intellect that
drew the attention of Unamuno and Baroja in the 1890s only emerged at
the beginning of the century in Martínez Ruiz's *Diario de un enfermo* and
La voluntad, in the wake of his association with Baroja and their conversations on Nietzsche and Schopenhauer. The Alicantine writer seems to
have mistrusted professional philosophy more than his cogenerationists.
He charged that Clarín was more of a philosopher ("podemos definir su
pensamiento como un *espiritualismo* laico"[1]), than a proper literary critic.
His evaluation of González Serrano's *Psicología del amor* reveals a preference for the modern social sciences over philosophy, which he considers
too abstract. *Psicología del amor*, according to Martínez Ruiz, is "obra de
filósofo, de pensador encariñado con ciertos procedimientos tradicionales
de investigación, más que psicología, es filosofía. Cabe hacer una psicología del *amor*. ¿Cabe hacer psicología de una abstracción? ¿Por qué no
Psicología del enamorado? Si no existe el libre albedrío, si no existe la voluntad (sino voliciones), ¿podrá existir el amor? . . . Leyendo a González
Serrano se percibe el *ritmo* filosófico de los grandes pensadores, el ritmo
de un diálogo de Sócrates y Fedro, al borde del Ilesos, sobre la fresca
hierba, a la sombra de los plátanos"(*OC* 1: 348-49).

The difference between Unamuno's and Martínez Ruiz's treatises on
the Spanish character is illustrative. While drawing on examples from
Spanish life and literature, Unamuno's *En torno al casticismo* (1895) is essentially a metaphysical essay on the nature of time, especially the relation of historical time to eternity. This concern began to emerge in
Martínez Ruiz's *La voluntad*, but his *El alma castellana* (1900) is a re-

searched work on cultural customs of the Spanish seventeenth and eighteenth centuries. Any metaphysical notion implied by the historical method centering on issues like fashion, courtship, convent life, mysticism and literary activity is secondary and unstated. This archeology of Spanish culture should not be overlooked as a major impetus of *La voluntad;* it overshadows the philosophical issues it raises in many chapters.

Martínez Ruiz preferred political theory in which he could see a practical application of metaphysics. The following are among the works of philosophy and political theory that he probably read in the family library: Voltaire's *Dictionnaire philosophique, Lettres choisies* and *Politique et legislation,* Mill's *L'Économie politique jugée par la science,* Hobbes's *Élémens de philosophie,* Pascal's *Pensées,* Taine's *L'Intelligence* and *Philosophie de l'art,* Proudhon's *Idée générale de la revolution au XIX siècle* and *Système des contradictions Economiques ou philosophie,* and Nordau's *Degénerescence.* The philosophical works in Azorín's personal library that bear early dates are of a varied nature; one finds a preponderance of excerpted "Thoughts of . . . ," many copiously annotated by their owner. The *pequeño filósofo* seems to have preferred the epigramatic kernel of a philosophical work to the labor of sifting through long and tedious argument (many longer works of traditional philosophy reveal very little marginal notation).

Martínez Ruiz's desultory university career included a specialization in metaphysics. He studied political law in Valencia with the Krausist Eduardo Soler y Pérez, and some of his interest in idealism may arise from his association with Soler (as well as from Pi y Margall). When Martínez Ruiz briefly attended the University of Salamanca after moving to Madrid in 1896, Unamuno sat on his examination committee, marking the beginning of a long and seemingly cordial (if paternalistic on Unamuno's part) friendship between the two. Compared to his Salamanca mentor, the future *pequeño filósofo* was interested in philosophy more as quick inspiration than as an opportunity to think critically and originally. By the mid-1890s, perhaps during his university years in Valencia, Martínez Ruiz became particularly attracted to the federalism of Pi y Margall, in which he found an integration of the reading he had done in metaphysics and practical politics. Pi y Margall's philosophical underpinnings were in Cartesian, Kantian and Hegelian idealism, especially his early *La reacción y la revolución,* which seems to have most impressed Martínez Ruiz.

That the Alicantine writer was very aware of Pi's rationalist orientation is evident in his 1895 tract *Anarquistas literarios,* where he wrote that Pi is "el símbolo de la razón."[2] As can be imagined from the sources mentioned, this work manifests certain contradictions and problems, particularly in the relation of the individual to the state. As a strong individualist, Pi placed the person, independent of life in the community, at the center of his system. All social progress was to be achieved by consensus. In "En casa de Pi y Margall," published in *Vida Nueva* (December 24, 1899) and incorporated almost verbatim into *La voluntad*, Martínez Ruiz sums up the Catalan thinker's philosophical position: "Pi es lo que Napoleón llamaría *un hombre:* consecuente, inflexible, lógico, remendadamente lógico, con la lógica perversa de un Julián Sorel, filósofo." Martínez Ruiz's interest in Pi's political philosophy contributed to the making of *La voluntad* in a variety of ways, chief among them Pi's own situation as a lofty and admirable theorist who ultimately had no impact on the realities of contemporary Spain. But Pi's idealism collided with the environmental determinists Martínez Ruiz was reading at the same time, particularly with Taine, whose emphasis on milieu in literary criticism was evident in Martínez Ruiz's early booklets on literary subjects (*Moratín, esbozo* [1893], *Buscapiés* [1894] and *La evolución de la crítica* [1899]).[3] His interest in environmental influences on behavior also emerged in his work on the anarchist theorizer Kropotkin and was reflected in his *Sociología criminal* of 1899 (prologued by Pi y Margall). In an *El País* article of January 6, 1897, he wrote, "Soy un determinista convencido,"[4] an assertion he would continue to make at least until 1902.

Also contributing to the conflicting philosophical sources that inform *La voluntad* was Martínez Ruiz's interest in Nietzsche's notion of the will. While Nietzsche's assertion of the individual's will to power contradicted environmental determinism, the notion of the eternal return, which so fascinated Martínez Ruiz and later Azorín, reinforces a view of the world that has limited possibilites for genuine change and renewal. Rather than projecting a distinct philosophical position on any of these questions, *La voluntad* marshalls a wide variety of narrative techniques to test a panoply of ideas and pit them against one another. The practice is reminiscent of a passage that Martínez Ruiz marked in his copy of Alfred Fouillée's *La Morale, l'art et la religion d'après Guyau* (1897): " 'Nous ne savons pas si le fond de la vie est volonté, s'il est idée, s'il est sensation, quoique avec la sensation nous approchions sans doute d'avantage du point central; il nous semble seulement probable que la conscience, qui est tout pour nous, doit être encore quelque chose le dernier des êtres, et qu'il n'y a pas dans l'univers d'être *pour ainsi dire entièrement abstrait de soi* " (underlining is Martínez Ruiz's).[5]

Martínez Ruiz seemed most concerned that pure philosophizing and abstract analysis constitute a deterrant to action, as he wrote of Urbano González Serrano in *Revista Nueva* on October 5, 1899: "El análisis paraliza en él la acción; pesa, mide, examina minuciosamente, duda en decidirse por una u otra idea." One wonders if this could not also be the problem of José Martínez Ruiz, as it certainly afflicts his character Antonio Azorín, protagonist of *La voluntad*. According to Martínez Ruiz, González Serrano tried to incorporate positivist notions into his philosophy, but ulitmately his position remained abstract:

El ansia de la crítica, llévale a la abstracción. Preferencias por la 'metafísica idealista' noto en sus primeros libros de la *Revista Filosófica* de París: hoy figura entre los mantenedores del Positivismo, pero quédale el gusto por las ideas abstractas. Ideas abstractas, independientes de toda contingencia son para él *deber, amor, altruismo, voluntad*. Por imborrable tiene el 'sentimiento del deber'; independientemente de espacio y de tiempo, pretende hacer la 'psicología del amor'; para nada considera en sus críticas literarias las circunstancias personales y de ambiente. . . . De avisados dicen que es dudar; y más parece que la duda es para González Serrano la 'blanda cabecera' del filósofo que 'el hastío y la amargura' del poeta.

Martínez Ruiz muted his critique of González Serrano, who had generously agreed to prologue his "Pasión" (1897) after Clarín refused to associate his name with the empassioned diatribe against the literary establishment.[6] Such had not always been his approach to writers with whom he disagreed or whom he did not respect. Unlike the more contemplative Unamuno, Martínez Ruiz was impatient and feisty, but by the time he wrote *La voluntad* he too was learning to submerge his hostility in the deflecting qualities of the novel and would soon mask it entirely behind the pseudonym Azorín. His earliest writing was literary criticism (at first strident and polemical), an aspect of the journalist's trade he would cultivate all his life. As Inman Fox has demonstrated, Azorín's impulse was primarily a literary rather than a philosophical one.[7] It took Martínez Ruiz less time than Unamuno or Baroja to find his writing vocation, but his search for a viable philosophical outlook was no less peripatetic. Recent research has uncovered early pro-Catholic tracts that preceded his collaborations in the anarchist press in the mid-1890s and the socialist-anarchist orientation of his *Sociología criminal* (1898).[8] Martínez Ruiz's (and later Azorín's) volatility and seeming lack of constancy in political and ideological affiliations have long been the subject of criticism, earning him condemnation in some quarters.

The philosophical confusion of the times goes far in explaining Martínez Ruiz's ideological inconstancy. In contrast to Unamuno and Baroja, the Alicantine writer's first vocational choice was a career in publishing. With no university or professional title to fall back on, he was more vulnerable than the others to a journalist's dependence on the good will of the publishing establishment. His earliest journalistic assignments were granted through the influence of an uncle who obtained for him the opportunity to review books for the Catholic press. In the articles he wrote for Catholic journals he scrupulously followed his uncle's advice to write within the confines of the ideology of the journals. Apparently he did not write entirely against his own inclinations, as attested in his attempt to interest Clarín in the works of his relative, the Catholic apologist.

Although it is difficult to determine if Martínez Ruiz's early interest in Catholic orthodoxy was genuine or if he felt it was required to succeed as a writer in Spain, the young man did learn a painful lesson about the need to conform to prevailing ideological norms when he was dismissed from his post at *El País* in 1896 for the unconventional opinions on private property and marriage he had expressed in his columns. The dismissal was an important motivation for his blistering attack on Madrid's publishing world in *Charivari*. Aware of Martínez Ruiz's penchant for controversial topics, in a letter of August 14, 1903, Baroja invited Martínez Ruiz to send articles to a newspaper recently founded by Picavea in San Sebastián, but warned him that they did not want "cosas fuertes sino artículos de crítica política o social hechos amablemente." The threat to his livelihood inherent in ideological nonconformity plagued him even in the last last days of his career. In the 1950s he refused to cooperate with an avid would-be biographer who had fallen afoul of the Franco regime. Azorín's only reply to the biographer's impassioned plea for Azorín's consent and cooperation was that he try to understand his awkward situation. (Azorín had experienced temporary exile during the Civil War and found it extremely difficult to exercise his journalistic profession abroad.) Azorín even distanced himself from Baroja during the Franco era, when many of the Basque writer's works were condemned by the censors.

For ten years (1890-1900) Martínez Ruiz devoted himself to journalistic essays on literature and politics, short tracts on literary topics and two longer essays of a sociological and historical nature (*Sociología criminal* and *Alma castellana*), none of which brought him the kind of acclaim he sought. In 1900-1902 he stepped back from the essay and called upon the dialogics of the novel to gain a space between himself, his mentors and their ideas. His reaction to the overintellectualizing of his predecessors (recall his critique of Clarín: "La vida para Alas es todo inteligencia. A la inteligencia lo sacrifica todo Clarín"[9]) was to employ a form radically opposed to both the realistic novel cultivated by Pereda, Galdós, Clarín and Pardo Bazán and the essay. His solution combines elements of both, although his first attempts in *Diario de un enfermo* and *Antonio Azorín* were abortive. An autobiographical confession that reveals a serious state of confusion, *Diario de un enfermo* is considered by some critics to be a proto-novel. The narration could perhaps be modeled on Unamuno's diary of his religious crisis of 1897, which Unamuno often showed to friends, although it was not published until much later.

If Baroja's *Camino de perfección* appropriated several genres from ealier periods to express a philosophical confusion, *La voluntad* is a disassembling and reassembling of all the major elements of the nineteenth-century realistic novel—its carefully woven plot, its descriptions, its character development, its pretensions to verisimilitude.[10] Even more than Baroja, Martínez Ruiz refused to tell a coherent tale; instead he stripped his novel down to the raw materials, the documents, that constitute a story and its subject prior to their incorporation into a metanarrative, a *grande histoire*, to use Lyotard's term. *La voluntad* most closely resembles a fractured *La Regenta*, which Azorín said was entirely too long and should have been reduced to one volume, although he dared make this assertion only some years after Clarín's death. Galdós's play *Voluntad* doubtless resonates here as well. If will was an uncomplicated and positive concept for Galdós, it is ambivalent and elusive in Martínez Ruiz's novel.

Martínez Ruiz marshaled the very same materials that Clarín drew upon in his masterpiece: 1) Restoration society in a provincial town dominated by the Church and its petty priests, 2) false intellectuals who prize fame over ideological constancy, and 3) a satirical view of scientific experimentation. Even the title of Martínez Ruiz's novel echoes Clarín's abstract, trisyllabic noun preceded by the feminine article. But *la regenta* refers to the social position of a concrete person, whose worldly and spiritual fortunes Clarín's novel gradually reveals, while *la voluntad* is a metaphysical concept, the nature of which constantly shifts and dissolves into ambiguity in Martínez Ruiz's novel. Within a meager plot, the characters engage in endless speech-making. Embedded in the discourses are all the contradictions and clashes of the several philosophical positions that Martínez Ruiz had been entertaining since his earliest days as a writer: Catholic orthodoxy, mysticism, the scientific method, positivism, anarchistic socialism, Kant's critique of pure reason, Guyau and Nietzsche (and perhaps Unamuno) on the nature of time and eternity, Nietzsche and Schopenhauer on the will and the intellect. The scenes dramatizing the several philosophies are arranged in blocks of text that do not flow one into the other but are juxtaposed to expose their oppositions.

The principal contradictions are between the religious life, represented in Azorín's fiancée Justina and her priest-uncle Puche, and the intellectual mode of Yuste and his disciple Azorín, who delight in discussing the latest philosophical issues, including Nietzsche, Schopenhauer and

anarchism. Within the religious realm, there is a further dichotomy between the genuine, favorably portrayed faith of Father Lasalde and the
vicious, dogmatic, life-denying faith of Puche. On the intellectual side,
conflicts arise over the nature of time and eternity and the tension between thought and action. Most of the contradictions on the intellectual
side are embedded in the character of Yuste, mentor to the protagonist,
Antonio Azorín.

Just as in *La Regenta*, the Church comes in for particular scrutiny in
La voluntad, but in a much more indirect way. In the first scene of Clarín's novel, a priest aided by a telescope spies from atop the cathedral
tower into the intimate corners of houses, gardens and streets where the
members of his flock display their natural human foibles and weaknesses.
With equal curiosity and powers of observation, Clarín's narrator moves
agilely and stealthily into and out of the consciousness of the characters,
sometimes switching viewpoints with nearly every sentence of a paragraph in a free indirect style that rivals Flaubert's. Empowered to discover
the inner motivations of every character, this all-seeing, all-knowing eye
or voice discloses the psychological and sociological rationale for Ana
Ozores's tragic dilemma. Martínez Ruiz's novel also opens with a birds-
eye view of the town, in which the church likewise assumes a prominent position, but no priest's spyglass lends a personal perspective to the
visual panorama. The reader has been abandoned before a depersonal-
ized scene.

The prologue of *La voluntad* is an account taken almost verbatim
from a nineteenth-century document chronicling the construction of a
new church. At the end of the prologue, there appears a seemingly unrelated history of ancient temples located on the same site. Here Martínez Ruiz employed what he called his archeological method, initiated in
his first play *La fuerza del amor* of 1901. If *Diario de un enfermo* follows a
more or less traditional confessional format to explore youthful frustration
in the face of ideological and professional confusion, *La fuerza del amor*
enlists pastiche or parody to the same purpose.[11] The play draws on elements (and I mention only the most obvious and easily recognizable) of
Golden Age *capa y espada* theater, the picaresque novel, the *Celestina* and
Don Quixote, abruptly juxtaposing them to create a very modern parodic
effect. Martínez Ruiz may have intended the piece to be a historical document, as each act is followed by a list of authors and/or works from which
its action was drawn. He seemed to indicate such a purpose in the preface
to the 1930 reprinting, but the artistic result is very different. When
Baroja called the piece unrepresentative of Martínez Ruiz's output, he

missed any parodic effect (or any similarities to his own methodology in *Camino de perfección*).

The abrupt juxtaposition of the new church and the ancient temples in archeological layers at the beginning of *La voluntad* suggests an Unamunian intrahistorical relationship between the spiritual lives of the occupants of that same piece of ground over the centuries.[12] Martínez Ruiz's church in both architectural presence and social function is not an emblem of individual clerical corruption in a particular society at a particular historical moment, as in Clarín's version of Restoration Spain. Instead, it points toward the eternal but futile desire to fill the metaphysical void. Clarín's heroine does not succeed in satisfying her spiritual longings, but Clarín's novel leaves open the possibility of such fulfillment for others; Martínez Ruiz's novel suggests that there are no metaphysical answers to life's dilemmas.

Juxtaposition (parataxis) rather than continuity (hypotaxis) is Martínez Ruiz's primary structuring device throughout *La voluntad*. The conflict between Church dogma and modern philosophy (and thus between the lovers Justina and Antonio) emerges in blocks of juxtaposed text. The two characters are introduced in separate chapters in which they each listen to a monologue by another character (Justina hears the Priest Puche, and Antonio, the intellectual Yuste; the assonance in the names of the two authority figures surely is intended to highlight the parallelism of the discourses). Puche delivers a personal sermon, replete with numerous biblical quotations, to a passive Justina, and in the following chapter Yuste expounds on ideas taken from Kant, Schopenhauer and Nietzsche before a silent Antonio. These received ideas are the primary shapers of the characters and their lives. Dominated by her uncle's conservative Catholicism, Justina breaks her engagement to the free-thinking Antonio and dies in a convent after a series of mystical experiences. Antonio lives for a time according to the Schopenhauerian intellectual ideal he has acquired in Yuste's company, but he eventually subordinates himself to a forceful woman whose dominating will has Nietzschean overtones. By alternating Justina's and Antonio's situations in contiguous (but temporally simultaneous) chapters, Martínez Ruiz postulates the unsuitability of each character's solution, as well as the inadequacy of the texts and ideas that informed them. Textual authority becomes the villain in the novel, but at the same time texts are the primary stuff of which the characters are made.

Todorov distinguishes between *sujet* and *discours*, the former being "the presentation of phenomena which occurred at a certain moment of time without any intervention on the part of the speaker" and the latter "speech act[s] supposing a speaker and a listener, and in the speaker an intention to influence the listener in some way."[13] *La voluntad* exhibits a lopsided distribution of *sujet* and *discours*. About half of its pages are devoted to articles, letters, quotations from books and long dialogues (or monologues) on philosophical and sociopolitical issues, in other words, what Todorov calls *discours*. The *sujet* is narrated in sketchy terms—Antonio Azorín's broken engagement with Justina, her subsequent death in a convent, Antonio's disillusionment with his journalistic career and his marriage to the strong-willed Iluminada. Absent is any novelistic building of personal anguish over or conflict in the vicissitudes of the protagonist's life.

Martínez Ruiz's incorporation of the actual documents (speeches and texts) that inform a character's life choices contrasts with Clarín's references to books in *La Regenta*. All the characters in Clarín's novel are identified in part by the kinds of books they read. Ana wavers between religious and secular works; her eccentric husband reads Calderonian drama, which his life ironically imitates; and Don Álvaro, the seducer, prefers the positivist philosophers, who assure him that there is no eternal damnation. Rather than constituting a character's consciousness, as they do in *La voluntad*, these books coincide with their *a priori* natures. Clarín does not quote passages of texts; references to written works are limited to titles and authors that reconfirm what we already know about a character. *La voluntad*'s characters have no natures prior to the texts they read and hear; the narrator supplies no information about family and childhood to elucidate a character's choice of reading matter. Further precluding any narrative attempt at rational retrospection is the unrelenting use of the present tense throughout the novel.

Martínez Ruiz's characters are caught in an existential web of continuous becoming, made and unmade by the words they hear and read. Paradigmatic textual juxtaposition, rather than narrative elaboration, reveals first Justina's unsuccessful choice of the religious life and finally Antonio's disillusionment with progessive intellectualism. Justina's failure initially makes Antonio's imitation of the intellectual life seem the more appropriate avenue. Yuste, on the surface, appears to be a more viable modern model than the priest Puche (Yuste has often been taken as Martínez Ruiz's mouthpiece in the novel[14]). A closer look, however, at the juxtaposition of ideas from one chapter to another and the omniscient narrator's voice, which introduces and interrupts Yuste's monologues, divulges the undermining of Yuste as a thinker. To this purpose Martínez Ruiz called upon certain nineteenth-century narrative devices that Clarín wielded so deftly, but rather than weaving a coherent narration with them, Martínez Ruiz summoned the devices intermittently, selectively and inevitably to diminish a character's authority, most often Yuste's.

Yuste and Antonio's relationship reflects many aspects of Martínez Ruiz's ambivalent relationships to older writers such as Pi y Margall and Clarín. He had a distaste for authority figures but found it necessary to cultivate them in order to achieve the literary success he sought. If the Yuste-Antonio Azorín pair is based on Nietzsche's "Schopenhauer as Educator," as has been suggested,[15] the inspiration was probably Lichtenberger's account of Nietzsche rather than the original *Thoughts out of Season*, which it is unlikely Martínez Ruiz had read by 1901. Lichtenberger points out that Nietzsche wrote on Schopenhauer as a mentor some time after he had already turned away from the ideas of the master. He wrote specifically of a phase that had passed, which is precisely Antonio's attitude toward his *maestro* in the second and third parts of *La voluntad*.

Félix Martínez Bonati and John Searle distinguish between "mimetic" or "pretended illocutionary acts" and other kinds of statements made by narrators.[16] Mimetic sentences containing no element of opinion or judgment establish the fictional world, the bedrock foundation of uncontestable truth within the context of the novel. Such is the first sentence of chapter 4 of *La voluntad*: "A lo lejos, en el fondo, sobre un suave altozano, la diminuta iglesia de Santa Bárbara se yergue en el azul intenso."[17] Martínez Ruiz employed these purely mimetic, world-presenting statements (just as did Clarín) to set up a situation in which a character's own words appear less veridical, thus latently exposing a character's hypocrisy.[18] For example, after Yuste invokes social Darwinisim and the unity of the physical and moral world authoritatively to deny the tenability of private property, the narrator informs us that Yuste has just read a journal article omitting his name from among the illustrious associates of a famous politician whom he considered a friend.

Thus the narrator reveals that Yuste's passionate speech is the product of a battered ego rather than a deeply-felt conviction. Later, Yuste, whose mood has improved, reverses his earlier radical stand, much to the surprise and consternation of Azorín, who has come ready to take the *maestro*'s part. The *maestro* now quotes passages from Plato and Tolstoy to substantiate his more moderate and conciliatory position, indicating that texts can be marshaled to formulate any truth. The narrator provides ample evidence of Yuste as a thinker who is often concerned more with the virtuosity of his expression than with the consistency of his ideological position. Rather than Martínez Ruiz's mouthpiece, Yuste embodies the fallacy of the intellectual role model and the tensions that inevitably exist between mentors and disciples. Yuste is a composite of Pi y Margall and Clarín (and perhaps others). The *maestro* epithet applied to Yuste had ambiguous connotations for Martínez Ruiz. He dedicated *Soledades* of 1898 to Clarín, calling him *maestro* on that occasion, but in 1897 he had published a short story entitled "El maestro" which depicts a younger writer patronized by an older one. If Yuste is Clarín, as some critics have suggested, such an equation is hardly a positive one, as Clarín is cited within the context of *La voluntad* as an example of "la hipertrofía que se nota en los escritores que viven en provincias cuando juzgan éxitos y fracasos ocurridos en Madrid" (96). Yuste is just such a writer; he has remained in the provinces, and, like Clarín, he turns to religious orthodoxy as he grows older.

In addition to the mimetic statements, Martínez Ruiz also occasionally had recourse to free indirect style, but unlike the Clarinian narrator who insinuates him or herself into the consciousness of the characters with liberal abandon, Martínez Ruiz's narrator coincides with a character's discourse very rarely and then only for a highly studied effect, again primarily to undermine another character's credibility. Yuste is subjected to this treatment on several occasions, underscoring his shifting intellectual posture and introducing a subtle antagonism between him and his disciple Azorín. Antonio Azorín is not so uncritical a follower of Yuste as has often been supposed. The free indirect method of revealing their antagonism allows Antonio to remain overtly a devoted admirer of his mentor (very much the way Martínez Ruiz did of Pi y Margall and Clarín). For example, when the narrator tells us that "el maestro, calmado con la apacibilidad de la noche, sonrió, satisfecho de su pintoresca asociación de ideas, y le pareció que sus paradojas de hombre sincero valían más que las actas de diputado y las carteras ministeriales de su frívolo amigo" (84), he adopts the perspective of Antonio who has just witnessed this "pintoresca asociación."

After a series of passages in which Yuste eloquently expounds on the futility of metaphysics, on eternity versus temporality and on social Darwinism, the following chapter begins with this observation by the narrator: "Este buen maestro— ¡habrá que confesarlo!—es en el fondo un burgués redomado" (98). The word *maestro* and the guilty sentiment implied by "confesarlo" associate this opinion of Yuste more with his disciple Antonio than with the objective narrative observer. On a few occasions, the narrator directly attributes to Antonio thoughts on Yuste's quixotic nature: "En tanto, Antonio piensa en que este buen maestro, a través de sus cóleras, de sus sonrisas y de sus ironías, es un hombre ingenuo y generoso, merecedor a un mismo tiempo—como Alonso Quijano el Bueno—de admiración, de risa y de piedad" (113). The ambivalence that Martínez Ruiz himself felt toward paternalistic authority figures like Clarín is masterfully embedded in these fleeting narrative moments.

Martínez Ruiz employed direct dialogue less often than Baroja and Unamuno to dialogize and diffuse the characters' ideas; Yuste's conversations with Antonio are really monologues. Though sparing with true dialogue, Martínez Ruiz did occasionally use it in *La voluntad* in a way that hints at a dialectical association of two philosophical positions. For example, in one passage Yuste blames all social evils on effects of the environment. Critics have taken Yuste's assertion as evidence that in 1902 Martínez Ruiz subscribed wholly to a social Darwinism deriving from Taine, Faure, Kropotkin and others, without considering that Antonio during the conversation categorizes the *maestro*'s ideas as *transformismo*. While not an overt contradiction of Yuste's thesis, Antonio's one-word summary emphasizes that Yuste is defending a theory that by 1902 had become something of a joke in intellectual circles and journals.

Martínez Ruiz further undermined Yuste in the contiguity of religious and intellectual lives of parallel chapters and by juxtaposing contradictory speeches at times within a single chapter and often in successive chapters. In his first intensely metaphysical speech to Antonio, Yuste affirms that "Todo pasa," while the "substancia universal perdura" (72), but a few sentences later he denies the existence of eternity, only to reverse himself in another passage saying that "La substancia es única y eterna." The whole issue of Martínez Ruiz and the subject of time is a thorny one, especially regarding the Nietzschean concept of the eternal return. The statements just quoted by Yuste are usually taken to be from sources such as Lucretius, Guyau and Nietzsche, but a review of Martínez Ruiz's earlier essays such as *La sociología criminal* suggests a different evolution. In *La sociología*, a summary of the major ideas (mostly of anarchists) about the relative responsibility of the individual and society for criminal acts concludes that "Nada es eterno; todo es mudable" (573). This same dictum is repeated in *Diario de un enfermo* and in "Ciencia y fe." Yuste's evocation of an eternal substance may also derive from Herderian notions held by Pi y Margall (Azorín mentions Pi's Herderian "sentido de la substancia, para el inmanente y eterna" in *Lecturas españolas*, 124) or from Unamuno's *En torno al casticismo*.

If Martínez Ruiz seems to favor mutability and change over essence and eternity in his essays, he did not give his character the same certainty;

he makes him look foolish with his fickle wavering between an idealist's insistence on transcendental eternity and the anarchist sociologists' negation of it. Nietzsche's notion of the eternal return, incorporating both change and permanence, does not occur to Yuste, but Antonio Azorín learns of Nietzsche's synthesis and mulls it over, only to decide that, if things do really recur at intervals as Nietzsche suggests, it is fortunate that we are unaware of it. Such awareness would make the world unbearable, and we would have to be supermen to overcome the inevitable (something his determinism precludes). This observation is hardly the uncritical acceptance of Nietzsche's notion of the eternal return usually ascribed to Martínez Ruiz. If he did have recourse to the notion of eternal recurrence in later literary works such as *Castilla* (1912) and *Doña Inés* (1925), it is more as a theme that allowed a particular kind of narrative construct than as a philosophical principle taken as truth.

In the same passage in which Yuste first addresses the problem of time, he emphasizes that all things pass, evoking the Kantian dictum that sensations are only a manifestation of the *substancia* and that "La imagen lo es todo." Both the "todo pasa" phrase and the "imagen lo es todo" are oft-repeated refrains throughout the novel in contexts that make these ideas sound increasingly ludicrous. When Yuste dies at the end of part 1, his last words are that he can confirm nothing, and the section ends with a drunk Antonio repeating the *maestro*'s refrain, "La imagen lo es todo." This phrase recurs often in the second part of the novel under similar circumstances. For example, an inebriated Antonio shouts, to the great astonishment of some café waiters: "Hay que romper la vieja *tabla de valores morales*, como decía Nietzsche . . . ¡Viva la imagen!" (215). In chapter 5 Yuste's interests turn to more materialistic subjects. He is now a confirmed determinist. Private property is the great evil; if the environment does not change, humanity cannot change. The physical and moral world are governed by the same laws (this after espousing a strict idealism in the previous speech).

Even greater confusion ensues in the next chapter, where Yuste attempts to combine both his desire for change and his wish for some sort of eternal continuity, a nostagia for Spain's traditional past. The dilemma is cast literally in the description of the tree under which Antonio and Yuste sit. An *árbol místico* shades them as they discuss political change and invent an allegory of three men who consult their elders about a reform plan. A figure representing Pi y Margall is cited as working in abstract generalities, while Salmerón wants to preserve specific rights. By the time the reformers confront all the abstracts and specifics of their mentors, their plan is reduced to nothing and they conclude with Panglossian irony that the present world is the best of all possible worlds. The refrain that all must change is evoked again, followed by the assertion that mysticism and tradition represent the best of Spain. Metaphysics is a human fantasy, a toy for men to play with. The chapter concludes with a story in which a Kantian philosopher and a carnival impresario agree that we cannot know the *noumena;* only *phenomena* are real.

Interwoven with chapters indicating Justina's progress on her *camino de perfección* are visits to Father Lasalde, a man of simple and enviable faith, and chapters on Quijano's unsuccessful rocket and torpedo experiments. Yuste begins to accept the priest Lasalde's faith when the priest responds to his refrain "Todo es lo mismo y todo cambia" with the observation that God is permanent.[19] Finally philosophy is reduced to nature. On a country outing, Antonio and Yuste see a "philosophical beetle" that has read the *Critique of Pure Reason;* it is "un filósofo perfecto" says Yuste, "¡cuántas cosas me diría que no me dice Platón en sus *Diálogos* ni Montaigne, ni Schopenhauer!" (160). In part 2 Antonio continues the "philosophy as nature" metaphor, although perhaps even more pejoratively, saying that a dog in the bar where he is drinking is wiser than Aristotle, Spinoza and Kant together. Perhaps such comments were part of Martínez Ruiz's and Baroja's stock of philosophical humor in their conversations, since toward the end of the second part of *La voluntad,* Silvestre Paradox's *perro kantiano* Yock makes an appearance.

Now Antonio follows in Yuste's footsteps, alternating idealism with materialism, and, like his mentor, he attempts to combine the two. In the fifth chapter of part 2, he proclaims himself to be a *determinista convencido,* saying that "todo es necesario y fatal" (218), but on the very next page "¡El mundo es una inmensa litografía de Daumier!" (219). He cannot accept Yuste's pronouncements on the eternal return; these theories, he says, were already stated by Toland and Lucretius. The philosophical companions he picks up in Madrid to replace Yuste are no more enlightening on the nature of life and the world. He visits Pi y Margall where talk turns to Comte's positivism, but on the way home he realizes that all of Pi's philosophizing has led to nothing. A visit to Olaiz confirms these sentiments, as Olaiz believes that revolution and democracy are a mistake and that socialism is crumbling; the future, according to Olaiz, lies with the individual.

In part 3, the juxtaposing technique suddenly ceases when Antonio decides to leave Madrid and the intellectual life to seek "real life." Much like the protagonist of *Diario de un enfermo,* he concludes that books teach nothing that is not already evident in life ("En filosofía, desde Aristóteles hasta Kant, ¿quién ha dicho nada nuevo?," *OC* 1: 262). Just as Yuste

gravitated toward the faith of Father Lasalde, for a time Antonio finds solace in reading religious books at a monastery where he has stopped to
rest. Here he sums up his philosophical position as encompassing absolutely everything he has read: mysticism, anarchism, irony, dogmatism,
Schopenhauer and Nietzsche. Finally he decides that overintellectualizing has paralyzed his will, a situation he attempts to remedy by returning to his village and marrying his opposite, the willful, domineering
Iluminada.

Antonio definitively refutes Yuste and his ideas by repudiating the
Yustian-style intellectual life and opting to live as a small-town, Casino-
frequenting gentleman, known to the locals as Antoñico. For more than
ten years Antonio has followed in Yuste's footsteps as a student of Kant,
Schopenhauer and Nietzsche, and their careers have many remarkable
similarities. But Antonio surpasses Yuste, who on his deathbed rejects the
whole European intellectual tradition in a verbal gesture: "no puedo afir-
mar nada sobre la realidad del universo... La inmanencia o trascendencia de la causa primera, el movimiento, la forma de los seres, el origen de
la vida... Arcanos impenetrables... eternos..." (179). Antonio does not
wait for death to unveil his disdain for intellectualism; he eschews it by
changing his vital posture.

Martínez Ruiz's iconoclastic narrative techniques that simultaneously
build and destroy characters' selfhood culminate in his own personal self-
immolation within the context of *La voluntad*. Several of Yuste's and Antonio's speeches are actually taken verbatim from journal articles that
Martínez Ruiz had published earlier under his own name. In assigning his
words to characters who have proven themselves inconsistent and unre-
liable, Martínez Ruiz erases his own previous intellectual position. A particular instance of this self-destructive mode occurs late in the novel.
After a very drunk and incoherent Antonio utters the exact words of a
Martínez Ruiz article, the narrator comments that "Verdaderamente, se
necesita beber mucho para pensar de este modo" (215).

As a novelistic character, Antonio Azorín remains an indistinct shadow
whose intellectual development (nominally the focus of the novel) con-
sists of a series of confrontations with the voices of different texts espousing a variety of philosophical and theological ideas. The ideas are
presented in a shifting, nonauthoritative narrative style that precludes any
determination of the ultimate truth sustained in the novel. Martínez Ruiz
achieved the enviable feat of having his philosophical cake and eating it
too, an achievement possible only in the multi-voiced novelistic genre.
The novel's heteroglossia provided Martínez Ruiz the forum he needed
to exorcise his former self and ideas before he underwent his next meta-

morophsis as Azorín, the passive and distanced observer of all things Spanish and human. *La voluntad* was the iconoclastic expression he was seeking to make his definitive break with the past: "¿No habría más en literatura? Galdós, Pereda, Palacio Valdés, Clarín, leídos de muchacho, no lograban equilibrar—menos, mucho menos, destruir—esta sensación que me producía los clásicos; eran ellos mismos una continuación directa de los clásicos; eran ellos mismos clásicos. ¿Y qué iba a hacer yo para salir de esta limitación? ¿Y es que esta limitación, como ya he dicho, no tenía su evidente superioridad? El horizonte lo tenía limitado; las potencias las tenía embargadas. . . . ¿Me resignaba yo a tal mancipación? . . . De pronto inicio un cambio de valores."[20]

La voluntad is a defiant work that challenges Galdós's simplistic view of the will in his play of similar title; it undercuts Baroja's solution to a will-less protagonist in *Camino de perfección*, and it undermines all philosophical and literary authority, especially that of would-be mentors Clarín and Pi y Margall. If Galdós's solution to an entire family's lack of will in *Voluntad* was for the strong Isidora (notice the assonance with *La voluntad*'s willful Iluminada) to assume control to everyone's approval and benefit, Martínez Ruiz presented this solution as less than satisfactory. Antonio degenerates into an unkempt has-been who is not respected by the townspeople. At the end of the novel, letters to Baroja from a dismayed Martínez Ruiz, who has visited Antonio, reveal that their former intellectual companion has become slovenly, no longer reads, writes or thinks, and spends his mornings at the beck and call of his wife and his afternoons at the local casino playing cards.[21] Martínez Ruiz's ending is also an answer to Baroja's solution to aboulia in *Camino de perfección*—Fernando's finding psychological equilibrium in marriage. Baroja and Martínez Ruiz both opposed the bourgeois institution of marriage, and Martínez Ruiz could not allow to go uncontested Baroja's failure to find a nonbourgeois resolution to his protagonist's quandary. If returning to village life is a positive experience for Ossorio, it is a decidedly negative one for Antonio Azorín. The letters from Martínez Ruiz to Baroja describing the ruin that village living has wreaked on Antonio are couched in a tone of moral superiority, implying that Baroja's solution to Ossorio's dilemma (a happiness predicated on eschewing city life, painting and intellectual pursuits) is untenable.

La voluntad was Martínez Ruiz's last anarchic cry against personal and literary authority before he himself took the *nom de plume* "Azorín," a name that echoes "Clarín," his mentor and nemesis. (José María Valverde wrote that Martínez Ruiz felt emancipated when Clarín died in 1901, and Anna Krause has suggested that Yuste's death may represent Clarín's.)

Did he announce with the onomastic change that he was now ready to assume the role of rapacious literary arbiter so recently vacated by the hollowed Asturian novelist and critic? In any case, the works that follow *La voluntad* have a markedly different quality from the earlier, more polemical works. This phenomenon has been thoroughly documented and analyzed in Azorinian criticism, but I shall briefly review *Antonio Azorín* (1903) and *Las confesiones de un pequeño filósofo* (1904) as epilogues to the story of Martínez Ruiz's development as a philosophical novelist.

In *Antonio Azorín* metaphysics is much less subtly dethroned than it is in the 1902 novel. Descriptions of Martínez Ruiz's native Alicante and his adopted Castile prevail (much to the advantage of the former). There are none of the long discussions of philosophical issues or clever narrative maneuverings to undermine an ideological position. The subject of philosophy does arise, but it is dismissed in a cursory, often humorous, manner. Schopenhauer, author of *La voluntad de la naturaleza*, is cited as someone who would probably find amenable the fact that spinach and parsley do not transplant well. The sight of a spider elicits the question: "¿Es un animal nietzscheano la araña?" (*OC* 1: 1019). Sarrió is reading *Diccionario general de cocina*, which he calls a transcendental and philosophical book; Azorín is referred to as no Spinoza, and a bishop who reads everything new believes that "Nietzsche, Schopenhauer, Stirner . . . son los bellos libros de caballería de hogaño" (*OC* 1: 1091). The bishop goes on to say that the young people who follow these thinkers are lacking "esa simplicidad, esa visión humilde de las cosas, esa compenetración con la realidad que Alonso Quijano encontró sólo en su lecho de muerte, ya curado de sus fantasías" (*OC* 1: 1091).

It is difficult not to see *Las confesiones de un pequeño filósofo* as the spiritual (if not actual) sequel to *Antonio Azorín;* rather than debating any philosophical ideas, the *pequeño filósofo* does attempt a humble view of things, reviewing his own development from childhood to adulthood first in his native region and then in Madrid. Now he does not even set up metaphysical ideas to undermine them: "Yo no quiero hacer vagas filosofías; me repugnan las teorías y las leyes generales, porque sé que circunstancias desconocidas para mí pueden cambiar la faz de las cosas, o que un ingenio más profundo que el mío puede deducir de los pequeños hechos que yo ensamblo leyes y corolarios distintos a los que yo deduzco. Yo no quiero hacer filosofías nebulosas; que vea cada cual en los hechos sus propios pensamientos."[22] The objects of attention are the small areas of life—days at school, childhood games, meals, the countryside, people's looks and behavior—that precede any grand philosophical abstractions formulated about them. If the little philosopher evokes eternal time, it is associated not with Nietzsche but with a cuckoo clock, "símbolo de lo inexorable y de lo eterno" (138), and if he thinks of the Infinite, it is upon catching sight of a certain kind of woman or when viewing the sea.

The first era of the Spanish philosophical novel had come to an end. The novelistic approaches of *Amor y pedagogía, Camino de perfección* and *La voluntad* that drew upon nineteenth-century narrative strategies (while simultaneously destroying them) in order to highlight the conflicts inherent in major nineteenth-century philosophies gave way to new forms as the Generation of '98 confronted a formidable new rival in José Ortega y Gasset.

5

UNAMUNO: LAST ATTACK
ON RATIONALISM

Unamuno and Azorín, whose writing careers were more diverse than Baroja's, did not publish any more novels until the second and third decades respectively (although each paid tribute to *Don Quixote* on the occasion of its third centenary in 1905). Baroja, however, found his professional *métier* in the novel and continued to produce longer works of fiction at the rate of one or two a year. The social criticism and philosophical disquisition combined with adventure story elements that forged *Camino de perfección* became a formula for novel writing in Baroja's prolific first decade, although philosophical discourse did not again play the central role it enjoyed in *Camino de perfección* until his last philosophical novel, *El árbol de la ciencia* (1911). Unamuno also returned to the philosophical novel in the second decade, finishing *Niebla* in 1913 or 1914, and in *Castilla* (1912) Azorín created a unique genre, the *estampa* (vignette or sketch), a kind of philosophical fable, often centering on the notion of eternal recurrence. The collection of sketches in *Castilla* is a social and literary archeology of Castile that represents an intrahistorical analysis of the political region that led Spain into the modern world.

Baroja's and Unamuno's philosophical fictions of 1911 and 1914 are also fossilizations of philosophical themes (especially reason versus will or life) that had once been raw and polemical but that now take on the patina of literary distance. In *El árbol de la ciencia,* Baroja marshaled every major thinker he had read in the past twenty years—Letamendi, Darwin, Bernard, Kant, Fichte, Schopenhauer, Nietzsche, Hobbes, Fouillée and Comte, among others—to create a melange of ideas and ideologies that jar against one another in the action and philosophical discussions. In *Niebla* Unamuno summed up Cartesian idealism and Kantian rationalism in his hapless character Augusto Pérez, who, like Andrés Hurtado of *El árbol de la ciencia,* is doomed by an inability to function in real life. Both books invent more personal and original structures and narrative devices and recur less to the imitation and parody of earlier types of fiction that shaped the 1902 novels.[1]

These last efforts in the discursive philosophical novel by members of the Generation of '98 respond to the philosophical and publishing milieu of the period 1907 to 1914. The major event in both arenas was the appearance and rapid rise in the Spanish intellectual scene of José Ortega y Gasset. Having spent much of his time from 1906 to 1908 studying with neo-Kantians in Germany, Ortega reintroduced the polemical assertion that Spain needed to Europeanize, to broaden its intellectual horizons and especially to include reason in serious Spanish philosophical discussion. Unamuno had struggled for twenty-five years to overcome his attraction to German idealism and English positivism, and Baroja had carried on a love-hate relationship with these orientations for some fifteen years, when suddenly this bright new star appeared on the Spanish intellectual horizon, resurrecting many of the philosophical problems the '98 authors had already worked through: an *a priori* basis for knowledge, the notion of the thing-in-itself, the world as image, the rejection of biologically centered philosophy in favor of reason, truth as a series of abstract relations. The members of the Generation of '98 had few years of hegemony between the time the previous generation had lost its ascendancy (Clarín died in 1901, and Galdós and Valera were clearly slipping in power if not prestige early in the decade) and the appearance of the new rival generation headed by Ortega, Ramón Gómez de la Serna and Ramón Pérez de Ayala.

From 1908 forward, Ortega engaged in public and private discussions with the members of the Generation of '98, especially with Unamuno, Baroja, Azorín and Ramiro de Maeztu. The young and brilliant upstart's attitude toward his seniors was a mixture of reverance and contentiousness. Ortega maintained complex relations with Unamuno and Baroja, but he also engaged with Azorín (although not so extensively, doubtless having less to say to the philosophically unsophisticated writer). Ortega criticized Azorín's writings in favor of the conservative politician Maura, saying that the *pequeño filósofo* lacked ideas and intellectual rigor. On this occasion Maeztu defended his cogenerationist by publishing an article in which he accused Ortega of intellectualism, although he admitted in a private letter to Ortega that he had never thought of Azorín as a serious thinker. Later it was Maeztu who attacked both Azorín for his establishment views and Ortega, who defended the former object of his criticism, saying that he was useful to the new generation's reformist aims. The crossfire between Ortega and the members of his circle and the older intellectuals provided ample inspiration for works of a philosophical nature on both sides.

Baroja's *El árbol de la ciencia* can be understood as an answer to Ortega's first major essay, the neo-Kantian "Adán en el Paraíso," and *Niebla* may have been inspired by Unamuno's hostility toward the resurgence of

Europeanism and philosophical idealism in Spain under the sponsorship of the young Ortega. Sparked by a letter of 1907 (the year Unamuno began *Niebla*), the polemics between Ortega and Unamuno became heated in 1909 when the letter was published (Unamuno again worked briefly on *Niebla* in that year). He finished the novel in 1913 immediately after *Del sentimiento trágico de la vida*, the last section of which refers to his differences with Ortega. Unamuno's copy of Ortega's *Meditaciones del Quijote* is not dedicated, suggesting that he was interested enough to buy a copy for himself. The marginal notations in it are uncharacteristic; perhaps out of haste or anger, Unamuno crudely underlined some passages in pencil and did not index the passages of interest on the front or back cover as was his custom (he was usually a careful reader and his notations most methodical). The envy theme of *Abel Sánchez* (1917) may also contain elements of this tussle, which became even more complex as Maeztu, Unamuno's earlier ally and a writer Unamuno believed he had mentored, sided with Ortega in the debate with Unamuno. Maeztu began writing articles about Unamuno from a safe distance in London. Despite Ortega's debt to Maeztu, to whom he owed his decision to take a university chair in philosophy (he dedicated the first three editions of *Meditaciones del Quijote* to him), the two also eventually had a falling out.

Paulino Garagorri's edition of Ortega's heretofore unpublished manuscripts on members of the Generation of '98[2] and E. Inman Fox's recent incorporation of these findings into a thorough reevaluation of the initial conception of *Meditaciones del Quijote*, provide convincing evidence that Unamuno, Baroja and Azorín were a major inspiration to Ortega in his first and perhaps most important book. Fox has demonstrated that the *Meditaciones* were to have been " 'meditaciones' sobre 'la manera española de ver las cosas' . . . las más importantes versaban, no sobre la obra de Cervantes, sino sobre la de Baroja y Azorín, no siendo el tercero y último ensayo de *Meditaciones del Quijote* sino parte de un escrito largo sobre la novela y la novelística *barojianas*."[3] The *Meditaciones* marked Ortega's retreat from neo-Kantianism and his embarkation upon a phenomenological project in which he understood Unamuno, Baroja and Azorín as part of his own horizon, his *circunstancia*. Although by 1912 Ortega began shifting away from rationalism, his relationship to Baroja and Unamuno early in the second decade (when *El árbol de la ciencia* and *Niebla* were completed) was that of a neo-Kantian thinker to those who had worked through idealism to a self-styled vitalism. It is likely that Ortega achieved his final solution to the life-reason problem (ratio-vitalism) as much through his interaction with the Spanish "vitalists" of the '98 as through his contacts with German phenomenology in Marburg.

Although *Niebla* is a complex work drawing on numerous philosophical sources, I believe that Ortega's painful (to Unamuno) reintroduction of the polemics of rationalism shortly before the Rector of Salamanca began work on the novel in 1907 provided the immediate, if not deep, motivation for undertaking the novel. Ortega's association with Unamuno is the earliest of his friendships-cum-antagonisms with members of the preceding Generation. Unamuno examined Ortega in Greek at the University of Salamanca in 1898, and Laureano Robles believes that their relationship was continuous from that time forward, although the epistolary trail is intermitent.[4] Ortega probably paved the way for Unamuno's collaboration on the prestigious periodical *El Imparcial,* directed by his father (one recalls Unamuno's bitter invective about the difficulty of placing articles there). Numerous studies chronicle their relationship,[5] which contains clues to Unamuno's renewed interest in his aborted novel about a rationalistic protagonist.

Mario Valdés, who worked at the Casa-Museo Unamuno before the first page of the *Niebla* manuscript disappeared, indicates that Unamuno wrote August 1907 on the title sheet.[6] Thus he assumes that *Niebla* was also completed in that year, but other evidence indicates the contrary: a letter of January 21, 1913, in which Unamuno wrote to a friend that he had just finished the novel,[7] and some notes written in 1910, accompanying the manuscript of *Niebla* in the Casa-Museo Unamuno, in which Unamuno outlined possible scenes for the novel. At the end of the notes, Unamuno pronounced the novel a failure, like others he had begun and abandoned.

Even in his earliest and more obsequious letters, Ortega marked his considerable differences with Unamuno's philosophical positions: "Acaso me diga usted que no hace falta saber para pensar; pero le he de confesar que ese misticismo español-clásico que en su ideario aparece de cuando en cuando, no me convence; me parece una cosa como musgo, que tapiza poco a poco las almas un poco solitarias, como la de usted, excesivamente íntimas (no se indigne), y preocupadas del bien y del alma por vicio intelectualista. . . . Corre por todos los ánimos de los intelectuales nuestros de hoy un viento de *personalismo* corto de miras, estéril, que es lo más opuesto a nuestras necesidades."[8]

The debate between Ortega and Unamuno left the arena of friendly sparring between an older and a younger man when Azorín published a private letter to him from Unamuno in *ABC* in 1909. In the letter, dated November 13, 1907, Unamuno railed against the new breed of intellectual (which he called *papanatas*), who saw the salvation of Spain in the importation of foreign science and ideas. Unamuno asserted that if he were offered the choice between Descartes and Saint John of the Cross, he preferred the latter. Not without reason, Ortega identified himself as one of the alleged *papanatas* and responded first with an indirect attack on "personalism," which could refer only to Unamuno, and on September 27, 1909, he published "Unamuno y Europa," in which he asserted that he was "plenamente, íntegramente, uno de esos papanatas; apenas si he escrito, desde que escribí para el público, una sola cuartilla en la que no aparezca con agresividad simbólica: Europa. En esta palabra comienzan y acaban para mí todos los dolores de España."[9] Unamuno considered resurrecting Don Fulgencio Entrambosmares of *Amor y pedadogía* to do battle with Ortega through a series of articles entitled "Don Fulgencio en Marburgo," but these were apparently never written. Instead, he returned to his abandoned novel *Niebla*.

In attempting to reconstruct Unamuno's reasons for beginning and then finally finishing *Niebla*, of interest are some of Ortega's statements in letters to Unamuno just before and during the time of its composition,[10] especially one of December 30, 1906: "La Humanidad es Idea: el hombre—lo único importante que existe en el Universo es Idea"[11] or "Yo me he metido en Matemáticas porque esos problemas de la física teorética me inquietan demasiado para no darles la batalla. Creo—como Cohen—que la filosofía como ciencia es función de la física; y no había por tanto nueva filosofía como ciencia—mientras no haya nueva física. Sobre la física del Renacimiento y su propia geometría hace germinar Descartes su trasmutación filosófica. Sobre el invento infinitesimal, su sistema Leibniz; sobre Copérnico, Galileo y Newton sale Kant con su nueva transmutación. Esto quiero yo ser: ¿es la física nuestra algo distinto de la newtoniana, y que por tanto posibilite y exija una nueva filosofía?" (12, January 27, 1907) or "desde que soy platónico todo me hace llorar" (14, February 17, 1907).

Did Unamuno have in mind his young antagonist when six months later he began the novel whose idealistic protagonist echoes Descartes and Kant? The possibility does not seem so remote in the context of a letter from Unamuno to Ortega written on November 21, 1912, shortly before Unamuno returned to the novel, this time to finish and publish it:

Estoy leyendo a la par la *Ethik* de Herrmann, y la *Logik der reinen Erkenntniss* de Cohen y la *Lógica* de Croce. Cohen, se lo repito a usted, no me entra: es un saduceo que me deja helado. Comprendo bien su posición, pero ese racionalismo o idealismo a mí, espiritualista del modo más crudo, más católico en cuanto al deseo, todo eso me repugna. No me basta que sea verdad, si lo es. Y luego no puedo, no, no puedo con lo *puro:* concepto puro, conocimiento puro, voluntad pura, razón pura... tanta pureza me quita el aliento. . . . Y no sirve razonarme, ¡no, no, no! No me resigno a la razón. (21)

Augusto's fate is one that Unamuno envisioned for all who cling to reason's treacherous promise, those misguided paths into which the German philosophers were leading young intellectuals, as he confided in a letter to Luis Zulueta on April 25, 1913. In this light, *Niebla* is a prophetic novel, offering a prophecy that doubles back upon itself.

Niebla was for Unamuno a continuation of *Amor y pedagogía*, but one, he believed, that was more artistically successful: "hace tres días he terminado una novela, o nivola fantástica y humorística y llena de cómicas crudezas, de desnudo, no de desvestido. Hace *pendant* a mi *Amor y pedagogía*, pero es más novela y más entretenida, creo."[12] The heightened comic tone no doubt derives from Unamuno's fervent reading of the English novel in the first decade.[13] Not only is *Niebla* artistically more satisfying, but the philosophical problems it poses and explores are more original than those introduced in *Amor y pedagogía*. As a philosophical novel that stands midway between the comic-burlesque of *Amor y pedagogía* and the embodiment of existential angst in the later novels, it begins ostensibly as an ironic critique of rationalism and ends with scenes of existential despair (though tinged with a comic irony lacking in the last four novels). Unamuno moved beyond the battles with Spencer and Hegel that underwrote his novel of 1902. Most importantly Kierkegaard's personalist philosophy, which Unamuno began reading in 1901 and continued to devour through 1906 as new volumes became available, provided him with a substitute for the rationalism and positivism he had discarded. Kierkegaard's *Either/Or* catapulted Unamuno out of his uneasy alliance with nineteenth-century thinkers like Krause, Hegel and Spencer, all of whom sought and believed they had found the "harmonious ideal"; for Kierkegaard, it was "either/or," not the "both and" of Hegel.[14] Unamuno left behind the dialectical and opted for the dialogical, eschewing synthesis in favor of opposition. He now saw traditional philosophy in general as a hopeless enterprise: "a series of inconceivable problems for which are given equally inconceivable solutions."[15] These ideas did not mature for Unamuno until the completion of *Del sentimiento trágico de la vida* in 1911, and he was unable to finish *Niebla* until after he had achieved a definitive position in that long essay.

In addition to the impetus given Unamuno by his quarrels with the Spanish neo-Kantianism of Ortega and his followers, *Niebla*'s composition is inextricably interwined with that of *Del sentimiento trágico de la vida*, which was begun as early as 1899 as a series of "diálogos filosóficos de plan vastísimo."[16] It was to draw on sociology and ethics to treat the unknowable finality of the universe and the concept of the deity, ending with the doctrine of the happy uncertainty that allows us to live. This early project, which is the antithesis of the "Nuevo discurso del método" that he was planning in June of 1892, became in the first decade "Tratado del amor de Dios." By 1907, however, Unamuno had abandoned the specific project of "Tratado del amor de Dios," which deals with logical arguments for the concept of God. In 1900 he temporarily suspended work on the "Diálogos filosóficos" to write *Amor y pedagogía,* and in 1907 he temporarily abandoned the "Tratado del amor de Dios" to begin *Niebla.*

By 1905 and the writing of *Don Quijote y Sancho,* Unamuno had become thoroughly aware of the conflict that existed between his desire for direct knowledge of concrete carnal, individual, unique, enduring life and nebulous eternity. So in 1907 he invented a character enmeshed in the fog of his own thoughts who fails miserably in his contacts with the "real" world. In *Don Quijote y Sancho* Unamuno evoked "hunger and love" as the two wellsprings of human life that became the will and the intellect in *Del sentimiento trágico de la vida* and the opposing forces in Augusto's Pérez's trajectory in *Niebla.* In passing, he scoffed at Descartes's project: "Otros vienen y nos dicen que no, sino que lo necesario y apremiante es podar nuestra lengua, que por dondequiera le asoman y apuntan ramas viciosas, y nos la quieren dejar como arbolito de jardín, como boje enjaulado. Así, añaden, ganará en claridad y en lógica. ¿Pero es que vamos a escribir algún "Discurso del método" con ella? ¡Al demonio la lógica y claridades!"[17]

In August of 1910, the year he returned to *Niebla,* he was also once again at work on "El tratado del amor de Dios," which in 1911 became *Del sentimiento trágico de la vida.* The first chapter was published in *La España Moderna* in December of that year. For Unamuno, the methods for the novel and the essay are not so dissimilar, as he believed *Del sentimiento trágico* to be a magnificent union of metaphysics and poetry. Sometime in 1912 he must have returned to *Niebla,* if as early as January 21 of 1913 he could declare that it was now finished. On February 11, 1913, however, he wrote to Jiménez Ilundain that he had renewed work on a novel that he had interrupted four years earlier, indicating that, like *Amor y pedagogía,* which was also prematurely declared finished, it underwent yet further revisions before publication in 1914.[18]

In *Del sentimiento* reason, or reflexive knowledge, which distinguishes the human species, is posited as a social product that owes its origins to language: "El pensamiento es lenguaje interior, y el lenguaje interior brota del exterior. ¿De dónde resulta que la razón es social y común?"[19] This idea was given a comic twist in Augusto's comments on language and in Augusto's dog Orfeo, who is empowered to speak at the end of the novel. There is a sensible world that is born of hunger and another world, the ideal, which is the child of love, so that living is one thing and knowing another, the two opposing each other in a way that echoes Hegel's notion that "all that is real is rational and all that is rational is real: "todo lo vital es antirracional, no ya solo irracional, y todo lo racional, antivital" (35). The ultimate truth can then be summed up as *"sum, ergo cogito"* (37). Augusto also deforms Descartes's famous dictum in several ways. Unamuno asserted in *Del sentimiento* that these opposites can be translated into will and reason, the former tending to appropriate the world while the latter seeks absorption by the world. Fused with ideas, the intellect does not need anything outside itself upon which to operate, while the will requires the material world. To know something is to make oneself into that which one knows; but to use it, to dominate it, it must remain distinct from oneself: "La consecuencia vital del racionalismo sería el suicidio" (107), prophesying Augusto's suicide at the end of *Niebla*.[20]

To remain vital, alive, one must maintain the duality of will and reason and struggle to keep one from dominating the other, as occurs in Descartes's system and all subsequent rationalisms. In fact, in *Del sentimiento trágico de la vida*, Unamuno embued the *Discourse on Method* with a tragic sense, and he replaced Descartes's unitary system with a duality in which the being is always conscious of itself. One must *serse* (which may sound like Kant's division of the noumenal and the phenomenal, but the *Critique of Pure Reason*, if not the *Critique of Practical Reason*, eventually privileges reason over the will). For Unamuno, the dichotomy between the interior and exterior selves gives rise to the *yo*. Hegel's abstract system had disregarded the subjective condition of knowledge on which Kant's position devolved (denying the possibility of self-knowledge), but Kierkegaard brought subjectivity back to center stage, relating knowledge and existence, and Unamuno goes even further than Kierkegaard in making self-consciousness an ontological baseline.

An additional philosophical impetus to finishing the novel in 1913 or 1914 may have been the biologically centered epistemology of Unamuno's friend Ramón Turró, a Catalan doctor, medical theorist and sometime philosopher who in 1912 published *Origens del coneixment: la fam*, refuting Kant's notion that one can never know the "thing in itself." Turró's argument provided the ideal counterweight to the Cartesian-Kantian (and Ortegian) rationalism Unamuno took as his central philosophical target in the novel. (There are several Turronian-sounding additions to the manuscript, written in a different color ink in the margins and on the backs of pages.) Turró argued that the indisputable proof of our direct knowledge of the world lies in the trophic sphere; we know that the objective world exists because we ingest it in the form of food, thus achieving the enviable feat of centering the origins of knowledge within the individual while simultaneously confirming the existence of the physical material world.

Turró accounts for the way we acquire knowledge as follows: The newborn baby or animal experiences a nutritive deficiency soon after birth, and being equipped with automatic motor activity, it moves toward the possible source of nutrition (the suckling movement), encountering the breast by trial and error. At first the newborn does not recognize the sensory attributes of this source, but after repeated experiences in satisfying hunger from the same place, a capacity for sensory perception and distinction begins to occur. After repeatedly receiving nourishment from its mother, a baby begins to recognize *a priori* the mother's physical features, her voice, the color of her dress. Once the senses identify these qualities in the hunger-quelling source, intellection takes place, and the subject forms mental images of the objects in the exterior world that satisfy internal needs. Intellection is thus the consciousness of a relationship between a trophic effect and its representation by means of sensorial impressions.

Unamuno wrote a prologue to the Castilian translation of Turró's book in 1916 in which he stated that he read *Orígenes* for the first time in its French version in 1914 (only the French version, not the Catalan, is present in his library). He was, however, clearly aware of Turró's ideas, which had been published fragmentarily in French and German in the first decade, well before finishing *Niebla*. A letter from Turró to Unamuno in 1913 thanks him for sending *Del sentimiento trágico de la vida* and alludes to their having already spoken either in person or by letter about Unamuno's sharing Turró's trophic theory of the origins of knowledge: "Nada tan cierto como lo que U. me dice acerca de que es una idea antigua en U. los orígenes tróficos del conocimiento. . . . Ya ve si lo había advertido."[21] It is possible that Turró's theory suggested to Unamuno the idea for Augusto's ludicrous death by overeating, which had not yet occurred to him in 1910; the notes indicate that Augusto was to commit suicide by ingesting poison. Other specific passages allude very directly to Turró.

Niebla is a novel about the acquisition of knowledge. In fact, knowing is ubiquitous and absurd; everyone knows everyone else (Eugenia's aunt knew Augusto's mother; Liduvina knows Eugenia; Mauricio knows Rosario), except for Augusto, who does not know any of them. Recall that knowledge was a topic Unamuno intended to take up in his philosophical treatise "Filosofía lógica," but he was unable to develop it at that time. Unamuno returned to epistemology in *Del sentimiento trágico de la vida*, and *Niebla* essentially embodies in a complex dialogic manner the ideas he tendered on the subject in that essay. The use of physiological language when discussing knowledge is more than mere metaphor in the 1912 essays:

Más es menester distinguir aquí entre el deseo o apetito de conocer, aparente-
mente y a primera vista, por amor al conocimiento mismo, entre el ansia de probar
del fruto del arbol de la ciencia, y la necesidad de conocer para vivir. Esto último,
que nos da el conocimiento directo e inmediato, y que en cierto sentido, si no
pareciese paradógico podría llamarse conocimiento inconsciente, es común al
hombre con los animales, mientras lo que nos distingue de éstos es el
conocimiento reflexivo, el conocer del conocer mismo. . . . más dejando ahora
para más adelante lo que de ello sea en las hondas entrañas de la existencia,, es lo
averiguado y cierto que en el orden aparencial de las cosas, en la vida de los seres
dotados de algún conocer o percibir, más o menos brumoso, o que por sus actos
parecen estar dotados de él, el conocimiento se nos muestra ligado a la necesidad
de vivir y de procurarse sustento para lograrlo. . . . Con términos en que la con-
creción raya acaso en grosería, cabe decir que el cerebro, en cuanto su función,
depende del estómago. [18]

Perhaps mindful of Turró's extreme theory of knowledge, which endows
the trophic sphere with primacy, Unamuno parodied in *Niebla* the idea he
took seriously in the essay.[22]

"Hay personas," writes Unamuno in *Del sentimiento trágico de la vida*,
"que parecen no pensar más que con el cerebro, o con cualquier otro órgano que sea específico para pensar; mientras otros piensan con todo el
cuerpo y toda el alma, con la sangre, con el tuétano de los huesos, con el
corazón, con los pulmones, con el vientre, con la vida" (18). *Niebla*'s protagonist, Augusto, suffers from the inability to integrate the physiological
and the mental modes of knowing. Augusto is a *nebuloso* (all the references
to *niebla* in the novel are associated with the protagonist) as was Unamuno
himself some fifteen years earlier when he projected his "Nuevo discurso
del método" and twelve years earlier when he drafted his *En torno al casticismo* with its ideas on the *nublo* of the eternal life of peoples. Augusto
says: "Los hombres no sucumbimos a las grandes penas ni las grandes alegrías, y es porque estas penas y esas alegrías vienen embozadas en una
inmensa niebla de pequeños incidentes. Y la vida es esto, la niebla. La
vida es una nebulosa."[23]

Unlike his methodology in *Amor y pedagogía*, in which opposing character pairs carry the satirical message, Unamuno abandoned Hegelian
dialectics altogether in *Niebla* to offer a more complicated design in
which the Cartesian rationalist Augusto (whose namesake St. Augustine,
like Descartes, had faith in the individual soul's knowledge of God) encounters a number of alternatives. Paparrigópulos is a Menéndez Pelayo-
style researcher who gets lost in endless detail. Like Entrambosmares
he combines positivism and idealism, and like Hegel he reduces all
life to form. The mystical anarchist Fermín is also divorced from life.
Other characters—Eugenia, her aunt Ermelinda, Rosario, Liduvina and

Víctor—represent varying degrees of the pragmatic or realist orientations. All female characters in *Niebla* cultivate the sensual and practical
dimensions of life, while most of the male characters emphasize an intellectualizing approach. Fermín is an anarchist, but in theory only; Paparrigópulos is writing a treatise on women without ever having had a
relationship with one, and Avito's experiences in *Amor y pedagogía* have
left him unable to live in the present. Eugenia says to her practical-
minded aunt that Augusto has no *entrañas:*[24] "Si es hueco, ¡como si lo vi-
era, hueco!" (81), and her uncle Fermín is no better ("Así como si no
existiese de verdad," 82), although confounding any neat scheme is Mauricio, who is pure body "a quien se le pasea el alma por el cuerpo" (81).
Contrasted to Augusto's Platonic or metaphysical love for Eugenia, is a
series of interpolated stories that relate the lives of people whose loves are
anything but Platonic and who have serious marital problems. The suggestion is that these people, unlike Augusto, exist because they are engaged with real life—creating a kind of text-metatext situation in which
the central character's story is commented on indirectly by the stories of
other characters.[25]

For much of the novel, Augusto's knowing is purely cerebral (he falls
in love with Eugenia *a priori*,[26] and he does not recognize her when he
passes her in the street), a bold contradiction of Unamuno's assertion in
Del sentimiento that mental knowledge cannot exist independently of the
physiological. In epistemological terms, Augusto's knowledge is unintegrated at the beginning of the novel and remains so until the interview
with Unamuno prompts him belatedly to attempt a remedy for his epistemological deficit. As the novel opens, his mother, with whom he has
lived well into adulthood, has recently died. Her maternal protectiveness
has kept Augusto from marrying and has shielded him from the need to
establish an independent relationship with the world. She has also in-
stilled in him a distaste for physiological knowledge by expressing dismay
at the contents of Augusto's university course in physiology: "Todo esto
es muy feo, hijo mío . . . no estudies para médico. Lo mejor es no saber
cómo se tienen las cosas de dentro" (77).

In the first scene, the epistemological infant Augusto stands at the
doorway of his home, a protective womb, from which he is about to be
expelled into a world where he will have opportunities to gain physiological knowledge. Augusto is apprehensive about the expulsion and extends
his hand out the door to test the weather. This action does not signify his
"taking possession of the world," says the narrator prophetically. In fact,
throughout much of the novel, Augusto fails to ingest the knowledge the

world offers him, mostly in the form of relationships with women. He is justifiably baffled when Eugenia accuses him of trying to buy her body by liquidating her debts: "¡Comprar yo su cuerpo... su cuerpo... ! Si me sobra el mío, Orfeo, me sobra el mío!" (80). Rather than gradually shifting from the initial random motor movements to intellectual knowledge outlined by Turró, Augusto leaps directly to intellection without passing through the physiological stage: "¡Mi Eugenia, sí la mía . . . ésta que me estoy forjando a solas, y no la otra no la de carne y hueso, no la que vi cruzar por la puerta de mi casa, aparición fortuita, no la de la portera!" (67).

He confirms his belief in abstract, *a priori* knowledge several pages later in musing about Eugenia, whom he has not actually met and whom he does not meet until chapter seven: "Y ¿cómo me he enamorado, si en rigor no puedo decir que la conozco? ¡Bah! el conocimiento vendrá después. El amor precede al conocimiento, y éste mata a aquél" (71). His *a priori* approach is succinctly summed up in Mauricio's apt epithet for Augusto—*predestinado*. Eugenia's uncle, Don Fermín, warns Augusto of the danger of such a beginning: "El único conocimiento eficaz," according to the eccentric Don Fermín, "es el conocimiento post nuptias . . . lo que en lenguaje bíblico significa conocer . . . no hay más conocimiento sustancial y esencial que ése, el conocimiento penetrante" (84). This comment is written on the back of the manuscript and in a different color ink, indicating that it was a later addition, perhaps inspired by Turró's rather simplistic notions of the physiological foundations of knowledge. By placing the statement in the mouth of the eccentric Don Fermín, Unamuno was perhaps gently mocking his Catalan friend. Later in the novel, Víctor and Avito, seeing their friend engaging in ever-increasing abstraction, urge Augusto to marry in order to bring him closer to reality. One of the keys that unlocks the door to knowledge is a physical relationship with a woman.

Following his friends' advice to marry, Augusto proposes to Eugenia, but once again lack of real life experience foils his intentions. When Eugenia's behavior toward him becomes baffling, he falls even further into the error of overintellectualization by deciding to study women scientifically. He seems to understand the scientific experiment in the same way that Turró did: as an attempt to fix the conditions of a phenomenon so that the results do not take the experimenter by surprise. Augusto is misguided as to the applicability of the scientific method outside the highly controlled conditions of the laboratory. His attempt to conduct an experiment in the laboratory of real life backfires, and he is converted from the experimenter into the experimentee—"la rana".[27] His three objects of study—Eugenia, the laundress Rosario, and Liduvina, the cook—represent three modes of acquiring knowledge about the world. Eugenia is the mental image ("su imagen me es casi innata," says Augusto, echoing Descartes [75]); Rosario emphasizes the sensory or phenomenalist ("un ser fisiológico, perfectamente fisiológico, nada más fisiológico" [150]), and Liduvina, who relates to him through his stomach, is the trophic mode. Augusto becomes aware of these women in the sequence just mentioned, inverting the order of Turró's epistemology. With Augusto, intellection takes place first; trophic knowledge comes last.

By contrast, the dog Orfeo, whom Augusto finds abandoned as a very young puppy, represents the correct epistemological arrangement in Turró's scheme.[28] Orfeo begins with purely physiological, trophic experiences and ends with intellectual analysis. When Augusto finds Orfeo by chance, the puppy begins his quest for knowledge in exactly the manner described by Turró, searching automatically for a nutrient-giving source ("buscaba el pecho de la madre" [78]). Unamuno details how Orfeo is supplied with his first life-giving (and therefore knowledge-producing) meals; Domingo, the servant, at first brings milk and a small sponge to facilitate suckling, and later Augusto buys him a baby bottle and nipple. As a being whose knowledge of the world is rooted in the physiological, Orfeo is incompatible with Eugenia, who represents the intellectual aspect of Augusto's unintegrated epistemological system. Therefore Eugenia demands that Augusto dispose of Orfeo before they marry. It is Augusto's one comfort when Eugenia jilts him that he may now keep Orfeo, his only bond with physiological truth. At the end of the novel, Orfeo reveals in his funeral oration for Augusto that he has developed an intellectual understanding of the world far superior to that of his master, whose life has just ended in bewildered despair. Orfeo says with an air of wisdom that Augusto never achieved: "¡Qué extraño animal es el hombre! ¡No está nunca en donde debe estar, que es a lo que está, y habla para mentir y se viste!" (183). Orfeo equates language with pure intellection (as does Unamuno in *Del sentimiento*), which he considers false knowledge and man's original sin. Orfeo dies precisely at the moment in which he achieves intellectual discourse and speech.

If love is the metaphor for the intellect in *Niebla*, eating is the metaphor for the physiological side of life. For example, Domingo interrupts Augusto's first reverie about Eugenia with a call to lunch, catapulting the would-be lover out of his mental fantasies. When the physical intrudes upon his mental world so abruptly, he wonders if it was the servant's voice or his own appetite, of which the voice was but the echo, that awoke him—again alluding to the possible tophic origins of all life experience. When Augusto tells Liduvina, the cook, that Eugenia is a pianist, the cook's reaction is typically pragmatic: "¡El piano! Y eso ¿para qué sirve?" (73). Later, Augusto calls Domingo to bring his breakfast while he daydreams about Eugenia and her musical profession: "La ciencia del ritmo son las matemáticas; la expresión sensible del amor es la música" (75). His calling for breakfast is spontaneous, unpremeditated, arising from an unreflected need: "Había llamado, sin haberse dado de ello cuenta, lo menos hora y media antes que de costumbre" (75). Love enlivens the appetite, muses Augusto, and after an ambivalent sensual episode with Rosario, whom he at first embraces passionately, then coldly dismisses, Augusto meditates on truth: "No hay más verdad que la vida fisiológica" (123). He finds this solution inadequate when it comes to love, and finally in despair he says to Orfeo: " 'vamos a cenar. ¡Esto sí que es verdad!' " (124).

Newly married and unable to impregnate his wife, Víctor nearly kills himself by overindulging in the carnal side of life; he overeats and engages in sex with alarming frequency. After his wife finally bears him a child, Víctor advises Augusto, who has fallen into a depression over Eugenia's treachery, to "devour himself" (165). According to Víctor, there are three possible attitudes toward life. In addition to the two conventionally recognized postures—to eat or be eaten—, he adds a third: to eat oneself, to be a spectacle for oneself and in so doing to become aware of the divisions of the self as a basis for a healthy equilibrium between them. The life out of balance is one that has not found the proper middle point between devouring (imposing one's mental construct on the world) and being devoured (the world imposing its form on the mind), between the rationalist and the phenomenalist (materialist) positions. Even in this, his penultimate hour, Augusto persists with his earlier rationalism. To Víctor's question "¿Qué te parece lo más verdadero de todo?" Augusto replies, "lo de Descartes; 'pienso, luego soy' " (168).

By ending his life through overeating, Augusto undergoes a radical shift from devoured to devourer, from the extreme rationalist to the extreme empiricist position. Just before indulging in his death feast, Augusto suddenly reverses his earlier faith in Descartes's dictum: "Soy, luego, pienso" (175). While he gorges himself, his philosophical position undergoes yet another metamorphosis: "Empezó a devorar el jamón en dulce. 'Pero si como—se decía—, ¿cómo es que no vivo? ¡Como, luego existo! No cabe duda alguna. ¡*Edo, ergo sum* [echoing Feuerbach]!' " (176). His desire to correct his epistemological defect by devoting himself entirely to the physiological (trophic) sphere comes too late and is excessive.

Perhaps rivaled in Spanish literature only by Calixto's ignominious fall from the garden ladder, the absurdity of Augusto's death by overeating emphasizes in a tragicomic manner his having failed to find the appropriate dualism. It is a dualism in which the mind and the body struggle as equals, not the Cartesian dualism in which the mind is the rudder within the body, which is subordinate to it. He has gone from the rationalistic extreme to the physiological extreme. The doctor who attends Augusto at his death says: "El corazón, el estómago y la cabeza son los tres una sola cosa." And Domingo ratifies the doctor's pronouncement: "Sí, forman parte del cuerpo. . . . Y el cuerpo es una sola y misma cosa" (179). In his 1916 prologue to the Castilian translation of Turró's *Orígenes del conocimiento: el hambre*, Unamuno overtly applied Turró's theories to his own view of self-knowledge: "Acaso la especial sensación íntima del yo, la sensación de sí mismo, léase del conocimiento de sí, va ligada al quimismo de nuestro ambiente interior fisiológico, que es la sangre."[29] In a 1916 letter, Turró thanked Unamuno for the prologue, which he said takes his rather crude ideas and converts them into something infinitely more subtle and complex.[30] What the Catalan writer did not realize was that Unamuno had already done just that in his landmark novel of 1914.

Most of *Niebla* (up to the interview between Augusto and Unamuno) continues the burlesque parody and ambiguous Carlylean overtones that Unamuno had developed in *Amor y pedagogía*. It has in common with Voltaire's version of the philosophical novel the satire of existing philosophical positions (the rational and the phenomenalist). But the tone of the novel, and therefore its genre, change radically during the interview beween author and character. Augusto begins to assert not only his fleshly existence but his control over that existence and even his power over his creator. At this point Unamuno interjects the Carlylean element absent in *Amor y pedagogía*—the passionate forging of a new philosphical position to replace those demolished through the satirical enterprise. The central notion of Unamuno's seminal essay *Del sentimiento trágico de la vida*—that existence is the agonistic struggle itself rather than its conclusion or resolution—becomes an integral part of a novel, exemplified in a character's life. Unamuno's same contribution to the philosophy of existence forms the underpinnings of *Abel Sánchez*, *La tía Tula* and *San Manuel Bueno, mártir* (in which he returned to the notion developed in *En torno al casticismo* of a universal consciousness of peoples or an eternal *intrahistoria*, here represented in the lake of Valverde de Lucerna). It works better as a literary image, however, than it does as a philosophical concept. Unamuno had begun writing *La tía Tula* before *Amor y pedagogía* and continued to work on it sporadically until at least 1905. He was unable to finish it until in *Niebla* and *Abel Sánchez* he had devised a proper form for his existential novel. He found that such material required dialogue—in a word, dynamism.

Kierkegaard's contribution to Unamuno's formula for the philosophical novel is twofold: The Danish thinker introduced him to the idea of thinking about the human personality as a viable philosophical problem and to the possibility of embedding that problem in a work of fiction. In *Either/Or*, one of Kierkegaard's most fictional works, the discursive prevails over the representational (as in Carlyle's *Sartor*). Its narrative qualities are elyptical and are clearly at the service of a philosophical idea with which the characters' lives are identified. Kierkegaard's model introduces a fundamental dualism, not only a philosophical dualism but a formal one. A and B of *Either/Or* represent two different, even opposing, ways of being-in-the-world that the Editor believes may be two phases of the same life, occuring in succession rather than simultaneously.

Kierkegaard denied the possibility of resolving the two positions, just as Unamuno (after 1912) rejected a solution to the struggle between reason and faith. Unamuno, whose characters are never as schematic as those of Kierkegaard, cast his philosophical dualism in a more truly novelistic mode than did the Dane. Even the fictional Editor of *Either/Or* (another device akin to Carlyle's) says that A and B are forgotten after the book is read and only their views remain confronting one another with no finite decision in particular personalities. Although none of Unamuno's characters ranks with the most unforgettable literary creations, certainly Joaquín Monegro and Manuel Bueno, if not Augusto Pérez or Avito Carrascal, are memorable in their own right, apart from the philosophical message their lives convey. At the end of *Niebla* and in the later novels, the dialogical device of "diálogo mucho diálogo," proposed by Víctor Goti in *Niebla* and practiced by Unamuno in all his philosophical novels, joins forces with his dualistic philosophy to create a new genre that I call the representational philosophical novel, a work that is truly a novel and yet is self-consciously philosophical in intent. It is the genre that Jean Paul Sartre and Milan Kundera have cultivated so successfully in more recent years.[31]

At the end of *Niebla*, Unamuno discovered a remarkable formula for eliminating the abstracting qualities of earlier philosophical fiction, an abstraction that was completely antithetical to the philosophical position he had formulated by 1912. Ontological despair, the anguished duality of existence, is wedded to the dialogics of the novel, especially to the speech of the characters. Unlike Carlyle, whose use of fiction to a philosophical purpose grew less subtle and less integrated with his ideas after *Sartor*, Unamuno's novelistic medium became ever more adequate to his philosophy in *Abel Sánchez*, *La tía Tula* and *San Manuel Bueno, mártir*. If, after 1914, he found a good solution to his novel-writing, he apparently still had not come completely to terms with his desire to gain the kind of fame Ortega was achieving with more traditional philosophical treatises. On November 6, 1913, he wrote to Jiménez Ilundain that he was engaged in preparing materials for a *Lógica*, a "lógica estricta, un libro de pura metafísica, sin sentimentalidades ni misticismos, rigurosamente racional. No una lógica escolástica y formal, ¡no! Mejor se titularía: *Deducción proyectiva de las categorías lógicas*" (443). God, the soul and immortality will have no place in this work, he goes on to say. But the treatise was never written. The last mention I have found of it is in a letter of March 20, 1916, to Jiménez Ilundain in which its composition is seen as one possibility along with *el quijotismo*, a novel or a biography. *Del sentimiento trágico de la vida*, which he also called a novel on occasion, stands in the complete works as the last (and only) treatise (and even that is more appropriately termed a long essay) to be followed primarily by philosophically inspired literary works—novels, poems, plays and essays.

Unamuno (especially his *Niebla*) remained central to the Spanish tradition of the philosophical novel for the next two decades, although more as a source of material and an object of parody than as a model for existential fictions. Thus he reappears in my analyses of Ramón Pérez de Ayala, Gabriel Miró, Rosa Chacel and Benjamín Jarnés, but in the next chapter, I turn to *El árbol de la ciencia*, Baroja's last grand novelistic effort to put rationalism (and Ortega) in its place. Given the similarity of purpose, Baroja's protagonist manifests many of the same characteristics as Augusto Pérez. He, like Unamuno's unfortunate idealist, also commits suicide, but rationalism proves very difficult to eliminate (especially the witty novelistic variety).

6

BAROJA: FAREWELL TO THE PHILOSOPHICAL NOVEL

If *Niebla* is obliquely related to Ortega's reintroduction of rationalism into Spain's struggle to gain a foothold in the Western philosophical tradition, *El árbol de la ciencia*, whose protagonist also contends with rationalistic-idealistic philosophies, is even more palpably associated with Ortega's neo-Kantian writings of the first decade. Ortega and Baroja met in 1906 when by coincidence they found themselves on the same train to Paris. Baroja was on his way to London for his first look at Dickens's England, and Ortega was returning to his studies in Germany. They shared a compartment on that train and conversed all the way from the Spanish to the French capital (Baroja, *OC* 7: 765 ff). Their friendship probably did not flower, however, until Ortega's return to Madrid in 1908 when he became more deeply involved in Spanish intellectual life as a professor and writer. For several years Baroja and Ortega saw each other in the cafés and *tertulias* and traveled together to various parts of Spain. In 1912 they both bought summer houses not far from each other in Vera in the Basque provinces, where they met frequently. One can only imagine the kinds of conversations they may have had, but their exchanges must have been mutually stimulating. Baroja called Ortega his friend and "en muchas materias maestro" (*OC* 4: 319). And Ortega, in recounting a trip they made together to the Sierra de Gata, hints at Baroja's powers of influence over him: "Quiso Pío Baroja, mi entrañable amigo, convencerme de que admiramos sólo lo que no comprendemos, que la admiración es efecto de la incomprensión. No logró convencerme, y no habiéndolo conseguido él, es difícil que me convenza otro" (*OC* 1: 339, n. 2).

Although their personalities were different (Baroja thought Ortega chaffed at his unsubmissive nature, and the Basque writer found Ortega's ambition and authoritarianism unpleasant), they gained much from their discussions. Baroja respected Ortega's mind, affirming that Ortega was Spain's only hope for a real philosopher and that he was one of the few Spaniards to whom he listened with interest. Ortega found in Baroja someone with a flair for philosophy: "La inspiración energética que le anima [a Baroja] es una inspiración filosófica, no literaria,"[1] and elsewhere he states that "Es el caso, en efecto, que Baroja me parece más bien un temperamento de metafísico que de novelista."[2] Although very different in their outlooks, they had many common interests that united them and distinguished them both from Unamuno: 1) admiration for German philosophy, beginning with Kant, who presented them both with problems of comprehension (recall that Baroja finally understood Kant thanks to Schopenhauer, and Ortega approached Kant through the neo-Kantian Hermann Cohen[3]); 2) comparisons of Spain and other Mediterranean countries to northern Europe, especially Germany, in which Spain fared poorly; 3) great respect for the possibilities of science, athough it began to tarnish for both men in the second decade;[4] and 4) a search for a rational explanation of life that avoids the limitations of traditional rationalism.

Several of their exchanges took published form, most notably in 1911 and in 1925. The 1911 public conversation centered on the superficiality of thought and sensuality in Spain and Mediterranean Europe as compared to northern Europe, where science and rationalism were the dominant modes of thought. Both Baroja's article "¿Con el latino o con el germano?" and Ortega's reply "Respuesta a una pregunta" (sent from Marburg) clearly prefer the latter. The second and more famous public dialogue concerned the nature of the novel. This dispute probably brought a chill to their friendship, which had begun to cool in 1916 when Ortega published an article focusing on Baroja's style as an example of national hysteria.[5]

It is possible that Ortega's discussions with Baroja were, if not as instrumental as his second visit to Marburg in 1911, at least catalysts in his shift from rationalism to ratio-vitalism during the years 1912-1914. The shift is evident in *Meditaciones del Quijote*, which was begun as a meditation on Baroja, whom Ortega found at this crucial juncture in his philosophical development especially antipathetic to *el raciocinio*. The two men personified the conflict between the '98's tendency to biological explanations and the new rationalism that had seduced Ortega: "Baroja quisiera conducirnos inmediatamente a una región donde sólo existen las fuerzas biológicas puras que, vertiginosas enfurecidas van y vienen azotando al mundo."[6] Salmerón points out that "Una primera vista sobre Baroja" reveals a very different attitude toward life from "Adán en el Paraíso" (both of the same year): "la palabra *vida* vuelve a su sentido 'nietzscheano,' a cobrar ese matiz de potencia, de anhelo y de intensidad que hallamos en escritos anteriores, a designar las fuerzas biológicas e instintivas."[7] Baroja was concerned about such a rapprochement at least as early as 1900 in the writing of *Aventuras y mixtificaciones de Silvestre Paradox*. Silvestre's philosophical treatise is an attempt to find a rational order for the universe that is superior to that of Kant or Schopenhauer. And *Camino de perfección*'s Fernando Ossorio, who overintellectualizes first his art, then his religious feeling, eventually opts for a completely natural and unintellectual life (perhaps erring on the side of life over reason). In the 1906 "Ciencia romántica," Ortega was convinced that "El individuo no ha existido nunca: es una abstracción. La humanidad no existe todavía: es un ideal" (*OC* 1: 38-39). What Fernando Ossorio rejects in *Camino de perfección* is the "cultura" that Ortega opposed to "natura" in essays such as "Renán": "todo lo que trasciende la naturaleza es cultura, es reflexión y artificio, es convención. La cultura en conjunto es un convencionalismo, eso son en último término las leyes lógicas, las normas de derecho las reglas morales y los ideales estéticos" (*OC* 1: 455-457).

Baroja's and Ortega's treatments of philosophy in the first decade, however, have some methodological parallels. In several essays written between 1904 and 1911, Ortega invented the mystical figure Rubén de Cendoya as an interlocutor, suggesting that he was not entirely comfortable with the rationalistic cloak he wore in his letters to Unamuno and in his early articles. Did Ortega feel the same need as members of the Generation of '98 to obfuscate his philosophical position in novelistic dialogics? In "Adán en el Paraíso" he changed the name of the fictitious expositor to Doctor Vulpius, professor of philosophy in Leipzig, thus creating some distance betweeen himself and the German sources of his idealism, and it is Doctor Vulpius who expounds on "life as a problem" for Adam, who must break life down into science, art and ethics in order to begin to find answers to the problem (interestingly, the three stages through which Fernando Ossorio passes on his way to discovering that he prefers living without precepts or abstractions).

While Ortega at last found his own philosophical voice in the 1914 *Meditaciones del Quijote*, Baroja continued to channel his voice through the refracted medium of multiple novelistic characters. The crossfire between Ortega and Baroja from 1908 until 1911, which perhaps catalyzed the philosopher's discovery of his mature philosophical position, inspired the novelist to yet another labyrinthine philosophical exposition in the novel. In *El árbol de la ciencia* (1910-1911), which came in the wake of Ortega's major neo-Kantian essay "Adán en el Paraíso" and suggestively resonated its biblical title, Baroja once again placed the problem of life and reason at the center a novel, this time even more deliberately and definitively than in *Camino de perfección*. In his last major philosophical novel, Baroja resurrected in Andrés Hurtado the introspective misfit character of the Fernando Ossorio type. Like Ossorio, Hurtado is a desultory medical student more interested in literature and philosophy than in medical practice. He too undertakes a quest, not so much for his physical and spiritual place in the world as for a philosophical orientation. He firmly believes that he must understand life intellectually and live according to a guiding ideology. That he is Ortega's Adam, seeking a solution to the problem of life, is suggested not only by his search, which takes him primarily to the German idealists, but by his name, which has three letters and a bisyllabic rhythm in common with "Adán." And the surname "Hurtado" recalls the Garden of Eden's forbidden fruit. Andrés, however, is not so fortunate as Ortega's Adam, who solves the problem of life with rationalistic constructs, for he is never able to integrate his abstract approach to life— either science or metaphysics—with real life. He tests a variety of philosophical positions, all of a mathematical or abstract (idealistic) orientation, and ends up momentarily achieving the wished for *ataraxia*, only to commit suicide when that attitude proves impractical.

Following his German source, Hermann Cohen, Ortega divides Adam's conscious into three areas: science, ethics and aesthetics. Neither the natural sciences nor ethics (moral science) can achieve their goal of adequately explaining life because their methodology always leads them toward the pole of abstraction—a set of general laws about what each individual thing has in common with others—thus precluding a comprehension of all the relations among things in their totality: "La ciencia convierte cada cosa en un caso, es decir, en aquello que es común a esta cosa con otras muchas. Esto es lo que se llama abstracción. La vida descubierta por la ciencia es una vida abstracta, mientras, por definición, lo vital es lo concreto, lo incomparable, lo único" (*OC* 1: 482). And the two general areas into which science divides the problem of life—the natural and the spiritual (or moral)—do not communicate with one another. Just as in natural science, in spiritual science the discoveries are only of relations, since the spiritual side of life is composed of states rather than of things.

Art is born of the tragedy of science; the province of art is precisely the unique and individual. Art overcomes science's inability to encompass all relations between things in their entirety, by producing a fictitious totality, "una *como* infinitud": "Por consiguiente, lo que debe proponerse todo artista es la ficción de la totalidad; ya que no podemos tener todas y cada una de las cosas, logremos siquiera la forma de la totalidad. La materialidad de la vida de cada cosa es inabordable; poseamos, al menos, *la forma de la vida*" (OC 1: 484). As Nelson Orringer argues, despite Ortega's having shifted Cohen's vocabulary to a more biocentric one, Ortega's philosophical position at this point remains essentially neo-Kantian, rendering life in the abstract: "¿Quién es Adán? Cualquiera y nadie particularmente: la vida" (*OC* 1: 492).[8]

In Baroja's 1911 novelistic representation of Paradise, the tree of science predominates, not only in the title of the novel but as the guiding motivation of his Adam, Andrés Hurtado. Like Ortega, he sets about solving the problem of life by clinging to *el árbol de la ciencia*, the tree of knowledge, the rational tree, which proves as disastrous for him as it did for the biblical Adam. Baroja did not offer his Adam the alternative of art as did Ortega (or as did Baroja to Fernando Ossorio in 1902), but he did offer the alternative of life itself, lived in a natural, pragmatic and unreflective way. Andrés's rationalistic position is attacked and modified by the narrator's ambiguous attitude toward the protagonist, by the viewpoint of Andrés's Uncle Iturrioz, the main opposing voice, who counters the protagonist's position with a combination of pragmatism and vitalism, and by Andrés's own inability to succeed in any but the intellectual and abstract arenas of life, a severe deficiency that leads to his death. In subjecting Andrés, who has so much in common with the neo-Kantian Ortega of 1910, to a vitalistic critique, Baroja indirectly countered his friend's philosophical orientation and foreshadowed the ratio-vitalistic position that Ortega assumed after 1914. Like a palimpsest lying beneath the surface of the philosophical dialogues between Andrés and his uncle are the conversations that Baroja and Ortega sustained during the years 1908-1910. If recent readings of Nordau and Nietzsche and conversations about the will with Martínez Ruiz were the inspiration for *Camino de perfección*, whose philosophical content is more latent, conversations with Ortega on the place of idealism in assessing the meaning of life informed the philosophical discussion in *El árbol de la ciencia*.

As in *Camino de perfección*, changes of locale are central to the plot of *El árbol de la ciencia* and to the protagonist's development, but *El árbol's* geographic shifts do not coincide with shifts in generic models as in the earlier novel. Baroja opted instead for a pattern in which the different locales that Andrés inhabits form isolated islands in the novel. Picaresque mobility and its reference to social and moral transformation are absent in *El árbol de la ciencia;* Andrés suffers fewer and more subtle permutations, perhaps reflecting Baroja's loss of his earlier faith in the power of environment to effect change. The number and length of the philosophical conversations increase substantially in *El árbol de la ciencia* (as compared to *Camino de perfección*), so that dialogue, specifically dialogue of a theoretical nature, assumes the function that genre types exercise in *Camino de perfección*. The arrangement of material is formalistic, alternating experiences and theoretical commentary in a rigidly symmetrical pattern, emphasizing the *a posteriori* forms that abstraction imposes on chaotic life.

The chaos of the picaresque is maintained only in the sections in which Andrés is observing raw life in the streets of Madrid or the villages of Spain, but these sections are carefully framed by philosophical discussion.

The novel is divided into seven parts that span the life experiences of Andrés Hurtado from his medical student days to his early death by suicide. The narration of these experiences is punctuated at predictable intervals by philosophical conversations between Andrés and other characters, most notably his Uncle Iturrioz. The longest of these dialogues occupies the entire fourth (and central) section of the novel. In *Camino de perfección* the philosophical dialogues are strategically placed as two columns or "legs" upon which the action rests; in *El árbol de la ciencia* the long central dialogue, which is related in content to all the other philosophical conversations and to the novel's action, is a hub from which other parts of the novel radiate like so many spokes of a wheel and upon which they pivot. The abstract nature of these conversations also underscores the life/intellect polarity that entraps Andrés. Significantly three of the four conversations between Andrés and his Uncle Iturrioz take place on a rooftop high above the teeming Madrid life below. If Andrés and his uncle represent, respectively, the extremes of idealism (in the mode of Kant and Schopenhauer) and pragmatism (with Nietzschean overtones), many of the other characters reflect various attitudes and lifestyles along the continuum in between. Aracil, Villasús and the money-lender are extreme opportunists, and many of the working class people Andrés observes live at a crude animal level; Luis, Andrés's younger brother, is physically weak and dies, Fermín Ibarra has physical disabilities but overcomes them. Hermano Juan is a very unNietzschean Christian saint, and Lamela is a pure idealist, living entirely according to his mental fantasies, ignoring all information of the senses.

In the first half of the novel, before the central conversation, Andrés is ill-defined as a character; he is primarily an observer who goes from experience to experience with no particular motivation or governing ideology. As the novel progresses, the events of Andrés's life become personal and unique. The early experiences—medical school, observations of people in the working-class neighborhoods of Madrid—are of a more collective and general nature (those of Adam as "cualquiera o nadie"). After the death of his younger brother in part 3, however, the experiences become more and more specific, ending with marriage, pending fatherhood and death. In the first conversation with his uncle at the end of part 2, he has no personal point of view; he is seeking an orientation, having just rejected the ideas of Letamendi, whose facile mathematical explanation of biology had seduced him for a time. In this early conversation, the uncle's materialistic, pragmatic position prevails. In answer to Andrés's desire to "sacar consecuencias de todas esas vidas" (the lives of the cruel, crude people he has observed in the working class sections of Madrid), Iturrioz provides a purely biological, Hobbesian explanation. That a spider eats a fly, a hyena devours a smaller animal, or a tree takes sustenance from the soil are the same as one man cheating another man. Echoing Nietzsche's disdain for all precepts and preconceived notions, he proclaims that justice is an imaginary concept that some people invent to suit their individual purposes; there exists, according to Iturrioz, no universal sense of justice.

Ortega maintained the same notion in "Adán en el Paraíso" but there endowed the abstractions with the authority of universal orientations of consciousness: Logic, ethics and aesthetics are "literalmente tres prejuicios, merced a los cuales se mantiene el hombre a flote sobre la superficie de la zoología, y libertándose en el lacustre artificio se va labrando la cultura libérrimamente, racionalmente, sin intervención de místicas substancias ni otras revelaciones que la revelación positiva, sugerida al hombre de hoy por lo que el hombre de ayer hizo" (*OC* 1: 473). Iturrioz's prescription for conducting one's own life in the face of the unsolvable dilemma of reconciling the vital and the abstract is either to abstain from involvement with life, assuming an indifferent, contemplative posture (a suggestion worthy of Schopenhauer), or to adopt the Nietzschean alternative, to tilt against a limited number of windmills ("se puede tener el quijotismo contra una anomalía; pero tenerlo contra una regla general, es absurdo"[9]). Paralleling the theme of life versus reason in *El árbol de la ciencia* is that of the particular versus the general (or abstract), one of Ortega's concerns in "Adán en el Paraíso" (i.e., science and ethics deal in generalities, while art and life are particular).

Although lacking its charm and witty irony, the narrator's attitude toward Andrés in *El árbol de la ciencia* has something of the ambiguity of *Aventuras y mixtificaciones de Silvestre Paradox*. The narrative attitude reveals more occult cynicism toward the main character than *Camino de perfección*'s narrator does toward Fernando. The narrator sympathizes with Andrés's sincerity and disgust for all forms of cruelty, mean-spiritedness and hypocrisy, but his willingness to indulge in corruption (for example, he asks his uncle to recommend him to his medical examiners) and his naiveté about the pitfalls of the ideologies he adopts undermine our faith in him. The early incident, in which Andrés's youthful faith in Letamendi's attempt to apply mathematics to biology is reduced to ridicule by his friends, establishes him as an uncritical ideologue and makes us skeptical of his defense of German idealism when he converses with Iturrioz. His pretense to sincerity is countered by the fact that he continues to associate with his materialistic companions Aracil and Montaner, even while professing to dislike them.

By the third section Luis succumbs to tuberculosis despite Andrés's attempt to save him by the most scientifically enlightened methods, and life begins to impinge painfully on Andrés. The death of his brother, the only member of his family for whom he really cares, and his readings in Kant and Schopenhauer equip Andrés for a more equitable exchange with his Uncle Iturrioz in the long fourth section. Now more philosophically sophisticated, Andrés announces to his uncle that he is searching for "Una cosmogonía, una hipótesis racional de la formación del mundo; después una explicación biológica del origen de la vida y del hombre" (124), and in so doing he sounds increasingly like the Ortega of 1910. Like Andrés, Ortega in "Adán en el Paraíso" divided science into two large provinces, the physical and the moral: "La ciencia divide el problema de la vida en dos grandes provincias que no comunican entre sí: la naturaleza y el espíritu. Así se han formado los dos linajes de ciencias: las naturales y las morales que investigan las formas de la vida material y de la vida psíquica" (*OC* 1: 482).

According to Ortega, moral science fares no better than natural science in an attempt to understand life; it is equally dependent on its methodology—its study of relations (a spiritual state cannot be studied in isolation; it can only be understood in relation to an anterior and a posterior state). It is thus also condemned to reside eternally in the realm of the abstract: "las ciencias morales, empero, están sometidas también al método de abstracción: describen la tristeza en general. Pero la tristeza en general no es triste. Lo triste, lo horriblemente triste, es esta tristeza que yo siento en este instante. La tristeza en cuanto vida, y no en cuanto idea general, es también algo concreto, único, individual" (*OC* 1: 483). Andrés centers his approach to life on these two branches of science—the physical and the moral—that are equally distanced from the vital core of life he hopes to uncover.

In the fourth and central section, entitled "El árbol de la ciencia y el árbol de la vida," Iturrioz continues to defend his earlier pragmatism, and Andrés wavers little from the Kantian-Schopenhauerian rationalism that he has recently embraced. Unlike his character Silvestre Paradox, who refrains from deliberately confusing his readers, Baroja indulged in a variety of techniques to derail the reader's attempts to find a single ideological strand. Iturrioz recommends that his nephew foresake the German metaphysicians and read Hobbes instead, saying that the English philosopher will not remove him so radically from life. His arguments draw on Nietzsche but are heavily shaded with a more Darwinian vocabulary and an occasional idea from Fouillée and Comte, particularly when it comes to summaries of his position.

Unswayed by his uncle's powerful arguments, Andrés defends his new idols. According to Andrés, reality is located in the forces of causality that operate in the dominions of time and space dependent upon the human mind. Truth is a set of relationships that remain constant due to reason and experience; truth is thus centered on the points upon which all agree. Operating within the same rationalistic frame of reference, Ortega stated in "Adán en el Paraíso" that "Cada cosa es un pedazo de otra mayor, hace referencia a las demás cosas, es lo que es merced a las limitaciones y confines que éstas le imponen. Cada cosa es una relación entre varias. . . . Hemos visto que un individuo, sea cosa o persona, es el resultado del resto total del mundo: es la totalidad de las relaciones. En el nacimiento de una brizna de hierba colabora todo el universo" (*OC* 1: 474-5, 484). In "Adán en el Paraíso" (and for Andrés), life is a system of relations that the mind interposes between itself and the rest of the universe.

For Andrés and for Ortega (in 1910) there are as many realities as there are minds to project them; the novelistic neo-Kantian says: "¿Qué duda cabe que el mundo que conocemos es el resultado del reflejo unido, constrastado, con las imágenes reflejadas en los cerebros de los demás hombres que han vivido y que viven, es nuestro conocimiento del mundo, es nuestro mundo?" (127). As a follower of Hermann Cohen, the nonfictional philosopher writes in "Adán en el Paraíso": "No existe, por lo tanto, esa supuesta realidad inmutable y única con quien poder comparar los contenidos de las obras artísticas: hay tantas realidades como puntos de vista. El punto de vista crea el panorama. Hay una realidad de todos los días formada por un sistema de relaciones laxas, aproximativas, vagas, que basta para los usos del vivir cotidiano. Hay una realidad científica forjada en un sistema de relaciones exactas, impuesto por la necesidad de exactitud. Ver y tocar las cosas no son, al cabo, sino maneras de pensarlas" (*OC* 1: 475).

Andrés defends science, using an argument very similar to that of Ortega. According to Andrés, science values observation and relates the diverse special sciences, constructing bridges between them, although these bridges are only hypotheses, approximations of truth. He concludes his arguments by reaffirming that science "es la única construcción fuerte de la humanidad" (131); it overpowers religion, moral systems, utopias and all the tricks of pragmatism. Iturrioz counters that it also overwhelms Man, a point which Andrés cannot deny. The two also agree that humanity needs rationalist constructions ("lies" in Iturrioz's assessment[10]) in order to live: "El instinto vital, dice Andrés, necesita de la ficción para afirmarse. La ciencia entonces, el instinto de crítica, el instinto de averiguación debe encontrar una verdad: la cantidad de mentira que se necesita para la vida" (131). Life and reason are indispensable to each another, but reason must be at the service of life (Iturrioz says that the problem with science is that it has grown away from life: "la habéis convertido en ídolo," 130). In putting science at the service of life, Andrés foreshadows Ortega's *Meditaciones del Quijote*, which establishes life as the radical reality, the foundation for the notion of vital reason that Ortega settled on later.[11]

At the end of the long central section, Andrés defends Schopenhauer's division between will and intelligence. Iturrioz points out that Andrés's division of life into two noncommunicating polarities is found in Genesis in the division of the Paradisiacal flora into the categories "tree of life" and "tree of knowledge." God told Adam he could have his fill from the tree of life but prohibited his partaking of the fruit of knowledge. According to Iturrioz, the Semitic races of the south followed this advice and refrained from revealing the workings of nature, but the northern Arians could not resist such temptation. Ortega, likewise, in his early article "Asamblea para el progreso de las ciencias" located the essence of Europe in the inductive method; he believed that this method distinguished northern Europe from Africa and other parts of the world. Andrés proposes that the northern European scientific mentality will eventually dominate over the materialism of the Semitic/Christian/Moslem south. Kant is the prophet of the north; he undertook to cut away the underbrush of the tree of life that was choking the tree of knowledge, and Schopenhauer, a later prophet, makes an even cleaner break between the two trees, eliminating even the tenuous interdependence between life and reason that Kant sustained. Schopenhauer clearly separated life and truth, will and intelligence. There is even a different narrative attitude toward "the prophetic Kant and Schopenhauer" in this section compared to *Aventuras y mixitificaciones de Silvestre Paradox*. In the 1901 novel the idea of prophethood is couched in burlesque terms; here it is placed in the mouth of the serious, even dour, Andrés.

Iturrioz cannot accept this division, so antithetical to his vitalistic position: "no creo que la voluntad sea sólo una máquina de desear y la inteligencia una máquina de reflejar. . . . No creo en esa diferencia automática que tú atribuyes a la inteligencia. No somos un intelecto puro, ni una máquina de desear; somos hombres que al mismo tiempo piensan, trabajan, desean, ejecutan... Yo creo que hay ideas que son fuerzas" (136). The notion of an *idea-fuerza*, which Baroja probably borrowed from

Alfred Fouillée, is remarkably similar to one that Ortega posits in an essay on Baroja: "¡Un ideal que fuera a la vez una espuela! La espuela ideal— símbolo de una cultura caballeresca."[12] If, as Inman Fox has suggested, this essay was actually written in about 1912 as part of the *Meditaciones* as they were originally conceived, Ortega's new posture would seem to owe a great deal more to Baroja than has heretofore been acknowledged.

By the end of the long central conversation with his uncle, Andrés finally admits that his position has not been sufficiently vindicated by ac- tual practice: "Cierto; fuera de la verdad matemática y la verdad empírica que se va adquiriendo lentamente, la ciencia no dice mucho. Hay que tener la probidad de reconocerlo... y esperar" (137). The difference be- tween Andrés and Ortega in 1910 is that the latter accepts the limits of science ("ese *ser* inagotable que constituye la vitalidad de cada cosa. Pero el método que emplea compra la exactitud a costa de no lograr nunca su empeño," *OC* 1: 484) but not the problems of rationalism. Andrés is se- duced by both. In 1910 Ortega found a complement to science in art. An- drés does not find such a corollary necessary, except that he does devote his medical school years to reading novels. Iturrioz suggests the measures of utility and faith instead of art to close the gap between lived reality and the reality revealed by scientific inquiry. Andrés stubbornly clings to his original position that scientific proof is the only valid one. Iturrioz ends his arguments by affirming that science jeopardizes life, and it certainly does in the case of Andrés, who succumbs in the end to the pressures of a life sustained only by intellectual pursuits. The two men finally agree that modern times require the founding of a "Company of Man" to re- place Loyola's Company of Jesus, echoing Fernando Ossorio's choice of marriage and family over his short-lived asceticism inspired by Loyola. The new company's aChristian bias suggests a Nietzschean inspiration, and a Religion of Humanity had once been suggested by the arch- Positivist Auguste Comte.

Andrés, thus equipped with his rationalistic baggage, sets out upon his career as a doctor, first in a backward village (part 5) and then in a Madrid clinic for prostitutes (part 6). The titles of the last three parts each contain the word *experiencia*, and each narrates specific life experi- ences that contrast with and even contradict the general principles of ab- stract science and philosophic rationalism. As his uncle had predicted, Andrés is ill-prepared for life and does not fare well in either the village or the clinic. He is able to maintain a certain equilibrium for a time by ab- staining as much as possible from the carnal side of life (in the village he eats only vegetables and fish, much to the consternation of the meat- loving villagers, and he shuns local social life). But human carnality does not allow him to remain aloof for long; it awaits an appropriate moment and invades Andrés's tranquility just when he thought himself well on the way to his desired state of *ataraxia*, "el paraíso del que no cree" (241). He becomes embroiled in the police investigation of a violent death, earning the lasting enmity of the other village doctor, whose interpretation of the event conflicts with Andrés's. His life in the village becomes unbearable, and he finally decides to return to Madrid. The night before his departure, he makes love to his landlady, briefly dropping the barriers he has erected between himself and his body. The experience makes him so ill that he is forced to stop for three days in Aranjuez before continuing on to Madrid.

Upon returning to the capital, Andrés engages in another brief conversation with his uncle, recounting his failure in the village. Andrés explains that he wanted to live an independent life in Alcolea, to do his work, to be paid for it and to be left alone. His uncle replies that he has attempted the impossible: "cada hombre no es una estrella con su órbita independiente" (199). Iturrioz makes a similar observation in *La dama errante* (1908), except that the statement in the earlier work has a more Nietzschean cast.[13] In 1911 Iturrioz's metaphor for one's position in society is more reminiscent of Ortega's astronomical example in "Adán en el Paraíso":

La vida de una cosa es su ser. ¿Y qué es el ser de una cosa? Un ejemplo nos lo aclarará. El sistema planetario no es un sistema de cosas, en este caso de planetas: antes de idearse el sistema planetario no había planetas. Es un sistema de movimientos; por tanto, de relaciones; el ser de cada planeta es determinado, dentro de este conjunto de relaciones, como determinamos un punto de una cuadrícula. Sin los demás planetas, pues, no es posible el planeta Tierra, y vice versa; cada elemento del sistema necesita de todos los demás; cada cosa se resuelve en puras relaciones. [*OC* 1: 481]

Rather than an abstract set of relations forged in the human mind, Iturrioz's metaphor refers to life lived in the world and in so doing approximates the notion of circumstance that Ortega discovered in *Meditaciones del Quijote*.[14] In his essay on *El árbol de la ciencia*, Ortega interprets Andrés in a way similar to Uncle Iturrioz:

La vida en general, y sobre todo la suya [Andrés's], le parecía una cosa fea, turbia, dolorosa e indomable. . . . De lo que llevo dicho se desprende que en ese *estar fuera de sí* consiste precisamente el vivir espontáneo, el ser, y que, al entrar dentro de sí, el hombre deja de vivir y de ser y se encuentra frente a frente con el lívido espectro de sí mismo. . . . Andrés Hurtado, el protagonista de *El árbol de la ciencia* no encuentra faceta alguna en el orbe donde su actividad pueda insertarse.

Vive como un hongo, atenido a sí mismo, sin adherencia al medio, sin cambio de sustancias con el dintorno. En nada encuentra solicitación bastante. Creemos un momento que la investigación científica va a absorber, por fin, su íntimo potencial. Más al punto notamos que si Andrés Hurtado busca el árbol de la ciencia es, no más, para tumbarse un rato a la sombra. *Nihil, nihil:* el mundo en derredor es un ámbito absolutamente vacio. Y en vista de ello, Andrés Hurtado se suicida mediante aconitina cristalizada de Duquesnel.[15]

Andrés does, however, share his uncle's opinion that he cannot exist outside his world, that he is himself and his circumstance, and he moves even closer to his uncle's philosophical position when he discusses his proposed marriage. Pretending the would-be bridegroom is one of his patients, Andrés asks his uncle's advice about the wisdom of a marriage between an arthritic, nervous young man and a weak, hysterical woman. The uncle counsels against the marriage invoking the potentially unfortunate offspring: "El delito mayor del hombre es hacer nacer" (233), comments Iturrioz reformulating the Calderonian maxim. Andrés argues, now from a pragmatic rather than a theoretical position (!), that the only guarantee for healthy children is healthy parents; all others should abstain from procreating. The two conversants are surprised to find that their earlier philosophical postures have been reversed: "—Me choca en un anti-intelectualista como usted esta actitud tan intelectual—dijo Andrés. —A mí también me choca en un intelectual como tú esa actitud de hombre de mundo" (233).

If Andrés accepts momentarily his uncle's assessment that he must live in consonance with his surroundings, he does not manage to incorporate that insight into his existence, and he soon withdraws almost entirely from all social contact after his marriage to Lulú. He leaves medical practice to earn a living by translating medical articles and synthesizing medical research. He arranges their apartment to allow all living to occur in one room, as he does not want any aspect of life relegated to an inferior part of the house. For these eccentric preoccupations Lulú affectionately dubs him *ideático*. Her unusual term of endearment reminds us that Andrés has retreated as far as possible from his circumstance; he is trying to live according to an entirely self-sufficient regime, once again disregarding the lessons he learned in Alcolea. Ortega interpreted Andrés's problem in light of the "yo soy yo y mi circunstancia" formula that became associated with his philosophy after *Meditaciones del Quijote*. He pointed out that Andrés refuses to involve himself in a world of which he does not approve: "Una repugnancia indomable a ser cómplice en esa farsa, a repetir en sí mismo—en su vida y en su obra—esos estériles lugares comunes, cuya única fuerza proviene precisamente de su repeticion, le obliga a adaptar una táctica nihilista. ¿Qué queda? Una isla desierta en torno a un Robinson. El individuo señero: *Yo.*"[16]

Although Baroja is never very explicit in sexual matters, it is suggested that Andrés also abstains from his marital duties, sex having the undesirable side-effect of producing children. He approaches that long-sought state of *ataraxia*, which has so far eluded him. But the world once again imposes itself upon him; Lulú wants to have a child, and Andrés finally succumbs to her tears. Their harmonious homelife is destroyed when the pregnant Lulú becomes jealous and irritable: "Ya no era aquella simpatía afectuosa y burlona tan dulce; ahora era un amor animal. La naturaleza recobraba sus derechos. Andrés de ser hombre lleno de talento y un poco ideático, había pasado a ser hombre" (243). Having to function as a complete man who engages with the natural as well as the intellectual side of life overwhelms him. First he begins taking morphine to escape the terrors of his impending fatherhood, and, when Lulú dies in childbirth, he takes poison and leaves behind both the tree of science and the tree of life.

The narrator has insinuated in a number of ways the inadequacy of Andrés's rationalism, but the ultimate condemnation of Andrés's position is couched in his failure to resolve the inherent conflict between the abstract cosmologies he professes so uncritically and the reality of life. Andrés's suicide does not inspire fear or pity; Andrés is too abstract and removed from life to evoke palpable emotion. Like the attendant doctor and uncle Iturrioz, whose statements close the novel, the reader is sorry that Andrés could not survive, but not surprised or unduly saddened. The narrator has prepared the reader well for this inevitable outcome. The vitalist-pragmatist Iturrioz, and Andrés, the rationalist, are juxtaposed in a way that suggests that neither position is wholly adequate but that both positions must be taken into account in any final solution. Life without reason, unreflective life, is chaotic and undignified (like that of the working-class people Andrés observes in Madrid), and reason without life is death. Like Ortega in *Meditaciones*, Baroja's narrator of 1911 rejects a Garden of Eden that gives greater credence to the tree of knowledge, while slighting the tree of life. *El árbol de la ciencia* reaffirms the lesson of Genesis but modifies it to include controlled consumption of the forbidden fruit. Recalling the procedure in *Camino de perfección*, the title of the work reminds us that solutions to the problem of life that were invented for past ages must be reevaluated in the twentieth century. Ortega heeded this warning, for shortly after 1911 he eliminated the concept of the consciousness from his philosophy to arrive at the notion of the problem of life as the problem of the human subject who tries to realize himself in his immediate circumstance. Adam as a symbol of the deficient consciousness vanishes, just as Paradise, the symbol of the universe of which we must gain consciousness, disappears. The tripartite orientation (natural science, ethics and art) is replaced by a plurality of perspectives on the problem of existence.[17]

The intertextual dialogue between Ortega and Baroja in 1910-1911 did not end with "Adán en el Paraíso" and *El árbol de la ciencia*. As Inman Fox has revealed, Ortega set to work immediately on his meditations on Baroja, although these were not published until 1915 and 1916, and then only fragmentarily. In the 1915 essay he appeared to carry over some of the aesthetics developed in "Adán en el Paraíso," especially in the critique of Zuloaga's painting, which he believed represented a sociological vision of Spain rather than individual lives. Ortega similarly faults Baroja's novel writing for being more of a national symptom than a work of art, calling it a case study in Spanish or Iberian national hysteria. Although this assessment could not have been very pleasing to the Basque novelist, it did not provoke an immediate public response. It could, however, have been one of the motivations for Baroja's unkind allusions to Ortega in *La caverna del humorismo* (1919). For example, he invented the word *almanaquegothismo* to refer to the elitism and aestheticism implied in Ortega's rejection of the Picaresque mode.

Thus began a rift between the two writers that was exacerbated in the 1920s in their dispute over the nature of the novel. Baroja's initial enthusiasm for Ortega as a philosopher who had the potential to lead Spanish philosophy out of the limitations of rational Kantianism waned with the years: "toda la filosofía moderna es poca cosa. La mayoría de los que la cultivan son profesores que quieren saltar por encima de las limitaciones que puso Kant al conocimiento humano y no pueden. No tienen ni la inteligencia ni la abnegación del filósofo alemán y van a ver si resucitan todas las fantasías antiguas y a encontrar una isla inexplorada para poner en ella su pabellón" (*OC* 7: 843-844). In later years, Baroja found Ortega to be merely cultivating a flamboyant and seductive style while sacrificing philosophical substance: "Si el novelista tuviera que dar una pragmática al filósofo, le diría: 'Nada de metáforas que en filosofía tienen aire de abalorios. Bastante cantidad de ringorrangos y de floripondios tiene el idioma de por sí para añadirle deliberadamente otros. Nada de orientalismos ni de color. Hay que tener en el estilo la austeridad de un Kant' " (*OC* 4: 312).

Many critics point to a decline in the freshness of Baroja's novels after *El árbol de la ciencia*, and the novelist himself considered the 1911 novel the apex of his literary career. The concealed debate with Ortega over reason and life that fueled *El árbol de la ciencia* appeared in later novels such as *El mundo es ansí* and *El gran torbellino del mundo*, but without the cohesive philosophical purpose of *El árbol de la ciencia*. Upon arriving at the notion of an equilibrium between the individual and his world at the end of Andrés Hurtado's story, there was little left with which to sustain novelistic tension. When characters are not viewed as either superior or inferior to their circumstances (according to Northrup Frye the principal motivating paradigms of narrative prose literature since the Romances of Chivalry and *Lazarillo de Tormes*), the traditional novel has indeed run aground. If Ortega was thinking of Baroja when he wrote in 1925 that the novel had died for lack of new themes, he would seem to have judged perceptively about the Basque novelist's specific case, if not about the novel in general. It is ironic that it is precisely Ortega's ultimate solution to the problem of life—an equilibrium between life and reason, between people and their circumstances—that paralyzes Baroja's novels after 1911.

The Spanish philosophical novel got a second wind, however, with the members of Ortega's generation. No little of their inspiration derives from a reexamination of the achievements of the '98 novelistic philosophers by their juniors, many of whose works center on an intertextual crossfire with *Amor y pedagogía*, *Camino de perfección*, *La voluntad*, *Niebla*, and *El árbol de la ciencia*.

7

THE GENERATION OF '14:
TAKING THE LEAD

If the philosophical and aesthetic consciousness of the Generation of '98 was formed in dissension with nineteenth-century ideas and literary figures, the Generation of 1914 coalesced in its awareness of and distancing from the Generation of '98.[1] All the members of the 1914 Generation wrote on one or all of the most prominent writers associated with the '98, muses who inspired both reverance and ridicule. While devoting serious attention to the '98 writers in essays, they mocked them in their novels.[2] Ideas and authors that had been problematic, even anathema, to the '98—Europe, rationalism, science, Krausism, Galdós, Clarín—return to favor in this Generation. The '98 wrestled with an ill-assimilated rationalism, which especially in Unamuno became a virulent anti-rationalism after 1900. The second generation was better prepared to accept rationalism both philosophically and artistically. The 1914 writers were not ambivalent about their vocations as literati or philosophers, producing literature or philosophical treatises without wavering between them as did Unamuno, Martínez Ruiz and Baroja (at least in their early careers). When the Generation of 1914 writers did engage in essay-writing, it was to address aesthetic theory (e.g., Pérez de Ayala's writings on drama, such as *Las máscaras*, or Pedro Salinas's *Reality and Poetry in Spanish Literature*). The Generation of 1914's novels are no less philosophical than those of the '98, but they are philosophical in a more integrated way; literature more clearly prevails. The philosophical questions they address in their novels are generally epistemological and aesthetic rather than metaphysical.

Ortega filtered the '98 debates about idea versus matter through literature in *Meditaciones del Quijote*. The result is a meta-metaphysics or a literary metaphysics, a metaphysics once removed, which is reflected in the philosophical fictions of the second generation. Second-generation works evince a cool reserve, a tranquil, detached vantage-point with no place for the passion and the pathos of *Amor y pedagogía*, *Camino de perfección*, *La voluntad*, *El árbol de la ciencia*, *Del sentimiento trágico de la vida* or *Niebla*. The first-generation writers took philosophy seriously, even while mocking it in their novels; they wrote satirical and burlesque works that originated in a deeply troubled spirit. The second-generation writers injected more levity and distance; philosophical thinking did not represent a crisis for them. Part of the lighter quality derives from the parodic double remove through which the original philosophical sources of the '98 are refracted. Ortega was "meditating" on Baroja and Azorín rather than on Descartes or other philosophers of the Western tradition. Ortega's eventual quarrel with German idealism was colored by his vision of the '98, just as the philosophical novel of his generation was often written with that of the '98 in mind. Ultimately it is a difference in levels of abstraction. The '98 struggled with philosophical idealism in the 1890s and rejected it by 1900. The '98 alternative to abstractions (Unamuno's anguish, Baroja's autobiographical elements) were judged by the following generation as "personalism": "toda su generación [that of Unamuno] conservaba el ingrediente de juglar que adquirió el intelectual en los comienzos del romanticismo, que existía ya en Chateaubriand y en Lamartine. No había pues, otro remedio que dedicarse a la pasividad y ponerse en coro en torno a don Miguel, que había soltado en medio de la habitación su yo, como si fuese un ornitorrinco."[3]

In an *Helios* review of Álvaro de Albornoz's *No liras, lanzas*, an incitation to political action in a declining Spain, Ramón Pérez de Ayala defended the use of *liras* rather than *lanzas*. Pérez de Ayala called for a universalism that transcended political borders: "Soy un poco supernacional en el espacio e inactual en el tiempo" (no. 9 [December 1903]: 513). The new lines of battle were drawn; the literary and philosophical approaches of the '98 were now considered passé. Along with that of Gómez de la Serna's *Prometeo* (another of the generation's self-defining journals), *Helios*'s title signaled the new universalism. Classical mythology replaced the personal and national interests of the '98, often expressed through an engagement with the Spanish literary tradition. (Mythical themes and figures are important to the novels of Pérez de Ayala, Gabriel Miró and Benjamín Jarnés.) *Helios*, with which Juan Ramón Jiménez, Pérez de Ayala, Ortega and Antonio Machado were all closely associated, was the early standard-bearer for the generation. An important part of its program was to provide its readers with current information about philosophical developments in Europe, since there was a dearth of specialized journals on the subject. The contents reveal an interest in the mystical, transcendental philosophies of Emerson, Carlyle and Maeterlinck, reflected in the search for totality in Juan Ramón's *Platero y yo*, Valle-Inclán's *La lámpara maravillosa*, Miró's *El humo dormido* and Pérez de Ayala's *Belarmino y Apolonio*.

Ortega further institutionalized the importation of new philosophical orientations in 1923 with the founding of the *Revista de Occidente,* whose express purpose was to disseminate European (particularly German) thought in Spain with translations of Freud, Cassirer, Dilthey, Keyserling, Schulten, Adler, Jung, Simmel, etc. Thus the new generation found inspiration in philosophical sources that were notably different from those of the '98. Instead of Darwin, Taine, Kant, Hegel, Schopenhauer, Spencer, anarchism and socialism, the new idols were Bergson, Simmel and Scheler. In the realignment of intellectual hegemony that took place in the second decade under Ortega's leadership, the antagonists of the first generation became allies to the second. The late Clarín and the other nineteenth-century realist-naturalists were restored to venerable positions, and Krausism enjoyed renewed influence through the establishment of the Residencia de Estudiantes in 1910. Both Miró and Pérez de Ayala also had close associations with Krausist thinkers in their native provinces. Krausism had certain affinities with the "totalism" that attracted the 1914 writers to transcendentalism. The new idealism derived from these several sources produced a conflict with the reluctant and confused positivism of the previous generation, especially its biological and social determinism, so thoroughly rejected by Ortega.

Emilia Pardo Bazán wrote an article in the March 1904 issue of *Helios* entitled "La nueva generación de novelistas y cuentistas en España." From her vantage point in *las nubes,* she did not clearly differentiate the aesthetics of the group who initiated the journal and the Generation of '98, but the authors in question had no trouble sorting themselves out. The relationship of 1914 writers to those of the '98 varied widely from author to author, but there was a generational fascination on the part of the '14 for the '98. A mentor and *confrère* of the Generation of '98, Luis Ruiz Contreras hinted at this interest in an article on Baroja published in *Prometeo,* one of the '14's early and important rallying points.[4] After a few anecdotal remarks about himself, he suggested that the article was solicited by the editors out of interest and curiosity about this central '98 figure: "Pero no divaguemos, y voy a satisfacer su curiosidad sobre aquellos jóvenes refiriéndole algunos recuerdos personales referentes a Pío Baroja" ("Pío Baroja," *Prometeo,* no. 14 [1910]: 46). Ruiz Contreras was clearly aware that his readers did not want to hear unqualified praise of the subject. He emphasized Baroja's ungenerous caricature of himself (he doesn't mention the novel, but it occurs in *Aventuras y mixtificaciones de Silvestre Paradox*), and he forthrightly pointed out the failures of the previous generation, while flattering his present editors (of the rivaling younger generation):

¡Qué lejos han quedado las miserias! Aquella generación, que luchaba por salir, ahora lucha por arraigarse; la empuja poderosamente otra generación más culta, más fortalecida, mejor preparada. Los jóvenes viejos han llegado a convencerse de que importa mucho que haya aquéllos a los cuales empujábamos como a estorbos inútiles. Y hoy, como ayer y mañana si vivo, repitiré lo que un día escribí: 'Los ignorados hoy, serán mañana los elegidos, como éstos eran los ignorados ayer y todos laboraremos para todos, porque la obra es grande y ninguno la empieza ni la termina; todos aportan su haz, todos enlazan su esfuerzo, como eslabones de la cadena que oprime al Universo y le hará esclavo de la obstinación del Hombre. [51]

Juan Ramón Jiménez in the July 1903 issue of *Helios* proclaimed Martínez Ruiz's Antonio Azorín a kindred spirit, and Gregorio Martínez Sierra indicated in the pages of the same journal that he felt like a very close friend of Antonio Azorín, but he could not agree with the character in matters of style. Martínez Ruiz's aboulic protagonist scorns style, while in true Generation of '14 spirit, Martínez Sierra believed that "el triunfo del escritor sobre el estilo no está en prescindir del estilo para alcanzar la claridad, sino en llegar a la claridad por medio de la perfección del estilo" (*Helios* 12 [1904]: 277). The admiration is evident, but so are the recognized and declared differences. At the instigation of Ortega, the younger writers organized a "Fiesta de Aranjuez en honor a Azorín" in 1913, and the author of the *Meditaciones* wrote the following dedication to Azorín in a gift copy of *Espectador VIII* (1934): "Para Azorín, con la devoción perpetua de Ortega." (Given the remarks he had made about the *pequeño filósofo* in private letters to Maeztu, apparently the same kind of hypocrisy evident in the literary world of the young '98 persisted into the new generation.)

The '98 were not better mentors to their juniors than their seniors had been to them, although the easier publishing climate in the second and third decades compensated for the lack of encouragement by older writers. The indifference of the established writers, however, was a serious impediment to Gabriel Miró, whose residence outside the Madrid Ortega circle created a disadvantage. His Alicantine compatriot Azorín chose to ignore Miró's early attempts to gain favor, perhaps out of envy. Miró's finely-crafted poetic prose more ably captures many of the nuances of Levantine life that Azorín himself was attempting to inscribe.[5]

Despite many instances of the new *jóvenes* seeking out the new *viejos*, the personal, philosophical and artistic differences were greater than the similarities. The general consensus among the 1914 was that the '98 did not live up to its promise. As early as 1904, in an article entitled "Plática" published under the pseudonym Clavígero, Pérez de Ayala answered

Unamuno's open letter against modernism: "El señor Unamuno y alguno que otro hijo putativo de su espíritu vienen repitiendo de algún tiempo para esta parte con abrumadora pesadez esta afirmación peregrina que nunca se han cuidado de probar. Si alguna vez se ha hecho cargo la literatura española de ideas y sentimientos que palpitan en la gran masa del público, es ahora en estos últimos años. El arte venía siendo puramente vago y ameno. Hoy ningún artista ejecuta su obra sin pensar en cuestiones y problemas más o menos trascendentales."[6] Pérez de Ayala's article "El '98" is similarly critical of the accomplishments of his predecessors.

In 1908, Ramón Gómez de la Serna joined the campaign against the older generation in *Morbideces*, which accused Azorín, Baroja and Valle-Inclán of kidnapping Larra and mortgaging their revolutionary capabilities. He also suggested that Baroja was not very original, having taken much of his material from Silverio Lanza: "¡Burlarse de la candidez de Silverio Lanza cuando ese es el mineral auténtico que Baroja ha fundido y refundido, el hierro virgen que el ha convertido en hierro colado!"[7] Ortega, who thought Unamuno was too personal and antirationalistic and that Baroja's style symbolized national hysteria, also opined that Azorín's attempts to reconstruct a sense of national identity failed because he lacked the necessary vitality to renew Spanish culture. Antonio Machado, who is often associated with the Generation of '98 but who is actually more philosophically allied with the 1914, wrote: "'¡Basta, Azorín!' 'Oh, tú, Azorín, escucha: España quiere/surgir, brotar, toda una España empieza."[8]

By the time Jarnés began writing his novels in the 1920s, the works and ideas of the Generation of '98 had become institutionalized jokes. Unamuno was transformed into the archetype of the ridiculous pedant in a number of Generation of '14 novels—just what Menéndez y Pelayo had represented in Unamuno's early works! His representation of himself as a kind of God in the author-character confrontation in *Niebla* received comic treatment in novels by Pérez de Ayala, Gómez de la Serna and Jarnés. María Zambrano indicated that Augusto Pérez had become a symbol of all that was rejected by her generation: "Son los famosos tipos—también tan españoles, tan de mesa de café, o despacho—de intelectuales inactivos. Es aquel personaje que nos presenta Unamuno en *Niebla*."[9] The relationship of Antonio Machado's character Juan de Mairena to his teacher Abel Martín is even more rich and complex than that of Antonio Azorín to Yuste. Like that novel's palimpsest of the Martínez Ruiz-Clarín-Pi y Margall relationships, it reveals Machado's ambivalence toward Unamuno.

Juan Ramón and Martínez Sierra may have felt a spiritual kinship with
Antonio Azorín in the early years of the century, but by 1907 and especially in the second and third decades the aboulia-ridden protagonist cultivated by Martínez Ruiz and Baroja was subjected to ridicule. The
Ossorio-Azorín-Andrés Hurtado type is parodied in Alberto Díaz de
Guzmán, the central figure of Ramón Pérez de Ayala's tetralogy, and in
several of Jarnés's and Gómez de la Serna's characters.

At the same time that epistemological issues replaced the metaphysical and ontological ones of the '98, questions of language and its relation
to perception and being emerged as novelistic concerns. Literature became an important realm in which to explore its own fundamental linguistic material, and in a number of '14 novels, metaphor edged out the
dialogue which was a crucial philosophical vehicle in the '98 novel. Ortega summarized (rather than prescribed, as is sometimes alleged) the
new aesthetics in *La deshumanización del arte* of 1925. In fact, his epistemology had a greater influence on the novels of his generation than did
his ideas about modern art and literature. His theory of aesthetics addresses art as a way of knowing, of forming ideas about the world. According to Ortega, the problem with knowing (or more precisely,
"conceptualizing") is that one cannot be living (i.e., receiving the stimuli
necessary for knowing) at the same time that one is knowing. Before it
can be known, life experience must be de-realized. Although Ortega employed the terms "dehumanized" and "de-realized" interchangeably in
this context, the former has taken on a pejorative connotation and has
frustrated criticism of the novel of his generation. As stylization or derealization *par excellence*, art aids the knowing process. Ortega maintained
that it is more effective as a means to knowledge than science itself: "De
la tragedia de la ciencia nace el arte. Lo natural es lo que acaece conforme
a las leyes físicas, que son generalizaciones, y el problema del arte es lo
vital, lo concreto, lo único en cuanto único, concreto y vital" (*OC* 1: 483).
The tension is no longer between science and idea, as in the '98, but between science and art, and art wins handily.

In *Meditaciones del Quixote*, Ortega posited the foundation of his epistemology in the primacy of perception. Humanity *is* its relationship to the
world around it as well as to things in it: "El hombre rinde el máximo
de su capacidad cuando adquiere la plena conciencia de sus circunstancias. Por ellas comunica con el universo: ¡La circunstancia! *Circunstancia*!
Las cosas mudas que están en nuestro próximo derridor!" (*OC* 1: 316).
The relationship is dialectical: "Hay dentro de toda cosa la indicación de
una posible plenitud. Una alma abierta y noble sentiría la ambición de
perfeccionarla, de auxiliarla para que logre esa plenitud. Esto es amor—el

amor a la perfección de lo amado" (*OC* 1: 311). Our relationship to things begins in the senses, in perception, but knowledge of the world (literally, the possession of it) is achieved only through conceptualization: "Sólo la visión mediante el concepto, es una visión completa; la sensación . . . nos da la impresión de las cosas, no las cosas. . . . Lo que hay entre las cosas es el contenido del concepto" (*OC* 1: 354, 351). True perception is not sensation but conceptualization: "De suerte que si devolvemos a la palabra percepción su valor etimológico—donde se alude a coger, apresar—el concepto era el verdadero instrumento u órgano de la percepción y apresamiento de las cosas" (*OC* 1: 353).

In art this necessary distance between the thing and the idea is, or should be, rigorously maintained, and this is what Ortega found of positive value in the new art of his age. In "dehumanization" ("derealization")—elimination of human forms and emphasis on style—there can be no confusion between life itself and the conceptualization of it. Art is a potentially powerful ally to understanding life: "Pues bien: pensemos lo que significaría un idioma o un sistema de signos expresivos de quien la función no consistiera en narrarnos las cosas, sino en presentárnoslas como ejecutándose. Tal idioma es el arte: esto hace el arte. El objeto estético es una intimidad en cuanto tal—es todo en cuanto *yo*" (*OC* 4: 256).

The aesthetics of the Generation of 1914 were by no means uniformly molded by Ortega's ideas, even though Ortega was an important catalyst to generational activities with the Liga de Educación Política (1913), his journals *España* (1915) and *Revista de Occidente* (1923), their attendant *tertulias*, and his book series—the biographies and Nova Novorum. The aesthetics of the novelists who were part of his circle were formed in a dialogue with other writers of the '14, with the '98 and with the European vanguard, as well as with Ortega.[10] The heterogeneous nature of the new generation was no different from the conglomerate characteristics that consituted the '98. There was dissension within the generation, just as there had been in the previous one. For example, Juan Ramón Jiménez called the *Revista de Occidente* the "Revista de Desoriente," and Ramón Gómez de la Serna clashed with Ortega over the aesthetics of Ruskin. The philosopher could not abide the English thinker's pragmatic approach to art, but Gómez de la Serna extolled the English aesthetician's views (if he did not practice them).

Ortega had few kind words to say about the novels of his contemporaries (who were, according to so many critics, slavishly following the aesthetic recipes of the master). Pérez de Ayala commented to Unamuno that Ortega had written him "poderosos elogios" of *Troteras y danzaderas* but had ended his letter by saying that the novel "no gravita."[11] Miró's *El obispo leproso* was the object of Ortega's acerbic pen, and the philosopher was ominously silent about the fiction of Benjamín Jarnés, his close associate at the *Revista de Occidente*. The only Spanish novelist he included in *La deshumanización del arte* was Gómez de la Serna, but he only mentioned his non-novelistic works. He understood, however, that Gómez de la Serna had shifted away from nineteenth-century realism with a new approach to perception:

Los mejores ejemplos de cómo por extremar el realismo se le supera—no más que con atender lupa en mano a lo microscópico de la vida—son Proust, Ramón Gómez de la Serna, Joyce. Ramón puede componer todo un libro sobre los senos— alguien le ha llamado 'nuevo Colón que hacía hemisferios'—o sobre el circo, o sobre el alba, o sobre el Rastro o la Puerta del Sol. El procedimiento consiste sencillamente en hacer protagonistas del drama vital los barrios bajos de la atención, lo que de ordinario desatendemos. (*OC* 3: 374)

Nonetheless, Ortega's ideas inspired thinking (and jokes) about art among his contemporaries, as well as a number of dialogues in their fictions.[12] The theme of the dichotomy between life and art appears in many of the generation's novels, in which the characters' *circunstancia* is generally neither a backdrop for nor a cause of their actions. The world is a place of perceptual and phenomenological discovery that occurs through a language that attempts to capture experience, the secret of things that so fascinated Gómez de la Serna. But the founder of *Prometeo* and ardent admirer of Ortega was not above a humorous gloss of Ortega's serious phenomenology: "Lo que menos merece la vida es la reproducción fiel de lo que aparenta suceder en ella. Es una mezcla de cochina e ideal realidad con cochina e ideal irrealidad; en una palabra, la cochinchina."[13] The playful aspect that Ortega noted in the new "dehumanized" art is everywhere in evidence in the novels of the Generation of 1914, some of it at the expense of Ortega himself. In *Troteras y danzaderas*, Pérez de Ayala placed the following dictum in the mouth of the guileless character Teófilo Pajares: "La vida es anterior y superior al arte" (*OC* 1: 791), and in *El curandero de su honra*, it is observed that man is more of an artist when he manages to feel and make others feel, to express with the greatest intensity his irrationality, his own life, as well as other irrationalities and other lives—to multiply for others the dimensions and pleasure of his own life.

Ortega and Ramón Pérez de Ayala met in 1903 or 1904 when the latter was studying for the doctorate at the University of Madrid. Ortega invited Pérez de Ayala, who had already begun publishing a few essays, to submit something to his father's prestigious *Los Lunes del Imparcial*. His first contribution entitled "Quería morir," a reminiscence of his native Asturias, contains the following passage, which draws a parallel between the ruminations of philosophers and those of cows: "Desfilaron por mi mente las ideas con vuelo tardo de ave vagabunda, porque el cerebro se emperezaba también. Era la pereza del Norte, pereza que es un recogimiento, pensativa, sesuda, parsimoniosa de acción, lentitud meditabunda; la pereza de los filósofos y de las vacas. Las unas sacan el jugo a su caudal rumiándolo; los otros buscan la esencia de la realidad especulando." It continues: "Estaba discurriendo musicalmente, según quería Hegel, y más tarde Schopenhauer; pero la misteriosa canción con la cual vibraba mi alma, como arpa en un acorde final negábase a brotar de los labios" (*OC* 1: xv). This irreverant description of the philosopher's enterprise characterizes many of the philosphical passages in Pérez de Ayala's novels; his attitude toward the pompous Ortega was likewise ambiguous, especially in light of his comic embodiment of Ortega in Antón Tejero of *Troteras y danzaderas*. Ortega probably learned as much from Pérez de Ayala as the novelist did from him. For example, the "Unas gotas de fenomenología" scene in *La deshumanización del arte*, proffered as a dramatic example of perspectivism, is similar to the death scene of Teófilo Pajares in *Troteras y danzaderas*.[14]

The dichotomy between life and art that Ortega recommended is a tragic flaw in many of Pérez de Ayala's characters. Teófilo Pajares succumbs to this malady, and Alberto Díaz de Guzmán nearly does. Alberto says to his prostitute friend Rosina: "Tú haces hombres, como se dice; yo hago literatura, artículos, libros. Si la gente no nos paga o no nos acepta, nos quedamos sin comer. Tú vendes placer a tu modo; yo, al mío; los dos, a costa de la vida. En muy pocos años serás una vieja asquerosa, si antes no te mueres podrida; yo me habré vuelto idiota, si antes no muero agotado" (*OC* 1: 556). Alberto converts the elusive and malicious Meg into an *objet d'art:* "Meg ya no era sino un objeto curioso de observación y un interesante tener artístico; había descendido de tirana a esclava, porque así como la forma domina el mal artífice y engendra la desarmonía de la obra, el buen artífice domina la forma y rige apaciblemente las leyes de la armonía. Alberto consideraba la vida como una obra de arte, como un proceso del hacer reflexivo sobre los materiales del sentir sincero, imparcial" (*OC* 1: 462).

Benjamín Jarnés toyed with Ortega's interest in the problem of perception by inventing characters who engage in paralyzing (and generally ridiculous) phenomenological observations at crucial moments in his lighthearted fictions. An early passage in *Locura y muerte de nadie* appears to take phenomenological observation seriously: "Ocurre hundirse en la entraña de un objeto sin haber paseado los ojos y las manos, voluptuosamente por regiones inexploradas de la piel. Se contenta con ver pasar por ella las efímeras caravanas del calor, tan enemigo del dibujo, del firme relieve. Sólo ve en ella lo que apenas existe, dejando lo duradero, su pura extensión, su frágil material encajada en los compartimentos del aire."[15] In a later scene, however, phenomenological attention to an object is cast in a humorous light. The protagonist, Arturo, goes to meet his married mistress, Matilde, as they had agreed, but Matilde is cold and distant. Arturo supposes that a servant must be listening or that the husband is expected soon. During the long, awkward scene, Arturo becomes perceptually fixed on a bowl of fruit; the entire continuity of action, the tension of this potentially explosive situation is dispelled by the phenomenological investigation of the fruit bowl: "Continúa la espera. Matilde es allí un objeto más. Se acerca a la pirámide de fruta, se sitúa en la baldosa exacta desde donde el azafate puede ser percibido con la máxima luz. El balcón está entreabierto, los visillos apenas empañan el cristal. Más lejos, sólo vería manchas inconcretas de color. . . . Abre la fruta tres horizontes, cada uno con peculiares deleites; el del color, el del aroma, el del contacto. Son los ojos espías vivaces de la voluptuosidad. . . . Arturo se enamora súbitamente de la fruta, pero quiere irla poseyendo por grados."[16] The passage continues in this vein for some five pages.

María Zambrano, sometimes considered Ortega's favorite disciple, almost invariably refers hagiographically to "Don José" in her writings. She may, however, have had a more ambivalent attitude toward her domineering mentor than even she herself realized. José Luis Aranguren cites a revealing passage about her departure from Madrid during the Civil War: "allí estaban, cuidadosamente ordenadas en unas cajas de fácil transporte, todos mis apuntes de los numerosos cursos de Ortega. . . . Nunca he logrado explicarme hasta ahora por qué corté mi gesto de recogerlos, por qué los dejé abandonados allí, en aquella casa sola, cuyo vacío resonó, al cerrarse la puerta, de modo inolvidable."[17] Her physical distance from the *maestro* and the psychological distance from his notes allowed her to develop her own original version of the *razón vital;* her *razón poética* focuses on the nature of language in reality, a topic that never really interested her mentor.[18]

Like María Zambrano, Juan Ramón Jiménez, Gabriel Miró and Rosa Chacel were more serious than others of Ortega's generation in their explorations of consciousness, perception and language, especially in *Platero y yo, El humo dormido,* and *Estación. Ida y vuelta,* respectively. All three authors add important dimensions to Ortega's fundamental notion of "yo soy yo y mi circunstancia"; memory and language become fundamental to one's cicumstance and are understood as important constituents of it. Time and the word are inextricably bound in their conception of language and in their individual styles. In extending the sense of world, they also extend the functions of traditional narration, inventing new genres that fuse narrative and philosophical qualities.

In a reply to the notion of dehumanization, Jarnés added his voice to those of his generation in venerating the ontological power of language:

La voluntad del estilo crea el mundo. Estilo es algo que el hombre consigue armonizando todos sus energías espirituales, algo que surge de este triunfo logrado contra las fuerzas contrarias que luchan dentro del espíritu. Estilo es cierto equilibrio de fuerzas conseguido por un hombre, no el mismo hombre.

No es razón ni pasión, sino equilibrio entre ambos.[19]

Language and the nature of being also receive serious consideration (although not without generous comic overtones) in Ramón Pérez de Ayala's *Belarmino y Apolonio.*

But the consummate linguistic pyrotechnist of the generation was Ramón Gómez de la Serna. Ramón, as he was known to his contemporaries, sought in his writing "el asa de la realidad para asirme a ella, para agarrarme."[20] And this was the prime purpose of his unique creation, the *greguería,* an innovative epigram invented between 1910 and 1912, combining humor and metaphor in an attempt to reach the essence of objects through language: "Lo que gritan los seres confusamente desde su inconciencia, lo que gritan las cosas."[21] The novelty of the *greguería* is a view of a thing that combines its traditional objective condition and a subjective human perspective (often perceptual) in one single, unified image: "Y" is, for example, the champagne glass of the alphabet. Gómez de la Serna's most original novels are one long *greguería* composed of many smaller ones: "La literatura se vuelve atómica por la misma razón por la que toda la curiosidad de la vida científica palpita alrededor del átomo, abandonadas más amplias abstracciones, buscando el secreto de la creación en el misterio del átomo."[22]

Along with Ortega (for whom he proclaimed the greatest admiration), Ramón provided important forums for generational dialogue in his journal *Prometeo* and the *tertulia* Pombo. *Prometeo* introduced Spanish intellectual and artistic circles to much of what was happening on the Parisian avantgarde. Ramón was friendly with Picabia and Tzara, and his journal was the first to publish Marinetti's "Futurist Manifesto" in Spain in 1909. Ramón facilitated a number of the vanguardist strategies by which his contemporaries—especially Jarnés, Salinas and Chacel—could elaborate their philosophical novels (and simultaneously parody those of their predecesors). Pedro Salinas's *Víspera del gozo* (1926), with its serious poetic language and surprising narrative twists, is perhaps one of the best examples of the second generation's achievement of a philosophical narrative that combines humor, image, metaphor and epistemological exploration.

In the last three chapters of this study, I explore the ways in which Pérez de Ayala, Miró, Jarnés and, more briefly, Juan Ramón, Salinas and Chacel shift the philosophical emphases of the novel in Spain onto new ground. The new territory they chart combines a focus on consciousness and language with frequent references to their differences with members of the previous generation.

8

PÉREZ DE AYALA:
PARODY WED TO
AESTHETIC THEORY

Born in 1880 in Asturias, Ramón Pérez de Ayala began his literary career
with articles in *El Progreso de Asturias* in 1901, the same year that his
professor Clarín died and about ten years after Unamuno, Baroja and Martínez Ruiz first appeared in the periodical press. Although he is frequently associated with the Generation of '98, especially in his early
novels,[1] his work betrays none of the anger and hostility toward the late
nineteenth-century authors, ideas and narrative styles that characterized
the earlier generation.[2] Pérez de Ayala returned to many of the values of
his grandfathers, while parodying the concerns and creations of his immediate predecessors. His education, while not ignoring the philosophical sources of the '98, emphasized classical philosophy and literature. He
combined his knowledge of the classics with his natural skepticism and
irony in his elaborate parodies of the Generation of '98 philosophical
novel. Pérez de Ayala's studies at the University of Oviedo from 1897 to
1901 brought him into contact with Krausism through his professors
Clarín, Adolfo Posada and Rafael Altamira among others. In the early article "Liras o lanzas" he wrote: "Albornoz y yo somos Krausistas. . . .
Ningún libro mejor que *El ideal de la Humanidad*, de Krause, para in-
querir cuál sea mi deber. Y así en los mandamientos de la Humanidad
(que no son más que 23) leo: 'Debes conocer, amar y santificar la naturaleza, el espíritu, la humanidad sobre todo individuo natural, espiritual y
humano' " (*OC* 1: 1129). The totalizing message embedded in the ending
of *Belarmino y Apolonio* recalls the Krausist ideal of universal harmony, as
does the serene transcendence of his aesthetics.

Pérez de Ayala's sojourns in England taught him to appreciate English philosophy, but without the agony that attended Unamuno's interest
in Spencer: "Si hay un orden de pensamiento nacional organizado de cultura de espíritu, que tenga unidad, es el pensamiento inglés, o si queréis,

la filosofía inglesa."[3] He thought the two major works of English philosophy that underpinned the British national character were Bacon's *Novum Organum* and Mill's *Logic*. He explained the foundations of English inductive-utilitarian thought as "De un lado, el anhelo de hacer la vida humana más plena, mejor; un ideal colectivo. Y de otro lado, una cierta parsimonia y cautela en la conducta individual con que se ha de contribuir a la consecuencia paulatina de aquel ideal, un sentido utilitario de la conducta."[4] He believed English utilitarianism had allowed the English people to engage in confident and vital action, but he contradicted this positive view of the English character in Alberto Díaz de Guzmán's portrayal of his alcoholic English friend, whose mentally retarded son commits suicide and whose daughter's morals are founded on complete self-obsession.

Having escaped the ponderous and conflictive philosophical debates that weighed so heavily upon the '98, thanks to his particular intellectual orientation and his education, Pérez de Ayala, like Don Melitón Pelayo, the character he invented in an early article entitled "La caverna de Platón," was "un poco filósofo y demasiado observador. . . . escrudiña la naturaleza de las cosas, en tanto aguarda la venida del esposo, que ha de ser, pienso yo, alguna intuición genial. Todo le sugiere profundas y trascendentales observaciones, rasgos humorísticos, referencias metafísicas."[5] The mystification with which Pérez de Ayala endowed all his fiction is evident in the character's name. Although it is one of Ayala's early *noms de plume*,[6] it also sounds like a modification of Marcelino Menéndez Pelayo, and the character's eclectic and ambiguous philosophical position echoes that of Fulgencio Entrambosmares. Pérez de Ayala's attitude toward his life and art was that of a detached observer. The name Plotino Cuevas with which he signed several early articles and his first novel *Tinieblas en las cumbres* is illustrative; while admiring the classics, he joked about his interest in classical philosophy with a humorous pseudonym that referred to the neoplatonic philosopher Plotinus and to Plato's famous example of the cave.

He shared with the '98 a preference for literature over the traditional philosophical treatise, and like the previous generation, he was irremediably attracted to literature with a philosophical purpose: "Todo arte literario que con dignidad lleve tal nombre, ha de ser en alguna manera filosofía, conciencia esencial de la vida" (*OC* 2: 560). He considered the fundamental problem of literature to be discovering the general principle in a particular case, finding continuity in change. These are philosophical problems that systematic philosophy cannot resolve: "La unificación de lo diverso y la inmutación de lo mudable son atinomías que sólo se concilian en el acto estético. Por eso la obra de arte genuina está embebida de un conocimiento de la realidad más filosófica que todas las filosofías tradicionales" (*OC* 4: 1125). Pérez de Ayala's literary approach to philosophical questions, however, was fundamentally different from that of the '98. He was the beneficiary of both the philosophical and the novelistic battles fought by Unamuno, Baroja and Martínez Ruiz in *Amor y pedagogía*, *Camino de perfección*, *La voluntad*, *Niebla* and *El árbol de la ciencia*. His style is less polemical and more narrative than theirs, as he was not struggling against traditional novelistic form. In the calm after the storm, he tranquilly culled pieces of the wreckage for his own unique creations both from the realist tradition, so odious to the earlier writers, and from the novelties offered by the '98. Not having directly confronted the implications of positivism or the obstacles put in the way of the '98's literary careers, he had no quarrel with Clarín and Galdós, and made generous use their omniscient, world-building, *a priori* storytelling methods, serenely combining them with the philosophical disquisition of the '98.

Although Pérez de Ayala did not share the '98's tendency to hostile relations with the previous generation or with his own, he was not above engaging in playful caricature of them in his literary works and in personal correspondence. He rendered an adoring homage to Clarín in a 1905 article entitled "El maestro" (and how different is his version of the *maestro* from Martínez Ruiz's!): "Cuando estudié Derecho natural con don Leopoldo, había un núcleo de compañeros míos que le 'adorábamos'. Ésta es la palabra, porque poníamos en nuestro amor y en nuestra admiración algo de respeto supersticioso y de culto fetichista. Su cátedra era un templo; sus reproches excomuniones o anatemas; sus elogios, gracia divina. . . . Los vinos de la vieja cepa mística castellana y los néctares de la metafísica de Kant, el último padre de la iglesia, añejos y generosos, rebosaban de su espíritu, y el bálsamo de su palabra tenía tanta unción que imprimía carácter en las almas adolescentes, de por vida, al ungirlas" (*OC* 1: xvii-xviii). The mysticism and Kantian metaphysics of the Asturian critic, such anathema to the '98, were now a divinely inspired balm, but in many of his novels he reduced Clarín's serious view of corrupt Restoration Oviedo (Vetusta in *La Regenta*) to a comic description of its brothels.

Pérez de Ayala honored Azorín with more critical attention than any other writer of his previous generation, and the pieces on Azorín have been collected to comprise an entire volume—*Ante Azorín*. Not surprisingly, Azorín inspired Pérez de Ayala to meditate on the problem of the will and on the nature of time. *La voluntad*, he wrote, was a violent reaction against the Spanish milieu: "La austeridad castellana y católica [que] agobia a esta pobre raza paralítica."[7] In his own early novels, Pérez de Ayala insisted less on milieu and more on an individual character's sensitivity as the source of his aboulia and spiritual crisis, and the intensely ironic tone of segments of these novels undermines the '98's sober portrayals of national will-lessness.

He commented on Azorín's penchant for using the present tense, a practice he said originated in Azorín's very nature, his need, like that of the classical writers, to capture the present as the only existing thing: "se ase y aferra desesperadamente al presente, reteniéndolo. Y de aquí el sabor clásico de la prosa de *Azorín*, porque, a juicio del clasicismo, sólo el presente existe; mejor dicho, una inteligencia y una sensibilidad cultivada sólo existen en presente" (115). He classified Azorín's views on time as outmoded because they did not take into account more recent theories (such as relativity). The new physics unchained time and space from the subjective formalisms of Kant and incorporated them into the same physical reality, something entirely alien to Azorín's focus on the eternal present. Pérez de Ayala praised his own contemporary Ramón Gómez de la Serna, who did understand time in terms of the new physics (163, 171). Just as Ortega's meditations on Azorín and Baroja inspired his philosophical position, thinking about Azorín's ideas and practices provided Pérez de Ayala an intellectual distance and artistic space to create works that would enter into a dialogue with those of the preceding generation.

Not only was Azorín an object of intellectual contemplation for Pérez de Ayala, he also became a friend after he went to Madrid in 1901 to broaden his horizons, and Azorín visited him in his native Oviedo in 1905. His friendly, yet ironic stance toward the *pequeño filósofo* is revealed in a letter to his lifetime friend Miguel Rodríguez-Acosta, to whom he gave the following excuse for not writing sooner: "llegó por estas Asturias el tácito y hermético Azorín, el cual se hospedó en mi casa y me enajenó diez días cabales desde la mañana a la noche. En todo ese tiempo no pude ni arrascarme los huevos, porque tenía casi que arrascárselos a él."[8] And the poem he composed on the occasion of Azorín's visit is hardly an elogium:

> Con el claro y rotundo monóculo en un ojo,
> en la mano el arcaico paraguas color rojo,
> luego la tabaquera, esculpida de plata,
> y, allá en lo íntimo, sorda misantropía innata,
> vagaste entre los hombres y los libros a cientos.
> Ahora te encuentras como cansado y sin alientos.
>   [*OC* 2: 148]

In speculating about the future in the same poem, Pérez de Ayala ironically concluded that "Llamarán a Unamuno, todavía chiflado,/ y Baroja, aunque rico, irá desharrapado" (*OC* 2: 151). Azorín is humorously (if not satirically) portrayed in the character of Juan Halconete in *Troteras y danzaderas*. His physical appearance represents a man whose convictions are not very reliable: "En el rostro de Halconete había siempre singular combate entre la boca, demasiadamente pequeña, y una sonrisa sutil que pugnaba, sin cejar, por abrirla y distenderla; y era esto de manera tan sugestiva y paradójica, que hacía pensar en esos chicuelos que conducen por la calle un gran perro atado con un cordel y el perro tira de un lado, el chico de otro, y andan en continuo vaivén, a ver cuál arrastra al otro" (*OC* 1: 609). In a discussion of the plans of Antón Tejero (Ortega) to save Spain through a liberal program, Halconete announces that he is a conservative, an assertion that launches Alberto Díaz de Guzmán upon a philosophical disquisition concerning the forces that move the world, summarizing in a nutshell the philosophical debates of the late nineteenth century that perplexed the Generation of '98. He outlines three philosophical positions, each of which has its corresponding political system: 1) man is fundamentally bad, the conservative position, 2) man is essentially good but is corrupted by society, the liberal position, and 3) man is neither, but rather an idiot, which gives rise to the *arribista* position. But observing Halconete, Alberto realizes that there is yet a fourth position regarding human nature, which is to refuse to concern oneself about *how* it is, accept that it is and simply enjoy it: "sentirse vivir, decorar el presente con las más suaves fruiciones; o sea, contraer la obsesión del tiempo que corre" (*OC* 1: 611). This fourth position engenders a peculiar ethics and aesthetics that combines a sympathy for the fragile and ephemeral with a great affection for that which time does not erase, for the things that gain stature with the passing of the years—old books, friends and wine, pleasures of the Epicurian.

Pérez de Ayala's commentary on Unamuno was less direct than his considerations of Azorín, perhaps because he knew him less well personally. He admired Unamuno as a poet; at least he dedicated *Troteras y danzaderas* to him with a phrase that greatly pleased the Rector of Salamanca: "Poeta y filósofo español del siglo XXI." (Significantly, the dedication is missing in the *Obras completas* version.) The only mark Unamuno made in his copy of the novel, published in Madrid by Renacimiento in 1913, was on page 32, where Alberto advises Teófilo to imitate the poetry of Unamuno, "el mejor poeta que tenemos y uno de los mas grandes que hemos tenido." But Unamuno, like Azorín, provoked Pérez de Ayala to consider the implications of fundamental '98 philosophical issues. Undoubtedly inspired by Augusto Pérez's indecision over whether or not to use his umbrella at the beginning of *Niebla*, he wrote in the article "El conflicto del paraguas" that the umbrella repesents the difficulty of determining the will without a prior determination of judgment.

Tocante a lo futuro, como el juicio opera sobre conjeturas, no cabe, racionalmente, que se determine. En el caso más sencillo, las conjeturas, son dos y opuestas entre sí. El juicio se inhibe; la voluntad vacila. ¿Qué hacer? Si la voluntad se inhibe también, indica un estado psicológico de la psique. Hay una enfermedad de la voluntad llamada 'abulia', que consiste en la inacción, a causa de la indecisión del juicio: En el no saber querer. En los individuos con exceso discursivos y racioncinantes es harto frecuente una disposición pasiva, que el vulgo atribuye a la pereza, y que es abulia, inacción por indecisión, como quiera que lo racional es que la voluntad se determine por motivos de certidumbre, y no de conjetura."[9]

Donald L. Fabian has noted Pérez de Ayala's inspiration in Unamuno's *Amor y pedagogía* for his "novela poemática" *Prometeo* of 1915. Fabian discusses the different emphases of the two novels, but he does not discuss the 1915 novelette's parodic stance vis-à-vis the Generation of '98's type of philosophical novel.[10] Part of the parody issues from mixing elements of various '98 novels in one, as Baroja also lends material to Pérez de Ayala's creative manipulation of the '98 novelistic production. The long philosophical dialogue so characteristic of both *Camino de perfección* and *El árbol de la ciencia*, as well as many of Baroja's other novels, is a strategic device in most of Pérez de Ayala's novels, garnering him the epithet of "novelista intelectual" by more than one critic.[11] The pure intellectualism of his novelized philosophical dialogues fades when seen in their ludic contexts and as a parody of the same practices by Baroja.

The first of these dialogues, occuring almost at the end of *Tinieblas en las cumbres*, is a summary rather than an integral structural part of a novel that otherwise devotes itself to narrating a young woman's fall into a life of prostitution. In fact, the narrator advises the reader to skip the dialogue if he or she is anxious to get on with the story line. Making fun of the '98's tendency to place inordinate weight on the philosophical dialogues, the narrator says in an italicized paragraph headed by the title "Coloquio supérfluo": "Calificamos este coloquio de superfluo porque sabemos que, en virtud de cierta trascendencia que en él va imbuida, ha de parecerles frío, baladí, y, por ende, innecesario, a la mayoría de nuestros lectores. Suplicámosles, pues que lo pasen por alto, asegurándoles, desde luego, que nada tiene que ver, con el asunto central de esta historia, y que pueden dejarle de lado en la lectura, sin que la preterición perjudique el interés de los acontecimientos, antes al contrario" (*OC* 1: 179). Pérez de Ayala reversed Baroja's use of philosophical dialogue in *Camino de perfección;* Fernando's conversation with Schulze about Nietzsche's program for a sane and healthy life comes early in the novel and initiates the protagonist's road to perfection.

Pérez de Ayala facilitated the reader's identification of Alberto Díaz de Guzmán with Fernando Ossorio: both protagonists lack philosophical direction in their lives, and there are many coincidences between the two men's respective encounters with a philosophical antagonist, the foreigners Schulze and Yiddy. Engaging Alberto in discussion on the way to observe an eclipse of the sun, the Englishman Yiddy provides a critical perspective on Alberto's existential malaise, just as Schulze does for Fernando (both encounters include a hike up a mountain). The similarities also underscore the fundamental difference in the philosophical message of the two dialogues. While Schulze extols the nature that Fernando ultimately embraces (choosing it over science, art and religion), Yiddy disparages nature with a decidedly anti-Nietzschean flair. Alberto's life trajectory is exactly the opposite of Ossorio's. The Asturian protagonist begins as an artist who prefers art to literature because it is closer to nature, and he ends by destroying his artwork and finally choosing the more artificial literature in *La pata de la raposa*. Yiddy describes Alberto's initial philosophical position: "El universo le parecía una inmensa nebulosa; esto es, una gigantesca esfera de neblina espesa, y de pronto se agrietaba, se agrietaba ante sus ojos de usted; parecía que iba a mostrarle su seno, su corazón, todo él cristalino y de lumbre, y exclamaba usted: '¡He aquí, he aquí el gran enigma del mundo, el pensamiento del orbe, que a mí se me revela por primera vez antes que a ningún otro hombre!' " (183). He warns him against the tendency to intellectualize nature: "Por eso, con perfecto conocimiento de causa le aseguro a usted que ese indecente vicio de metafisiquear y neoplatonizar a solas con la naturaleza es el peor de los vicios, el que conduce a más miserable vida" (184). After a mystical experience in which he felt at one with nature, Yiddy eschewed intellectualizing and gave himself over to skepticism and sensuality. But Alberto remains unconvinced; he insists that nature depends upon humanity for its meaning.

If Pérez de Ayala alludes to Baroja in the earlier parts of the dialogue, Unamuno's concerns take over toward the end of it in an uncanny premonition of the major themes and images of *Niebla*.[12] As the fog closes in ever more densely, Alberto wonders aloud to Yiddy if our consciousness survives death intact. He concludes that "Acaso la conciencia no sea otra cosa que fenómeno huidero; pero por él todos los átomos del inmenso conjunto han de pasar, a su vez, sólo con el fin de que posean y afirmen esta verdad sublime: 'Soy la conciencia del universo.' Y cuando el hombre lo comprende así, es realmente parte de Dios en el Universo" (213). After his spiritual crisis on the mountaintop, precipitated by the solar eclipse he has witnessed in an advanced state of inebriation, Alberto (like Unamuno in his religious crisis of 1897) wishes to return to the simple faith of his childhood.

At the beginning of *La pata de la raposa*, Alberto, like Ossorio, repudiates art, which he says has led him into a Schopenhauerian desire to forget life (Baroja created the quintessential Schopenhauerian life-denying Andrés Hurtado in the same year). But Alberto goes further than either Antonio Azorín (also devoted to reading Schopenhauer in his youth) or Andrés Hurtado and throws all the books of the "viejo lúbrico y cínico" into the patio, and determines that in future his only texts will be his cat and dog. It is also significant that his servant, who in his free time has read all the philosophical works in Alberto's library, treats him with cool cynicism when he loses his fortune. After realizing that he lives only through aesthetic perceptions, never really coming in direct sensual contact with life, he determines to "animalizarse" (262), which he proceeds to do through a series of studies on the moral character of his domestic animals. The absurdity of his essays is perhaps rivaled only by Silvestre Paradox's philosophical treatise (and the connection is enhanced when we recall that Silvestre owns the Kantian dog Yock). Alberto's dog Sultán represents Christian morality ("El perro y el semita son los únicos animales que creen en un ser superior a ellos," 266), and again Alberto seems to presage Unamuno in *Niebla* when he recalls a story about Pope (Unamuno owned a copy of the first edition of *La pata de la raposa*): "La ética judía, como la del perro, es de origen teológico (ética judía = ética cristiana = ética canina), la moral es emanación divina. Dios es el legislador de la conducta del hombre, y éste de la del perro. Recuérdese la inscripción que Pope—creo que fue Pope—puso en el collar de su perro: 'Yo soy vuestro perro, Señor; pero cuyo sois vos el perro señor?' " (266).

Alberto is also inspired to write an ode to an ant that has metaphysical overtones (recall Antonio Azorín's speculations on the Kantian beetle):

> ¿No tienes dudas ni teorías,
> hormiga? ¿Temes el sordo abismo
> del no ser?
> . . . .
> —Sí, trabajas todos los días.
> Lo sé. Mas ¿no profesas el hormigocentrismo?—
> . . . .

—Ya; cuidas del mañana con mira terrenal.
Eres dichosa porque nunca miras al cielo.
No sabes del bien ni del mal.
No sientes melancolías
ni la horrible desolación
del que ve que se acaban sus días
y en su boca se hiela la canción. [*OC* 1: 270, 271]

Although the reader has not been privileged to "see" one of Alberto's paintings as in the case of Ossorio, he/she suspects that, given the high esteem in which he is held as a painter, his new career as a literary-philosophical writer is a comic aberration. Like Fernando Ossorio, he takes up the life of a picaresque adventurer, but his philosophical encounters (unlike Fernando's) are comic and transitory—a prostitute who quotes Voltaire and an innkeeper with a store of folk wisdom. In his room at an inn, the Voltairian prostitute becomes the muse that inspires him to write philosophical poetry: " 'Si dos minutos la existencia/ ha de durar, según Voltaire,/ brindemos uno a la sapiencia,/ y antes demos otro al placer' " (321). The poetry inspired by the prostitute is better and more serious than the dialogue with the ant.

Contrasting sharply with Fernando Ossorio and Antonio Azorín, Alberto chooses to join the circus and live its ludic world as an alternative to the artistic life. Unlike the serious searching of his '98 counterparts, Alberto's artistic talent is turned to making comic sculptures before the circus audiences and acting out various satirical skits for which he is eventually jailed. A long passage in the circus portion of his adventures is dedicated to a series of letters that he writes to Halconete (Azorín). Alberto's early letters contain numerous philosophical meanderings prompting Halconete's request that Guzmán write him "lances de [su] vida actual, y que deje de lado las filosofías espontáneas" (340). Alberto observes that "lo primero no es sino pretexto o arbitrio para lograr lo segundo" (340). Pérez de Ayala has Halconete complain that Guzmán indulges in precisely the same errors as Azorín's early novels, which allow philosophical commentary to overshadow the story. Alberto humbly accepts the advice of his friend: "Usted me aconseja y yo voy a seguir el consejo con toda docilidad. Sea, pues, esta carta un mero documento narrativo" (340). And Pérez de Ayala himself follows Alberto's example in the third volume of his tetralogy (one presumes untutored by Azorín). *La pata de la raposa* lacks even the one philosophical dialogue found at the end of *Tienieblas en las cumbres* (unless one counts the homespun conversation on the problem of finding a basis for moral judgment that Alberto sustains with Tita Anastasia). Unlike Antonio Azorín and Yuste, who discourse on socialism as a theory, Alberto only considers socialism as an alternative political system when he himself is destitute.

Eventually artistic contemplation (if not art or literature) saves Alberto. After three years in Madrid, he has earned a small amount of literary fame (though not the remuneration he had envisioned), but his artistic enjoyment is genuine: "se recogía dentro de sí propio, con los párpados cerrados, a gozarse en los deleites intelectuales y estéticos de sentir destilada en su espíritu la realidad y no la realidad hermética e inerte de la materia, sino una realidad templada, traslúcida y expresiva. Recreación" (444). It is precisely the ability to observe life from an artistic, rather than "real," perspective that extricates him from the potentially disastrous marriage he is considering with an immature, untrustworthy, but captivatingly beautiful English girl. By converting Meg into an object of artistic contemplation, he is able to withdraw from the magnetic field in which she has held him. The conclusion of his story is very different from either that of Fernando Ossorio or Antonio Azorín, whose blood brother he is so often thought to be. Both of the '98 protagonists marry and retire to family life in a village, one happily, the other oblivious to the destruction it has wrought on his intellect.

After his escape from Meg, Alberto returns to his village to marry his sometime fiancée Fina (who, like Justina, had considered the convent) to find that she has died of a broken heart after his last abandonment of her. So Alberto is excluded from sharing the fate of Antonio Azorín and Fernando Ossorio. Neither does he commit suicide in despair when his hope of marital felicity is precluded (as do Augusto Pérez and Andrés Hurtado). Pérez de Ayala quietly closes the door to the '98 solutions to the problem of the philosophically disoriented protagonist, and he comments obliquely on these solutions at the end of *Troteras y danzaderas*. Alberto advises Bériz, a would-be poet and member of the bohemian group that protagonizes the novel, to give up Madrid's unstable literary world and return to his village to marry his girlfriend. At the end of the novel Alberto receives a letter from Bériz, who is miserable in the village and longs for the literary circles of Madrid (an echo of the letters Martínez Ruiz writes to Baroja at the end of *La voluntad* describing the intellectual decline of Antonio Azorín in his village). A German whose mistress is pregnant seeks Alberto's advice about an abortionist, recalling Andrés Hurtado's uncle in *El árbol de la ciencia:* "Engendrar a un ser es condenarlo a la muerte y, lo que es peor, al sufrimiento" (*OC* 1: 795). And Travesedo comments in Hurtadian fashion that "La vida es mala. No hay otro remedio sino el suicidio cósmico que aconseja Hartmann" (797).

These echoes of '98 existential angst, in which Schopenhauerian pessismism is replaced by a ludic tone and a nontragic ending, effectively overturn Baroja's serious message.

Written in 1912 after *La pata de la raposa*, chronologically, the action of *Troteras y danzaderas* comes toward the end of the earlier novel's plot. Alberto spends three years in Madrid after leaving Fina to make the fortune upon which their marriage plans depend and before he breaks with Fina to go to England, where he becomes infatuated with Meg. *Troteras y danzaderas* is Pérez de Ayala's portrait of the Madrid literary scene of his own Generation of 1914, which parallels Martínez Ruiz's descriptions of an earlier literary Madrid in the second part of *La voluntad*. Many scenes in *Troteras* also reflect the bohemian life of Madrid portrayed in *El árbol de la ciencia*: the concrete depictions of the sordid lives of Madrid's poor, their prostitution of their daughters, the seedy *pensiones*, the *picardía*, etc. A major difference between Pérez de Ayala's novel of 1912 and Generation of '98 philosophical novels is that the irony is directed toward the author's contemporaries who hold particular philosophies rather than toward canonical European philosophical positions.[13]

Rather than concentrating on Alberto's struggles and disappointments in seeking his *métier* in life (as is the case in *La pata de la raposa*), here the central perspective is deflected onto the modernist poet Teófilo Pajares and the vicissitudes of his love affair with Rosina, the prostitute of *Tinieblas en las cumbres* whose story occupied a central place in that earlier novel. In *Troteras y danzaderas* philosophical conversation assumes the major proportions that it enjoyed in the '98 philosophical novels, a place Pérez de Ayala had denied it in the first three volumes of the tetralogy. As in *El árbol de la ciencia*, the plot moves from vignette to vignette of Madrid life, each offering the opportunity for philosophical commentary. This commentary, which focuses on issues of aesthetics, is integrated into individual scenes and does not form the punctuated asides it provides in Baroja's novel.

Rosina and Pajares in a visit to the Prado Museum discuss the different realities of poetry and painting; not surprisingly, Teófilo believes that painting is ancillary to rhetoric. Alberto reads Shakespeare's *Othello* to the prostitute Verónica, an experience that inspires a theory of tragedy that rivals Aristotle's (prostitutes in the tetralogy turn out to be the most spontaneous and sympathetic philosophical commentators). When Alberto describes to Antón Tejero (Ortega) his theory, which centers on the difference between living one's life and living an artistic work, Tejero is certain Alberto has read those ideas in certain German theoreticians and is amazed to learn that Alberto's source for the theory is a prostitute. (Since Ortega at this point in his career had dwelt on aesthetic issues derived from the neo-Kantians, it is evident that Pérez de Ayala did not confine his mockery to members of preceding generations.) Another scene in which Teófilo witnesses a man rapidly win and lose large sums of money in the casino dramatizes the theory of tragedy Alberto has developed, as does Teófilo's attempt to reduce the pain of Rosina's rejection by converting it into a theatrical work. When Rosina returns to him and they renew their love affair, however, Teófilo is unable to write. Verónica's becoming a professional dancer also gives rise to aesthetic considerations about dance that explore the ideas of the playwright Monte-Valdés (Valle-Inclán), who only believes in the visual sense.

Most of the characters are mild, straightforward parodies, good-humored portraits that point out eccentricities of Pérez de Ayala's friends and acquaintances of his Madrid literary circle (Ortega, Azorín, Eduardo Marquina, Maeztu, Valle-Inclán). But, Don Sabas, the aging conservative government minister who keeps Rosina as a mistress, is presented in a narratively ambiguous way. He is a repulsive power figure representing backward politics and corpulent, aging vanity whose opulent life contrasts strikingly with the hand-to-mouth existence of the struggling artists and writers. Rosina's daughter does not like him: "Los niños . . . tienen el don de rehuir instintivamente aquellos individuos cuyo contenido ético es antivital" (534). His ethics are egocentric: "el egoísmo es la medula espinal del espíritu humano. Cuando ejecutamos aun las acciones más generosas, no tenemos otro móvil que el egoísmo" (526), but he is partially redeemed when he wisely contradicts certain untenable positions of more sympathetic characters.

Sabas has a sense of humor and is capable of irony. He named Rosina's pet fish "Platón," explaining that "Platón era un filósofo, y que todos los filósofos son como peces en pecera, que ellos toman por el universo mundo, y que los filósofos son castos e idiotas, como los peces" (515). As a joke and probably because he is genuinely hungry, Angelón Ríos swallows *Platón*. Sabas's comment is typically ironic: "Y es que toda filosofía . . . tarde o temprano no sirve sino para alimentar el amor carnal" (522). In general Don Sabas has a negative view of the intellect, and, like the narrator in *El árbol de la ciencia*, he links it to humanity's downfall, but in a much more comic way than in Baroja's novel: "Todos los males del hombre, ¿no cree usted, señor Pajares?, se derivan de un mal original: el de tener epidermis. Parece a primera vista que el mal original es la inteligencia, entendiendo por inteligencia la manera específica y necia que el hombre tiene de conocer el Universo; pero si en lugar de epidermis tuviéramos un caparazón como este animal privilegiado, o un derma-toesqueleto como la langosta, nuestra inteligencia sería de distinto y aun de opuesto linaje" (533).

Sabas is a more serious and sympathetic commentator on Spain than Rainiero Mazorral (Ramiro de Maeztu), who delivers a speech on the need for Spain to Europeanize. Here Pérez de Ayala parodies Maeztu's perennial theme (one character points out that Halconete had already said it all and another that it is a less eloquent repetition of Tejero's ideas). In conversation with Alberto, Sabas proposes as an alternative to Mazorral's uninspired communication that Spain's problem is lack of an ideal. Guz-mán, usually ready for argument, agrees with Sabas (not recognizing that Sabas's assessment of Spain's problem had also been suggested by the Generation of '98—Ganivet's "ideas madres" and others).

Teófilo complains to Alberto at one point that "Vosotros los mestizos de literatos y filósofos, se os figura que nadie sabe nada de nada" (628). Perhaps recognizing that Teófilo has a point, Pérez de Ayala abandoned the *Troteras*-style philosophical novel, which, like those of his predeces-sors, interjected philosophical discourse (*discours*) at the expense of the *sujet*. In his next set of three novels entitled collectively "novelas poe-máticas de la vida española," the philosophical and political message is embedded in a set of complex literary devices that includes alternating poetry and narrative.[14] As he did in the tetralogy, in *Prometeo* Pérez de Ayala created a melange effect by mixing references to the people and texts of his own generation and to those of the Generation of '98. He com-bined elements from Baroja's *El árbol de la ciencia* and Unamuno's *Amor y pedagogía*, of very different tone and philosophical underpinnings, and couched the mixture in a highly artificial epic-homeric apparatus. The complex intertextual and personal references create a joke on the type of philosophical novel cultivated by Pérez de Ayala's predecesors.[15] Aside from the obvious mythological reference, the title also coincides with the important generational journal *Prometeo* founded by Ramón Gómez de la Serna, a vehicle for promoting the Generation of 1914's idealistic goals for Spanish political regeneration and for introducing Spain to the latest Eu-ropean artistic theories. Another parodic reference to the generation's writing is conveyed by the title of the first chapter: "Rapsodia a manera de prólogo," an unveiled reference to Ortega's "Ensayo de estética a man-era de prólogo," with which Ortega prefaced Moreno Villa's *El pasajero*.[16]

The intertextual relationship between *Prometeo* and *Amor y pedagogía* subverts the philosophical intent of Unamuno's novel. Avito Carrascal's positivistic attitude is contradicted at every turn by his wife's religious ori-entation, an education that does not prepare Apolodoro for the slings and

arrows of real life. If Apolodoro's dilemma is attributable to the conflicting philosophies by which he is raised, Prometeo's situation has no such
evident cause. Unamuno's serious critique of philosophical positions
through novelistic devices is at the heart of Pérez de Ayala's parody; it is
the narrative method rather than the philosophy that is *Prometeo*'s target.
The intertext takes on parodic overtones in the hyperbolic use of classical
references as epithets for the principal characters. In the opening sections, Marco is Odysseus, and his wife, Perpetua is Nausikaa (Unamuno's
Forma and *Materia* in *Amor y Pedagogía* raised to the level of absurdity).
Unamuno himself is also the target of mockery during Juan Pérez/Marco
Setiñano's peripatetic career. After ruminating on a course of action for
his life, Juan Pérez leaves his native Italy for Spain, where he believes
he will find unlimited possibilities. After an odyssey around the country
that frustrates his hopes, he arrives at a city in the center of Spain where
he meets the wise man Teiresias, who has a face like an owl (a resem-
blance often cultivated in caricatures of Unamuno).[17] In open mockery of
the author-character confrontation in *Niebla*, Teiresias tells Marco that he
has lost his humanity: "Infortunado, has venido a unas regiones adonde
no se puede llegar sin haber perdido la humanidad. Ya no eres hombre, ni
podrás recobrar tu estado de hombre. Serás, de aquí en adelante, un recuerdo de hombre" (*OC* 2: 608-609). The protagonist's original name is
reminiscent of Augusto Pérez of *Niebla*, except that Pérez de Ayala strips
the character of a distinctive first name. (Parody of Augusto Pérez and
Unamuno's author-character interview became a stock resource in the
Generation of 1914 novel, reappearing in fiction by Gómez de la Serna
and Benjamín Jarnés.) Significantly, after changing his name to Marco de
Setiñano, the character becomes a professor of Greek (like Unamuno) at
the University of Oviedo.

   Juan/Marco realizes that he has failed as a man of action but believes
he can reverse his failure by marrying and producing a child with heroic
qualities. Here the similarities with *Amor y pedagogía* begin. Unamuno's
Avito Carrascal failed in his attempt to father the perfect child through the
scientific method, whereas Setiñano does not succeed because his understanding of history is faulty. The novel begins with an exposition on Carlyle's notion that heroes are products of their times. If the Spanish times
are not propitious to heroism, Setiñano's plan is doomed from the outset,
but ultimately it is not the Spanish times that cause the sad demise of
Prometeo. He had the misfortune of being born a crippled and retarded
hunchback. In Pérez de Ayala's version of planned heroism gone awry, '98
deterministic philosophy has no place, nor does the Nietzschean will to
power. Marco willed Prometeo as hero, but the Nietzschean "superman"

he produces mocks his hubris. In answer to Ortega's notion of vital reason (the wedding of thought and action that underlay all of his ambitious political programs such as the Liga de Educación Política), thought in *Prometeo* not only fails to beget action, it begets nothing.

Similar parodic treatment is accorded Baroja's *El árbol de la ciencia*. Before his transformation, Juan Pérez seeks counsel from an uncle about the course of his life in an interview that is a succinct version of the conversations between Andrés Hurtado and Iturrioz (and of the dilemma over action versus contemplation that infuses many of Baroja's novels). Juan wants to be both an "hombre de pensamiento" and an "hombre de acción," which the uncle points out is contradictory: "No se compadece lo uno con lo otro. El pensamiento es rémora de la acción" (*OC* 2: 604-605). Like Andrés Hurtado (and Ortega), Juan insists that thought is a stimulus and a motivating force. But the mixing of elements from Unamuno into the Andrés Hurtado-Iturrioz model subverts the consequences of Andrés's ignoring his uncle's advice. Neither Juan/Marco's failure nor the tragedy of his son is the result of the philosophical positions entertained in the novel's dialogues.

Pérez de Ayala's other two "poematic" novelettes, *Luz de domingo* and *La caída de los Limones* and his longer *Luna de miel, luna de hiel* and *Los trabajos de Urbano y Simona* are allegories of contemporary Spanish life, with less overt philosophical content, but he returned to the "philosophical novel" in 1920 and to a direct engagement with the philosophical positions of his predecesors and contemporaries in *Belarmino y Apolonio*, arguably his best effort in the narrative genre. *Belarmino y Apolonio* is a highly structured novel in which the philosophical positions of two characters (on the nature of language) are developed on one level of the narrative while a second story of the seduction and subsequent prostitution of a young girl is narrated, much as Rosina's story is in *Tinieblas en las cumbres*, for its natural human-interest qualities. These two levels of narrative are futher complicated by the first two chapters, which serve as a comic philosophical prologue.

Once again Pérez de Ayala appeals to the reader's love of a story-line in the nineteenth-century realistic mode, but he counters its appeal by the long intervening tale of the two rival philosophical positions. The personal stories of Apolonio and his son Pedro Caramanzana, and of Belaramino and his adopted daughter are completely separate from the philosophical commentaries or metacommentaries at the beginning and ending of the novel. Pérez de Ayala's practices avoid what the ghost in chapter 2 calls a cyclopian novelistic perspective in which the author is a god who creates an entire universe (a position that parallels Unamuno's depiction of the author's role in *Niebla,* as well as Ortega's notion of the author in *Notas sobre la novela*): "El novelista es como un pequeño cíclope, esto es, como un cíclope que no es cíclope, sólo tiene de cíclope la visión superficial y el empeño sacrílego de ocupar la mansión de los dioses, pues a nada menos aspira el novelista que a crear un breve universo, que no otra cosa pretende la novela."[18] Ortega's notion of the necessary distance between life and philosophy and life and art is parodied here, as the novel indulges in many narrative mechanisms that interrupt the reader's immersion in the story.[19]

Pérez de Ayala again marked his distance from Unamuno, Baroja and Azorín in the opening pages of his masterpiece, but this time he employed very different weapons. In the tetralogy his technique was to mock by similarity—a protagonist with preoccupations similar to those of the '98 "heroes," loosely formed "picaresque" formats and long philosophical commentaries that echoed '98 forms. In *Belarmino y Apolonio* he appealed directly to farce and exaggeration. The first two chapters form a preamble to the novel that summarize and parody the favorite themes of Unamuno, Baroja and Azorín. The ideas of the '98 writers are pronounced by a character who does not live them (as do the '98's characters). Don Amaranto de Fraile is a member of the same club of eccentric philosophers as Silvestre Paradox, Fulgencio Entrambosmares and Antolín S. Paparrigópulos, but Baroja's and Unamuno's eccentric thinkers have a more direct (and not very positive) influence over other characters' lives. Life, which is such a grave problem for Unamuno and Baroja's characters, is the subject of the following commentary by Don Amaranto: "Cada vida es un drama de más o menos intensidad, cada vida es, asimismo, una sombra inconstante y huidera" (72). There is an enormous difference between an Augusto Pérez who suffers this dilemma personally and Don Amaranto de Fraile, who glosses it after dining at his *pensión.*

Don Amaranto's unconventional "filosofía de las pensiones" adds a layer not found in the '98 ironic approaches to philosophy because it includes consciousness of its own method. If Baroja's characters (especially Andrés Hurtado) live in *pensiones* where they observe humanity and attempt to arrive at some conclusions about its nature, Pérez de Ayala's Don Amaranto is conscious of his procedure as a philosophical method. For Don Amaranto "[l]a Naturaleza es un libro ciertamente; pero un libro hermético. La casa de huéspedes es un libro abierto. . . . Eso es una casa de huéspedes: la caverna de las sombras" (64, 72). A long discourse by Don Amaranto on the differences between theology and science is evidence that Pérez de Ayala was thinking of *El árbol de la ciencia* when he invented the "filosofía de las pensiones." Don Amaranto seems to be commenting on Andrés Hurtado's dilemma when he states that "[e]n la edad científica un sólo árbol se multiplica en tantos árboles como ciencias, y ninguno es el árbol verdadero" (70). The important difference between the two novelistic comments on the philosophical inadequacy of science is that Don Amaranto disappears from the rest of the novel after these prophetic statements. As the central figure of Baroja's work, Andrés Hurtado suffers the consequences of the inefficacy of the "árbol de de la ciencia" to sustain life. Taking philosophy seriously is dangerous in Baroja's novel; most of Pérez de Ayala's characters do not take philosophy seriously, and even Belarmino, who is a serious philosopher, does not die from it.

The allusions to *El árbol de la ciencia* do not end with Amaranto's brief appearance. One of the principal characters is named Pedro Caramanzana, possibly a nod to Andrés Hurtado's name freighted with biblical significance. Once again the reference is parodic; Baroja's character shuns all sensual pleasure offered by sex and food, while Pedro (whose priestly vocation underscores the irony) enjoys the Epicurean life. He eats extraordinarily well, even during Lent, and he is guilty of seducing and abandoning his childhood sweetheart. The sensuality of this character is a parodic inversion of all the ascetic types that populate the '98 philosophical novel, including Antonio Azorín, Fernando Ossorio and Augusto Pérez. Pérez de Ayala underscored the difference by juxtaposing Belarmino and Apolonio, who live completely outside everyday reality, and their children Pedro and Angustias, who live very much within it. In the dialogue between Pedro Caramanzana, the priest, and Don Celedonio, a republican, there are echoes of the discussion between the priest and Fernando Ossorio in Yecla and Antonio Azorín and Yuste in *La voluntad*, with the important exception that the '98 versions of the confrontation between atheism and religion are devoid of humor. Pérez de Ayala's dialogue on the subject is characterized by copious wit:

> —Pues los cristianos primitivos—dijo el señor De Obeso, rebajando el tono y batiéndose en retirada—eran republicanos.
> —Eran más; eran anarquistas. Pero, en fin, así como aquellos cristianos, partiendo de la idea de Dios, llegaron a la de república, bien puede usted tomar el viaje de vuelta, y, partiendo de la idea de república, llegar a la de Dios.
> —Para ese viaje no necesito alforjas—concluyó don Celedonio. [80]

The second chapter, entitled "Rúa Ruera, vista desde dos lados," begins with a passage echoing the *tradición eterna* that preoccupied Unamuno and Azorín: "De la zona profunda, negra y dormida de la memoria, laguna Estigia de nuestra alma, en donde se han ido sumergiendo los afectos y las imágenes de antaño, se levantan, de raro en raro, inesperadamente viejas voces y viejos rostros familiares, a manera de espectros sin corporeidad" (90). Unamuno first developed the notion of an eternal national character in *En torno al casticismo* of 1895 and resurrected it as a literary image in *San Manuel Bueno, mártir* published nearly ten years after *Belarmino y Apolonio*, but without the irony with which Pérez de Ayala endowed it. Pedro Lario of the same second chapter of *Belarmino y Apolonio* is a good Spencerian, as was Unamuno in his university years; Lirio the anti-Spencerian reflects the later Unamuno. Lario is characterized by the Unamunian habit of self-contradiction: "Pero concedo que me contradigo con frecuencia. ¿Y qué? Así me siento vivir. Si no me contradijiese y obedeciese a pura lógica, sería un fenómeno de la naturaleza y no me sentiria vivir" (95).[20]

Pérez de Ayala's literary portrayal of philosophical positivism is much more distanced and comic than the "tragedia burlesca-grotesca" with which Unamuno approached it in 1902 in *Amor y pedagogía* (the chronicle of the terrible destruction of both father's and son's happiness). In *Belarmino y Apolonio*, the positivist Pedro Lario only appears in the preamble, not in the *logos* of the novel, and he has no direct or indirect influence over the lives of the characters. The chapter's declared intention to describe the Rúa Ruera, site of the novel's action, is diverted to a parody of the nineteenth-century novel's penchant for pictorial detail. In the process it also subverts the '98 novel's preference for philosophical dialogue over world-building description by focusing on a philosophical discussion that has no integral relationship to the story of Pedro and Angustias. The discussion does, however, relate to the "perspectival" way in which the story is told, and Don Amaranto's comments on language are part of the thematics of language at the heart of the novel.

While alluding to the philosophical contradictions of the august Rector of Salamanca, the chapter's confrontation of positivism and anti-positivism also refers to the conflict between Ortega and Unamuno. Ortega was the harbinger of logic, Unamuno an anti-rationalist, and the hostility between the two men was widely commented on within Ortega's circle. It is said, for example, that Ortega left the *tertulia* at the *Revista de Occidente* whenever Unamuno appeared, as he could not abide Unamuno's egotism. The prologue also prepares for the philosophical conflict between the two rival shoemakers Belarmino, a Platonist, and Apolonio, the Aristotelian, who could also be incarnations of the Rector of Salamanca and the professor of philosophy at the University of Madrid. Belarmino in his mystic hermeticism is a kind of Unamuno, while the flamboyant, public figure is reminiscent of Ortega's style (or Belarmino, in his use of difficult philosophical vocabulary is Ortega, and Apolonio, in his passionate egotism, Unamuno). Pérez de Ayala's penchant for playful allusions was endless. The two shoemakers are also reminiscent of the Cain and

Abel envy theme that Unamuno explored in *Abel Sánchez*. In Unamuno's novel of envy, as in *Belarmino y Apolonio*, one character is the passive soul naturally sought out by the public, the other is the passionate extrovert who never receives the public recognition he seeks. The existential pathos of Unamuno's Cain is, however, notably missing in this ludic Cain, and the denouements are vastly different. At the end of Pérez de Ayala's novel, Cain and Abel embrace and accept each other as complementary halves of a whole, while Unamuno's Joaquín murders Abel (at least in the moral sense).

The shoemaking profession of Belarmino and Apolonio may have been inspired by Baroja's *La busca*, as well as by real life counterparts documented in Andrés Amorós's introduction to his edition of the novel. In *La busca* there are two rival shoemakers, and a sign appears over a shoe repair shop that reads: "A la regeneración del calzado," a sentence that evokes the following commentary on the part of the narrator: "El historiógrafo del porvenir seguramente encontrará en este letrero una prueba de lo extendido que estuvo en algunas épocas cierta idea de regeneración nacional, y no le asombrará que esa idea, que comenzó por querer reformar y regenerar la Constitución y la raza española, concluyera, en la muestra de una tienda de un rincón de los barrios bajos donde lo único que se hacía era reformar y regenerar el calzado" (*OC* 1: 278). Pérez de Ayala turned this idea into a vast metaphor in which two shoemakers and the society that surrounds them serve as a hyperbolic representation, not only of the evils of Spain but of human folly in general, above all its desire to understand the meaning of life through philosophy and literature. Pérez de Ayala's two shoemakers are extreme cases—one a philosopher, the other a dramatist—that demonstrate the inefficacy of either of the two discourses to offer practical solutions to life's dilemmas: unrequited love, ill will, abused political power or changing economic conditions.

It is on this point that Pérez de Ayala's most important philosophical novel differs fundamentally from those of his immediate predecessors. The Asturian novelist focuses on the problem of language, rather than on the problems of existence, knowledge, the will and reason that had preoccupied Unamuno, Baroja and Martínez Ruiz, and which he mocked in the tetralogy without tendering an alternative. Even while couching the ideas about language in humorous, satirical terms, *Belarmino y Apolonio* is prophetic.[21] Several of the linguistic ideas suggested in the comic positions of the characters are reminiscent of Heidegger on language and being, of Wittgenstein on private language, and the later development of both these thinkers in the work of such contemporary French writers as Foucault, Althusser and Derrida. Belarmino's mystical idealism and lack of experience in the material world have much in common with Augusto Pérez, but the two differ on the subject of language. Augusto scorns language because it lies and never coincides with truth, while Belarmino affirms that language is the world, the entire and only reality: "El diccionario, en su opinión, era epítome del universo, prontuario sucinto de todas las cosas terrenales y celestiales, clave con que descifrar los más insospechados enigmas. La cuestión era penetrar esa clave secreta, desarrollar ese prontuario, abarcar de una ojeada ese epítome. En el diccionario está todo porque están todas las palabras; luego están todas las cosas, porque la cosa y la palabra es uno mismo; nacen las cosas cuando nacen las palabras; sin palabras no hay cosas" (169).

Like that of Heidegger, Belarmino's philosophical method centers on language, the word: "Pues el aquel de la filosofía no es más que ensanchar las palabras, como si dijéramos meterlas en una horma [reminiscent of Heidegger's practice of inventing new composite words such as 'Being-in-the-world'[22]]. Si encontrásemos una sola palabra en donde cupieran todas las cosas, vamos, una forma para todos los pies; eso es la filosofía como la apunta mi inteleto" (111). Like Heidegger's, Belarmino's ontology of the word exists on a different plane from the logocentric themes of pure existence, reason and will associated with the '98. It situates itself in a world that is entirely linguistic. But the heart of the linguistic theme in *Belarmino y Apolonio* is the division between public and private language, so much in the Wittgensteinian vein. Although Pérez de Ayala was in England on several occasions, I have not been able to substantiate that he was aware of Wittgenstein's lectures and teachings. The problem of language's social nature, however, was widely discussed at the time. Pérez de Ayala posits the problem of an individual, private language as opposed to language as a social entity by having Belarmino develop a language that only he can understand, while endowing Apolonio with the opposite extreme—a penchant for speaking in dramatic verse, a very public form of language. Ultimately, the novel rejects the notion of a viable private language, as did Wittgenstein; the experiment in which El Estudiantón and his friends test Belarmino's linguistic invention proves that language is iterable, and El Estudiantón manages to learn Belarmino's language up to a point.

For Unamuno, Baroja and Martínez Ruiz the individual subject and its will represented the basis for all philosophical investigation, while Pérez de Ayala reorients the thematics of the philosophical novel toward an intersubjectivity (of the kind later defended by Foucault and Derrida). Perhaps Pérez de Ayala's most important contribution to the Spanish philosophical novel in *Belarmino y Apolonio* was to introduce as its principal theme the very material of which novels are constructed, their language. He thus inverted the '98 custom of subordinating the philosophical problems taken from Kant, Schopenhauer, Nietzsche and others to their own personal and social preoccupations. If the '98 employed literature without a self-consciousness of method as an alternative discourse to the philosophical treatise, it privileged literary discourse. Pérez de Ayala questioned both literary and philosophical language as avenues to truth by inventing ridiculous characters of each persuasion.

In the next chapter, I take up two philosophical narrators who, like Belarmino, endow language with ontological status. Both Juan Ramón Jiménez in *Platero y yo* and Gabriel Miró in *El humo dormido* (and other narrations) abandoned the realm of comedy and satire (though irony remains an important part of their aesthetics) to elevate language in their own styles and in their thematics to a privileged category. While Pérez de Ayala undermined the possibilities of language through the ridiculous figures that represent different aspects of it, Juan Ramón Jiménez and Gabriel Miró, not only restored to it the unquestioning faith of realism to reproduce an *a priori* reality, they granted it the power to be reality.

9

JUAN RAMÓN JIMÉNEZ AND GABRIEL MIRÓ: *KÜNSTLERROMANE*

Pairing Juan Ramón Jiménez, known primarily as a poet, and Gabriel Miró, exclusively a narrator, makes most sense at the philosophical level. The philosophical concerns revealed in *Platero y yo* (written between 1906 or 1907 and 1914, the definitive version published in 1917) and *El humo dormido* (written in 1917 to 1918 and published as a book in 1919) are remarkably similar. Both works defy generic categories by mixing lyricism, philosophical observation and fable in a series of vignettes narrated in first person. Each vignette contains a philosophical message that builds toward a comprehensive theory of how consciousness welds memory and language to constitute reality.[1] The collective effect is a *Künstlerroman* that portrays the artist as a young man and chronicles his growing consciousness of the power of language. If philosophical dialogue laced with irony, parody and parodox carries the burden of metaphysical and epistemological messages in the works I have discussed thus far, Juan Ramón Jiménez and Miró embedded their philosophical issues in a lyrical narrative voice that substitutes metaphor and fable for the metonymic associations employed by the other novelists. The lyrical narrator, however, cannot always resist an expository or more explicit rendition of his meaning, as Edmund King remarks of *El humo dormido:* "The argument is implicit, of course, and slightly explicit . . . else it could not be inferred. But its very latency, its subordination to the truth of experience, the quality of experience is, while at first puzzling to the reader, ultimately discovered to be part of the charm of Miró's art."[2]

The affinities between the philosophical interests of Juan Ramón and Miró are not as easily explained as those of other members of the second generation. Miró is the only author of the second wave whose intellectual formation was not closely associated with the Madrid circles involved in such publications as *Helios* and *Prometeo* (although he sent articles to the latter from Alicante), Ortega's journals and *tertulias* and the Residencia de Estudiantes. He did have in common with Juan Ramón a connection to Krausist ideas, although his contact with Krausism came later than Juan Ramón's and was less intense and sustained. Perhaps more significantly for their ideas on memory, language and consciousness, both authors had an early and important introduction to French, especially symbolist, thought and literature of the turn of the century. Richard Cardwell (*The Modernist Apprenticeship*) has documented Juan Ramón's interest in symbolism, and Ian Macdonald's catalogue of Miró's personal library notes Miró's reading in nineteenth-century French authors.[3]

La lámpara maravillosa (published in 1916) by Juan Ramón's good friend Ramón del Valle-Inclán, also very familiar with late nineteenth-century French literature, reveals many ideas similar to those of the Andalusian and Alicantine authors. Valle, like Juan Ramón and Miró, affirmed a pre-linguistic consciousness: "La contemplación es una manera absoluta de conocer, una intuición amable, deleitosa y quieta, por donde el alma goza la belleza del mundo, privada del discurso y en divina tiniebla";[4] associated language and memory: "Son las palabras espejos mágicos donde se evocan todas las imágenes del mundo. Matrices cristalinas en ellas se aprisiona el recuerdo de lo que otros vieron" (101); and endowed the artistic use of language with a mystical, religious power that is particularly akin to Juan Ramón's view of language. Leo Cole's study on Juan Ramón's religious instinct qualifies his poetry as symbolist because it "attempts to convey a spritual essence which lies in the word after it is abstracted from the material objects of the external to which it refers." Cole understands Juan Ramón's view of language as Platonic; words "allude to a kind of Platonic Idea on which the concrete objects of the physical world depend for their meaning."[5]

The sources of both Juan Ramón's and Miró's ideas on language and reality are, however, diverse and diffuse, and include a healthy dose of native intuition. Mervyn Coke Enguídanos mentions Juan Ramón's knowledge of Nietzsche, the Vienna Circle and Wittgenstein in constructing arguments for the "universal Andalusian's" ongoing ambivalence about language's ability to represent an external reality faithfully.[6] My own perusal of Miró's library has located a number of volumes indicating his interest in theories of language and consciousness: M. l'Abbé de Condillac, *La Logique ou les premiers développements de l'art de penser* (Paris, 1789), 56, bears a line in the margin marking: "l'on dirait que la connaissance de la nature est une espèce de divination que se fait avec des mots"; José Ortega y Gasset, *El Espectador* VII (Madrid: Revista de Occidente, 1920) bears no marks, but its pages were cut; in André Suarès, *Variables*

(Paris: Émile-Paul Frères, 1929), 215, Miró marked "Par *conscience,* j'entende toujours la reflexion de la pensée sur elle-même, et jamais le sentiment moral du devoir ou du péché"; David Katz, *El mundo de las sensaciones tactiles,* trans. Manuel G. Morente (Madrid: Revista de Occidente, 1930) is cut but contains no pen marks. Also showing cut pages but bearing no marginal notations are Max Scheler, *El puesto del hombre en el cosmos,* trans. José Gaos (Madrid: Revista de Occidente, 1929), containing a chapter on "La reducción fenomenológica como técnica para anular la resistencia (realidad, resistencia, conciencia)"; J. Hessen, *Teoría del conocimiento* (Madrid: Revista de Occidente, 1929), the first part of which is entitled: "Investigación fenomenológica preliminar"; Hans Driesch, *El hombre y el universo,* trans. R. Cansinos-Asséns (Madrid: M. Aguilar, n.d.), containing a section "La conciencia y su papel en el universo"; and Gustavo Pittaluga, *La intuición de la verdad y otros ensayos 1915-1925* (Madrid: Caro Raggio, 1926), containing a chapter on "Recta percepción de la realidad." Many of these volumes were published too late to have exercised any influence on Miró's ideas on language. Rather they indicate an interest he had already cultivated. That Miró gave early attention to the theory of literature is evident in his copious annotations of Menéndez Pelayo's *Historia de las ideas estéticas en España* (Madrid: Dubrull, 1891).[7]

Miró and Juan Ramón did not meet until shortly after Miró had composed *El humo dormido,* but it is clear that Miró had long admired the precocious Juan Ramón, who achieved acclaim in Madrid literary circles long before he did. In a letter to Oscar Esplá of 1919 on display in the Sala Gabriel Miró of the Biblioteca Gabriel Miró in Alicante, he mentioned how important it was to him to finally establish meaningful contact with Juan Ramón. He had been introduced to the poet by Gregorio Martínez Sierra at the publishing house Renacimiento, but they did not exchange words because Miró, embarrassed by his own provincialism, refrained from addressing the more sophisticated Juan Ramón. He feared they would never become friends, but Oscar Esplá arranged for an exchange of books and letters: "Estoy muy contento," wrote Miró, "yo creí que Juan Ramón y yo no seríamos nunca amigos; creí que ya no nos encontraríamos. Tú nos has cogido a los dos de las manos, y después nos has dejado juntos." Even though the friendship did not flourish in the long run, they did share a lifelong, albeit independent, concern with how language mediates consciousness and world.

The consensus among critics who have approached *Platero y yo* from a philosophical point of view is that its orientation is essentially Krausist.[8] Juan Ramón's early and continuing contact with Krausism has been well documented, beginning in his school years in Seville with his teacher Federico de Castro. Although, Dr. Simarro, with whom he lived from 1903 to 1905, widened his philosophical interests to include Voltaire, Nietzsche, Kant, Wundt and Spinoza, he also introduced Juan Ramón to the Institución Libre de Enseñanza, where he met and became a fervent admirer of Francisco Giner de los Ríos, the Krausist educator. Juan Ramón's close association with José Ortega y Gasset, first through *Helios* and later at the Residencia de Estudiantes, was another important source of his interest in German idealism,[9] but Ortega's interest in German phenomenology (beginning in 1911 and finding its way into the *Meditaciones del Quijote* of 1914) would have come too late to have any impact on *Platero y yo*, which, by most accounts, was begun in 1906 or 1907.[10]

The Krausist interpretation of *Platero* emphasizes the themes of education and intrahistorical time and the book's use of religious motifs and images of universal harmony. The linguistic representation of subjective consciousness and memory, both implicit and explicit throughout the narrative, however, goes beyond issues taken up by Krause or his Spanish disciples Sanz del Río and Giner de los Ríos. These concerns draw Juan Ramón closer to the realm of twentieth-century philosophical orientations, such as that of Heidegger, for whom language, consciousness and being merge. Significantly, both Leo Cole and Mervyn Coke Enguídanos locate Juan Ramón's mature vision of the nature of language in his poetry collection *Eternidades* of 1916-1917, a book considered to have Heideggerian overtones.[11] Cole points out that the earlier works merely personify nature according to the subjective mood of the poet, whereas by 1916 his view of the relationship of world to poetic language invests the latter with self-sufficiency. Coke Enguídanos asserts that "It is with the collection of poems called *Eternidades* that JRJ first articulated his preoccupation with the Word" (44). Neither Cole nor Coke Enguídanos noticed (concentrating as they do on the poetry) that *Platero y yo* chronicles Juan Ramón's awareness of this philosophical shift. It captures that moment when the poet is becoming self-conscious about his craft and is formulating a theory of how raw experience is transformed into the poetic word.

The process is embodied in a series of observations by a poet-narrator as he travels about his native countryside in the company of his donkey. Like Augusto Pérez of Unamuno's *Niebla*, the protagonist ("el poeta") of *Platero y yo* selects an animal—a nonlinguistic entity—as the audience for his monologues. Augusto's orations in the company of Orfeo are, however, relatively rare, greatly outnumbered by Augusto's conversations with other characters, whereas most of the poet's observations are either directed to the silent animal (the vocative occurs in nearly half of the 138 vignettes) or focus on him as a subject. In fact, the narrative voice, which has not been adequately studied to date, undergoes subtle shifts from scene to scene, demarcating the narrator-protagonist's relationship to reality.[12] There are at least four different narrative situations: 1) a homodiegetic narrator focuses on Platero as object (e.g., sections 1, 5 and 12); 2) a homodiegetic narrator describes a scene in which, if Platero appears, he is not the center of interest (e.g., sections 3, 4, 9, 14 and 15); 3) a homodiegetic narrator addresses Platero in the second-person vocative one or more times in vignettes that often contain a childhood memory or a philosophical observation (e.g., sections 8, 10, 11 and 13); and 4) the homodiegetic naration becomes autodiegetic (e.g., sections 7 and 19).[13] Adding to the narrative complexity are shifts between a synchronic time-frame (the poet's observations of scenes from his present wanderings about the countryside with Platero) and diachronic memories of childhood in similar locations.

The constant movement from one narrative situation to another (most of the vignettes occupy one page or less) acts as the focuser on a lense, drawing the reader closer to the poet's own consciousness and then distancing him/her once again. The technique effects a movement something like phenomenological intentionality between consciousness and its objects. Platero's presence in the poet's musings can be understood metaphorically as the poet's prelinguistic consciousness (a philosophical concept later developed by Maurice Merleau-Ponty in *The Primacy of Perception* and elsewhere, but rejected by other French thinkers such as Derrida, Foucault and Lacan). Platero's animal status is signalled by lack of language; he has no place in *la miga* (school) where the ABCs are learned by rote. His realm is nature, unadorned by linguistic apparatus: "No, Platero, no. Vente tú conmigo. Yo te enseñaré las flores y las estrellas. Y no se reirán de ti como de un niño torpón, ni te pondrán, cual si fueras lo que ellos llaman un burro, el gorro de los ojos grandes ribeteados de añil y almagra, como los de las barcas del río, con dos orejas dobles que las tuyas."[14]

Immediately after the poet removes Platero from the proximity of language (the ABCs at school), the poet is directly associated with words; he is named "El loco." The crazy poet is alienated from the rest of humankind by his closeness to nature, but at the same time language interposes itself between him and the landscape he prefers over society. As he enjoys the "placidez *sin nombre*" (91, my emphasis) of the natural surroundings, a linguistic refrain intrudes stridently and insistently upon the "serenidad armoniosa y divina" of nature:

Vestido de luto, con mi barba nazarena y mi breve sombrero negro, debo cobrar un extraño aspecto cabalgando en la blandura gris de Platero.

Cuando, yendo a las viñas, cruzo las últimas calles, blancas de cal con sol, los chiquillos gitanos, aceitosos y peludos, fuera de los harapos verdes, rojos y amarillos, las tensas barrigas tostadas, corren detrás de nosotros, chillando largamente:

—¡El loco! ¡El loco! ¡El loco!

...Delante está el campo, ya verde. Frente al cielo inmenso y puro, de un incendiado añil, mis ojos —¡tan lejos de mis oídos!—se abren noblemente, recibiendo en su calma esa placidez sin nombre, esa serenidad armoniosa y divina que vive en el sin fin del horizonte...

Y quedan, allá lejos, por las altas eras, unos agudos gritos, velados finamente, entrecortados, jadeantes, aburridos:

—¡El lo... co! ¡El lo... co! (91)

The struggle between language and nature emerges again in chapter twenty ("El loro"). The French doctor's parrot repeats at cross-purposes the phrase he has obviously learned during the doctor's consultations: "—*Ce n'est rien*. . . ." The parrot, upon pronouncing these untimely and inappropriate words, is associated with flowers: "En una lila, lila y verde, el loro, verde y rojo iba y venía. . . . Y el loro, entre las lilas: —*Ce n'est rien*. . . *Ce n'est rien*. . ." (106, 107). The strangeness of the French language emanating from a parrot highlights the incongruence of the linguistic utterance. The French language again signals disharmony with nature in a later passage in which the poet and Platero enjoy a day in the countryside. Platero grazes free of encumbrance while the poet reads Ronsard under a tree. Ronsard's words form a chorus to the poet's own experiences with nature, but nature manages to overwhelm language when a bird's activity interrupts the poet's reading. In the section "La luna," nature similarly intrudes while the poet reads a verse from Leopardi to the moon. Platero has the last word, or rather gesture (his ability to express is limited to gesture and braying): "Platero la miraba fijamente y sacudía, con un duro ruido blando, una oreja. Me miraba absorto y sacudía la otra" (177). Words, especially when codified in the dictionary, can falsely interpret nature. For example, the poet finds the term *asnografía* an offensive way of referring to the animal who forms such an integral part of his consciousness. He writes in the margin of the dictionary after the definition of *asnografía* "*se debe decir, con ironía ¡claro está!, por descripción del hombre imbécil que escribe Diccionarios*" (149). The word *desasnar* used by the mayor to refer to school boys also displeases the poet.

Platero, the natural, nonlinguistic entity, becomes one with the poet at intensely homodiegetic moments conveyed in lyrical language: "Caía la tarde de abril. Todo lo que en el poniente había sido cristal de oro, era luego cristal de plata, una alegoría, lisa y luminosa, de azucenas de cristal.

Después, el vasto cielo fue cual un zafiro transparente, trocado en esmeralda. Yo volvía triste. . . . ¡Alma mía, lirio en sombra!—dije. Y pensé, de pronto, en Platero, que, aunque iba debajo de mí, se me había, como si fuera mi cuerpo, olvidado" (109). In "La verja cerrada," one of the rare segments in which Platero is entirely absent, even as a silent listener, the poet recalls being shut off from reality. His dreams and thoughts ran on "sin cauce" as he looked longingly through an iron gate for which there was no key: "fui, mil veces, con la mañana, a la verja, seguro de hallar tras ella lo que mi fantasía mezclaba, no sé si queriendo o sin querer, a la realidad" (110). If Platero speaks, it is "hablando con miel," in keeping with his constant association with nature (carrying butterflies, flowers; his eyes mirroring the sun and rain).

Nature and language also achieve harmony in "El pino de la corona" where the autodiegetic mode and vocative references to Platero converge: "Donde quiera que paro, Platero, me parece que paro bajo el pino de la Corona" (129). The pine tree is a constant that has not changed over time, coinciding in the present with the poet's memory of it. The experience culminates in language: "La palabra magno le cuadra como al mar, como al cielo y como a mi corazón" (129). The pine tree, which on other occasions was "el mejor sostén" of the poet's linguistic creation, his poetry, does not always cooperate to achieve these magic moments: "Nada me dice hoy, a pesar de ser árbol, y árbol puesto por mí. . . . Un árbol que hemos amado tanto, que tanto hemos conocido, no nos dice nada vuelto a ver, Platero. Es triste: mas es inútil decir más. No, no puedo mirar ya en esta fusión de la acacia y el ocaso, mi lira colgada. La rama graciosa no me trae el verso, ni la iluminación interna de la copa el pensamiento" (134). In another ecstatic moment of unity and perfection bound up in language, the poet observes a child at a fountain "en grupo franco y risueño, cada uno con su alma"; although there is not a single tree, his heart is filled with "un nombre, que los ojos repiten escrito en el cielo azul Prusia con grandes letras de luz: Oasis" (131). And the word *pozo* is ideal for "well": "¡qué palabra tan honda, tan verdinegra, tan fresca, tan sonora! Parece que es la palabra la que taladra, girando, la tierra oscura, hasta llegar al agua fría" (144). The well, so perfectly identified with its signifier, is capable of uniting the poet mystically with the heavens: "—Platero, si algún día me echo a este pozo, no será por matarme, creélo, sino por coger más pronto las estrellas. Platero rebuzna, sediento y anhelante" (144).

Toward the middle of the book (section 60), after chronicling his mature struggle to harness language in the shaping of reality, the poet recalls a story from his childhood. He bought a rubber stamp bearing his name and town with which to imprint worldly things ("libros, blusa, sombrero, botas, manos," 157). The child's naive desire to possess the world by printing his name on things has become more subtle in the mature poet's attempts to mediate the distance between himself and nature through language. The poet experiences nostalgia for his childhood imaginative powers that did not insist on verbal expression—words and poetry. His children's books contained representations of a brook as it naturally was but upon which the poet imposed his imagination, a truer poetry: "Y onda uno semiciego, mirando tanto adentro como afuera, volcando, a veces, en la sombra del alma la carga de imágenes de la vida, o abriendo al sol, como una flor cierta y poniéndola en una orilla verdadera, la poesía que luego nunca más se encuentra, del alma iluminada" (165). As an adult, he now views his world through books, even literary movements: "¿No me has visto nunca, Platero, echado en la colina, romántico y clásico a un tiempo? . . . Y yo estoy cierto, Platero, de que ahora no estoy aquí, contigo, ni nunca en donde esté, ni en la tumba, ya muerto; sino en la colina roja, clásica a un tiempo y romántica, mirando, con un libro en la mano, ponerse el sol sobre el río" (184).

Ultimately, the vocative itself, the name Platero ("¡Platero! ¡Platerón! ¡Platerillo! ¡Platerete! ¡Platerucho!" 180), which has been evoked consistently throughout the narrative, acts as the poet's sense of self in language. In "El eco" (section 101) the poet shouts "¡Platero!" at a rock, which echoes "¡Platero!" When Platero brays and the echo repeats his bray, the burro attempts to escape, leaving the poet alone with his infernal words and repetitions, but words prevail on this occasion: "lo he ido trayendo con palabras bajas, y poco a poco su rebuzno se ha ido quedando solo en su rebuzno, entre las chumberas" (204). Toward the end of the book (section 125), the poet expresses disgust at apologues that employ talking animals: "Los pobres animales, a fuerza de hablar tonterías por boca de los fabulistas, me parecían tan odiosos como en el silencio de las vitrinas hediondas de la clase de Historia natural" (229). He would never put words in Platero's mouth; the silent animal must always remain as pure pre-linguistic consiousness.

Nature/Platero cannot ultimately be reconciled with the poet and language: "Claro está, Platero, que tú no eres un burro en el sentido vulgar de la palabra, ni con arreglo a la definición del Diccionario de la Academia Española. Lo eres, sí, como yo lo sé y lo entiendo. Tú tienes tu idioma y no el mío, como no tengo yo el de la rosa ni ésta el del ruiseñor" (229). And the butterfly a few pages later has the good fortune to "volar . . . pura y sin ripio" (235). Platero dies, leaving the poet alone with his poetic language, inspired by the natural things that Platero represented: "Platero, ¿verdad que tú nos ves? Sí tú me ves. Y yo creo oír, sí, sí, yo oigo en el poniente despejado, endulzando todo el valle de las viñas, tu tierno rebuzno lastimero... " (237). The poet's creation remains as a constant struggle between the pre-linguistic experience and the need to express it in language that may not prove adequate. He achieves the goal only through the metaphorical death of sensorial, nonlinguistic experience, leaving it as a memory which can assume linguistic shape. If the perfect union of consciousness, memory, world (nature) and language has eluded the poet, his Krausist desire for transcendence is fulfilled. Platero is the past, but "¿qué más [le] da el pasado a ti que vives en lo eterno, que, como yo aquí, tienes en tu mano, grana como el corazón de Dios perenne, el sol de cada aurora?" (251). The belief in a mystical union between a human subjectivity and a power greater than itself, so thoroughly undermined in Baroja's *Camino de perfección* and Martínez Ruiz's *La voluntad*, is reaffirmed in Juan Ramón's narrative that posits a silent narratee and a speaking subject, Platero and I, nature and the word.

Like *Platero y yo*, Gabriel Miró's *El humo dormido* is a series of seemingly autobiographical vignettes centering on a narrating subject's memories of childhood, especially those experiences that have shaped his aesthetic consciousness. Miró's narrator, however, is more sanguine about the power of language from the very beginning of the narration. Words are what weld experience and memory into a definitive reality, and Miró's philosophical message, while extraordinarily well embedded in narrative flesh, is at times more explicit than Juan Ramón's. The opening paragraph of *El humo dormido* expresses poetically, but unequivocally, the linkage of time, memory, consciousness and language. I quote it in full as it contains all the important philosophical-narrative elements that Miró developed in the rest of the book:

De los bancales segados, de las tierras maduras, de la quietud de las distancias, sube un humo azul que se para y se duerme. Aparece un árbol, el contorno de un casal; pasa un camino, un fresco resplandor de agua viva. Todo en una trémula desnudez.

Así se nos ofrece el paisaje cansado o lleno de los días que se quedaron detrás de nosotros. Concretamente no es el pasado nuestro; pero nos pertenece, y de él nos valemos para revivir y acreditar episodios que rasgan su humo dormido. Tiene esta lejanía un hondo silencio que se queda escuchándonos. La abeja de una palabra recordada lo va abriendo y lo estremece todo.

No han de tenerse estas páginas fragmentarias por un propósito de memorias; pero leyéndolas pueden oírse, de cuando en cuando, las campanas de la ciudad de Is, cuya conseja evocó Renán, la ciudad más o menos poblada y ruda que todos llevamos sumergida dentro de nosotros mismos.[15]

As in *Platero y yo*, a pre-linguistic experience precedes language's intervention, but language here is accepted as an integral part of the discovery of reality, "la abeja de una palabra" (Valle employs the same metaphor for language in *La lámpara:* "abeja cargada de miel," 49). But Miró departs radically from Juan Ramón's emphasis on individual voice and memory by including a collective dimension in his concept of memory and language (as does Valle in *La lámpara:* "lenguaje es lámpara donde arde y alumbra el alma de la raza," 82). These "autobiographical" vignettes are not memoirs in the traditional personal sense; they are designed to call up the collective voice that resides in all of us (Valle's expression of the collective voice also calls upon an aquatic metaphor: "Se sienten en sus lagunas muertas las voces desesperadas de algunas conciencias individuales, pero no se siente la voz unánime, suma de todas y expresión de una conciencia colectiva," 82). For Miró memory is collective, incorporating self and world; thus literature is also a communal enterprise that includes the writer and the reader in their respective literary traditions. Miró projects these complex notions through shifts in narrative voice that enlist the reader in subtle ways—the passive-reflexive and first-person plural rather than the standard subjective "I" of autobiography—and through generic strategies that ask the reader to call upon his or her experience with the collective genres inspired by the Bible and folklore.

There are several sources for Miró's notion of a universal memory that links him with the members of his own generation and with those of the previous one. Miró's personal library contains a copy of Carmen de Burgos's Spanish translation of John Ruskin's *The Stones of Venice.* The subtitle of one of the sections of Ramón Gómez de la Serna's introduction to the volume is "El huso dormido." Not only is the title similar to Miró's, but Gómez de la Serna's explanation of Ruskin's mission is equally suggestive. His introduction begins with a quotation from the Grimm brothers' tale "Un sueño largo," reminiscent of Miró's penchant for parable and fable in *El humo dormido:*

'Comenzó a correr las habitaciones abandonadas, hasta que llegó a una torre muy elevada. Subió una estrecha escalera de caracol y llegó a una pequeña puerta. En la cerradura estaba puesta la llave. Al darle una vuelta se abrió su hoja y vio en el cuarto una anciana con un huso, hilando muy de prisa su lino. —¡Buenos días, abuelita!—dijo la Princesa—.

¿Qué haces aquí?... —Estoy hilando—contestó la anciana bajando la cabeza.' "[16]

Gómez de la Serna followed with the story of Ruskin's search in Westmoreland for a special cloth that was in former times woven from a particular kind of wool. He finally found an old woman in the village who still had an ancient spindle of the kind used to make the woolen material, and he ordered a number of spindles fashioned on the original model. Ruskin employed the townspeople to recreate the earlier type of cloth under the tutelage of the old woman. If one were unaware that Gómez de la Serna was describing Ruskin's approach to his work, he could easily be discussing Miró: "Ruskin no es nunca un teórico, cuenta con pisar el paisaje que alaba, con entrar en él, lo ve todo vivo, asequible, tibio, móvil, y por eso en las cosas más petrificadas encuentra la brisa que juega con ellas, la luz que las anima y la vida que se las adentra . . . escucha las distancias y tiene una idea del tiempo y de la vida en que todo se encaja, que le atraen la atención y el deseo de reanimarla toda con su voluntad de director artístico" (l-li). Valle in *La lámpara maravillosa* also invokes the *huso* as an agent of the collective unconscious: "Las crónicas, leyendas, los crímenes, los sudarios, los romances, toda una vida de mil años parece que se condensa en la tela de una araña, en el huso de una vieja, en el vaivén de un candil. Sentimos como en el grano de polvo palpita el enigma del Tiempo" (161-162). The stones of Toledo evoke meditations about memory similar to those Ruskin finds in the stones of Venice: "Toledo es a modo de un sepulcro que guarda en su fondo huesos heroicos recubiertos con el sórdido jirón de la mortaja, y cuando todas sus piedras se hayan convertido en polvo se nos aparecerá más bello, bello como un recuerdo" (165). Perhaps Miró and Valle were both captivated by Carmen de Burgos's translation of Ruskin, which appeared so close in time to the composition of their own books of aesthetic theory.

Is "el humo dormido" an "huso dormido"? Does Miró search out and find the sleeping spindles, the keys to a universal Alicantine consciousness that can be awakened by his sensitivity to the appropriate word? Proust is supposed to have learned the importance of place to memory from his intensive reading of Ruskin between 1899 and 1906, and it is entirely possible that his Spanish counterpart followed in his footsteps a few years later. But Miró did not have to rely on foreign sources to discover the concept of an eternal tradition in a particular place. Between 1910 and 1916 (when Ruskin's book was probably translated into Spanish), Miró would have been conversing with at least two key proponents of the idea—Miguel de Unamuno and the Krausist historian Rafael Altamira.

Unamuno's concept of *intrahistoria*, as Ciriaco Morón Arroyo points out, differs from that of Rafael Altamira and Ramón Menéndez Pidal in that it derives from the German rationalist notion of *volksgeist*, whereas Altamira and Menéndez Pidal base their ideas of the *tradición eterna* on naturalistic psychology. This distinction is important for understanding Miró's explorations of universal consciousness in *El humo dormido*. Like that of his compatriot Rafael Altamira, Miró's version of the *tradición eterna* is less idealistic than Unamuno's, but Unamuno was the only critic who has discussed the concept of a universal consciousness in Miró's work. In his introduction to the Edición Conmemorativa volume of *Cerezas del cementerio* he commented: "Y todos estos vivientes que traman el paisaje, que son paisaje, son, como el mochuelo de Poblet [Miró had stopped to study with microscopic interest a little owl that he and Unamuno found in the monastery of Poblet on their visit there in 1916], fragmentos de la Conciencia Universal, y figuras, figuras de la Pasión de Dios."[17]

Even though Unamuno wrote to Menéndez Pidal in 1920 that he was distancing himself from the notion of *volksgeist*, the *tradición eterna* of *En torno al casticismo* echoes insistently in his final paragraph on *Las cerezas del cementerio*:

Que Miro llegó a la contemplación de cómo se funden el espacio y el tiempo, y por ese camino al hoy eterno. Llegó a contemplar 'perdido, olvidado o malquerido el pobrecito instante de lo actual' en 'la augusta serenidad divina... del Hoy eterno', 'escuchó'—como el Félix de esta novela—'los pasos de otra vida, llegada del misterio, caminando encima de su alma,' sintió las 'aguas lentas, calladas y resplandecientes' del 'amplio río' de nuestra pobre vida temporal que se desvanece 'entre nieblas azules', sintió que 'se le deslizaba la vida como una corriente por llanura' y una sensación 'tan clara, tan intensa del olvido!' " [xiii]

Perhaps during that excursion to the monastery of Poblet in 1916 (two years before the composition of *El humo dormido*), Unamuno and Miró discussed the effects of time and change and the relative merits of individual values versus eternal permanence, while viewing the "stones of Poblet" just as Ruskin did in his meditations on Venice.

Rafael Altamira is another possible source for Miró's interest in a *tradición eterna* during the several years before he composed *El humo dormido*. Although Ian Macdonald states that Miró had none of Altamira's books in his library and that no proof exists that he read him, there is circumstantial evidence as to the likelihood of his familiarity with Altamira's philosophical orientation. Miró doubtless had long been aware of Altamira, the Alicantine native son, who had left his *patria chica* as a young man to take a professorship of history in Oviedo and who had authored numerous articles and books. Most prominent among them are *De Historia y Arte* (1898) and *Historia de España y de la civilización española* (volumes 1-3 published from 1899 to 1906 and volume 4 in 1911), in which he defends a Krausist version of history as *Kulturgeschichte*, the study of social, economic and cultural activity of the *pueblo*, the collective entity, rather than politics.[18] Altamira's *La psicología del pueblo español* (1899) tenders the theory of the *notas constantes* of Spanish history, very much in the vein of Unamuno's *roca viva* or *tradición eterna*, except that the *notas* are rooted in particular psychological features of the Spanish people. It thus recognizes individual contributions to culture more concretely than does Unamuno's *intrahistoria*.

If Miró had not previously been aware of the particulars of Altamira's ideas about history, he caught up quickly when the prodigal son stopped in Alicante after a trip to America in 1910. Miró wrote at least three articles on Altamira for that occasion, and in a note appended to one of them he indicated that he produced his humble essay before learning that Guardiola Ortiz intended to publicize (*vulgarizar*) Altamira's ideas in a series of lectures. Surely Miró was present at these lectures in 1910, since he corresponded with Altamira from January 28, 1908, through January 16, 1914, to request assistance in gaining an entrée to the publishing world. Perhaps more importantly, Miró's close friend Francisco Figueras Pacheco corresponded with Altamira from as early as August 1904; it is likely that Miró read some of Altamira's works aloud to his blind friend from Figueras Pacheco's own copies, as he did other texts.

If the first edition of *La psicología del pueblo español* of 1899 escaped Miró's notice, he was doubtless aware of the second edition published in Barcelona in 1917 during his residence there (and the year he probably began composing *El humo dormido*). Mauro of *El humo dormido* is an Altamira-style historian, one who, in Altamira's words, should have "un juicio tranquilo y perspicaz, un instinto fino y aguzado para ver los hechos y darles su lugar y valor propio en los tiempos, y un sentimiento profundo de lo vivido para resusitarlo a sus ojos como si viviera de nuevo."[19] When the narrator of *El humo dormido* accompanies a group of friends to the hillside caves where Moors and Christians had once engaged in battle, Mauro brings medieval history alive for the younger boys: "La voz de Mauro iba proyectando la memorable jornada que originó esta ermita" (104). The ironically portrayed Don César of *El abuelo del rey* and *Alba Longa* of *Nuestro Padre San Daniel* and *El obispo leproso* are examples of what a historian should not be.

With these theories of history in mind, the singular use of voice in *El humo dormido* is more comprehensible, particularly in those places where the border of the individual historical-present consciousness frays and blends with the universal, eternal one. Miró's personal contribution to the notion of universal consciousness and memory was to place language and literature at the center of the human experience of them. The opening paragraph or prologue quoted earlier suggests that language forges the connection between personal and universal consciousness. The past is not concretely ours until language (the bells of Is) brings it within the range of our personal consciousness. The narrative person in *El humo dormido* is inconsistent; an autobiographical "I" frequently dissolves into a collective "we" that incorporates the narrator's companions in some instances and in others suggests a pact between the narrator and the reader. On occasion the first person narrative voice (be it singular or plural) disappears entirely and the narration is carried by the impersonal passive-reflexive construction, a narrative situation that invites narrator, reader and characters to participate in the action as equals. The verbal imagery (of which the term *el humo dormido* is a prime example)—"la abeja de una palabra recordada lo va abriendo y lo estremece todo"—moves us toward a universal collective memory through language, which is a social, collective phenomenon. In *El humo dormido*, Miró was exploring the possibilities of the text—the written word, literature—for revealing the self's relation to other and for the retention of that relationship in memory.

The collective, eternal voice of the opening paragraph quoted above extends through the three exempla that initiate the narration: the stories of the harmonium, the *hidalgo* and the footsteps of the stranger, each of which explores a dimension of the problem of individual perception and a truth one suspects lies beyond that limited perception. These tales, which serve as an overture to the book, reduce the personal focus to a minimum. The autobiographical "I" appears hardly at all, and there is no indication that the events narrated contribute to "I" 's story. This is the realm of collective, literaturized memory. The last of the three initial scenes or vignettes concludes the exposition of Miró's theory of perception and memory in the universal "we" voice. We do not normally see what is unfamiliar, says the narrator, but one day, for whatever reason, our attention may fix on a stranger. In our memory, the image of that person remains stronger than his actual physical presence because sensual experience always repeats itself without deepening, while remembered experience is clearer and more refined. The extraordinary experience that is able to reach the depths of memory is like "la palabra que no lo dice todo sino que lo contiene todo" (60). Thus memory and language are wed in their potential for containing the ultimate reality, and a biblical text is invoked to confirm this truth: "Siempre se alza ese hombre entre el humo dormido... Y el rumor de sus pisadas trastrona las palabras del *Eclesiastés*, porque si hay cosa nueva debajo del sol, del sol y de la tierra hollada; todo aguarda ávidamente nuestra limitación; todo se desgarra generoso y se cicatriza esperándonos... " (61).

These words, which remind us of the discrepancy between the message of Ecclesiastes and the way life really is, prophesy the shape of the rest of *El humo dormido*, a series of Bible-like tales that constantly involve the reader in the experience of collective memory. Words (texts) are the supreme pneumonic device, especially the great classic texts such as the Bible and *Don Quixote*, which are embedded in the Western collective memory. The "I" and "we" voices are employed with almost equal frequency in the ensuing vignette, "Nuño el viejo," but "I" dominates in "Don Marcelino y mi profeta" until it is dissolved into the collective "we," precisely when *humo dormido* is evoked at a key moment toward the end of the vignette. Don Marcelino and the narrator go to a house where an old woman has been murdered: "Desde la leja les acechaba el gato; junto a un confín, la tortuga, inmóvil y cerrada bajo su bóveda, oiría el trastorno siniestro. Los dos guardaban la imagen de la verdad feroz. Participaron de la soledad del crimen sin interrumpirla, quedando a nuestros ojos como esculpidos en una estilización humana, porque llevan la angustia de un secreto de los hombres... Y ya los animales que viven en las casas trágicas, en las casas desventuradas, se quedan siempre mirándonos entre el humo dormido" (73-74).

The only other vignette in the entire work that issues from the "I" perspective is "La sensación de la inocencia," which like the "Don Marcelino" episode is diffused into a more general consciousness in sentences such as: "Parece que entonces rebulle y suena en nuestra alma el aleteo de una ave que dormía y se remonta en busca de otros horizontes" (93). In each of the instances of "I"-narrated vignettes, the point of the story is to establish the interrelatedness of consciousness. Nuño, Marcelino, Ordóñez, and Ordóñez's mother all define the "I" narrator in some way, establishing his sense of self and the limits of his own consciousness.

The remainder of *El humo dormido* is narrated in a collective "we" voice that refers most immediately to the narrator and his friends, but this "we" shades into the universal collective "we" through the collective literary genres—parable, fable, legend—in which the episodes are cast. The vignettes centering on Don Jesús are the most parable-like. In "Don Jesús y la lámpara de la realidad," Don Jesús tells several stories to explicate his theory of reality as perception.[20] The young narrator and his friends ("I"/"we") watch from outside the grillwork on the windows as a conversation about the nature of reality unfolds in a series of folkloric tales. The magistrate proclaims that reality is the same for everyone, but Don Jesús contradicts the magistrate by reciting the tale of the assembled canons of Pamplona who determined that Adam and Eve spoke in the Basque language: "Y desde que los canónigos se alzaron de sus bancas hasta que mudasen de parecer, fue una realidad el eúskaro en el Paraíso" (118). Another of Don Jesús's tales involves a poor mute boy who said nothing by way of thanks when given the leftover candy from Don Jesús's saint's day celebration. The young Don Jesús, unaware of the boy's handicap, remarked that gratitude is mute, but when he learned of the boy's condition he felt that his pronouncement had mutilated him. Upon finishing the story, Don Jesús turns up the lamp, "la lámpara de la realidad," which has the power to illuminate truth through words or tales whose universal nature subverts their subjective narrative voice to a collective purpose. The reader, like the young boys peering in on the scene through a window, is drawn in by the familiar format of the biblical or folkloric genre and forgets the distance between his or her own world and that of the text.

One of the best examples of the way in which traditional textual types are incorporated into *El humo dormido* is the section entitled "Don Jesús y el Judío errante." Both its narrative form and its content, which fuse the Bible, *Don Quixote* and the narrator's personal history illustrate the importance of the written word to memory and reality. When an adult warns the children that a tall, wizened, itinerant Englishman may be the wandering Jew, the unfamiliar is transformed into the familiar by equating the stranger with a well-known figure from the Bible. The man soon becomes *el Judío errante* to all the townspeople: "Pero 'aquel judío errante' que nos ha hecho incurrir en 'literatura', según dicen los mismos literatos, no traía barbas semitas, ni sandalias, ni túnica, sino que iba afeitado y usaba gabán, sombrero gris de castor y un junco con puño de hueso" (125). Physical reality and literary reality meet in the consciousness, and the literary reality becomes the pneumonic touchstone calling up this stranger who might not otherwise have occupied an iterable space in the narrator's memory.

The textual aspects of the image created by this impoverished Englishman take on even greater complexity as he is always associated with reading the *Quixote*, especially the passage in which Don Quixote is pronounced dead after the brutal beating by Maritornes's muleteer lover. At first the Englishman grows sad upon reading the passage, but he eventually laughs at the squad leader's mistaken interpretation of the scene. Don Jesús, who has befriended the Englishman, explains to the young boys how literature works. The stranger's initial reaction to the text was a product of seeing Don Quixote as a tragic character in the context of the novel, but in the second stage of his reaction, which now involves memory, he compares Don Quixote to himself, a poor foreigner lodged in a third-class *pensión* with a "camastro pavoroso que semejaba enceparle entre sus palpos y rodajas de hierro" (126).

At the end of the vignette, the Englishman (the wandering Jew-cum-Don Quixote) lies dying, and Don Jesús assumes the role of his biblical namesake as he undertakes to save the soul of this Protestant foreigner. The Englishman's last words to Don Jesús and the curious neighbors who surround him in his death throes are those of the squad leader at the inn in *Don Quixote:* "¡Ciérguese la puegta de la venta; miguen no se vaya nadie, que han muegto aquí a un hombre!" (136). In his own mind he has become that literary figure whose image is so much a part of his mental apparatus. In remembering himself, he remembers himself as literature. The "wandering Jew" episodes demonstrate that reality is memory and language (literature).

"I" am only "I" in the context of other (the communal "we"), and "my" reality becomes evident only in retrospect and through language: " ...Y entre el humo dormido, sigue pasando don Jesús, con los hombros doblados, como si trajera un atadijo del 'Judío errante', y le buscara el cielo que le corresponde. Pero el Judío errante quedóse tendido, muerto y sepultado, y don Jesús le ha sustituido, errando siempre por la misma ciudad" (137). The collective mind uses literature, the tale of the wandering Jew, to domesticate the stranger and bring him into the realm of the familiar. "El oracionero y su perro" concludes the book as it began, with a parable. The coda, "Tablas del calendario entre el humo dormido," seals the collective nature of consciousness through the eternal yearly Easter ritual, especially its literaturization in the Bible. Ritual and literature are, after all, the vehicles for and reinforcement of collective memory.[21]

The early "I" voice narrating particular incidents in the child's experiences cedes to the collective "we" of the boy and his friends. In turn, the collective consciousness eventually fuses with the universal, eternal consciousness—the rituals and legends—of the *pueblo* as a whole. If for Unamuno particular historical and biographical events were but small ripples on the sea of eternity, Miró preferred Menéndez Pidal's or Altamira's version of a *tradición eterna* in which individual consciousness is not entirely lost in the universal ocean. The narrator does affirm early on that there is "algo nuevo bajo el sol." Miró realized the difficulty of defining the border between an individual instance of *humo dormido* (personal recollection) and the *humo dormido* of the eternal collective consciousness, but language is the element common to both. Words seal and make real personal recollection, and literature is the medium of universal consciousness.[22]

The centrality of a philosophy of language unites Miró and Juan Ramón Jiménez with three younger narrators of their generation—Ben-

jamín Jarnés, Pedro Salinas and Rosa Chacel—whom I discuss in the next
and final chapter. These three writers were, however, more closely associated with Ortega's circle and the Master's concerns: his repudiation of
'98 philosophical interests, the intersection of individual and circumstance and theories of avant-garde aesthetics. The tone of their novels,
which also concern consciousness and language, is decidedly different;
they introduced a levity not found in *Platero y yo* and *El humo dormido*,
which respectively endow language and artistic expression with sacred
and ontological powers.

10

SALINAS, CHACEL, AND JARNÉS: THE VANGUARDIST PHILOSOPHICAL NOVEL

While Pedro Salinas, Rosa Chacel and Benjamín Jarnés continued to explore the same philosophical issues of perception, consciousness and language that had absorbed Juan Ramón Jiménez and Gabriel Miró, the younger writers, whose careers all began in the vanguardist 1920s, recast these problems in a light-hearted, playful mode. They continued to subvert conventional genre models through fragmentation and unorthodox narrrative techniques begun by the '98 and intensified by Miró and Juan Ramón, but the philosophical purpose of these devices is leavened with humor. If Miró and Juan Ramón embarked upon a quest to find linguistic means to express the relationship between consciousness and the world, Salinas, Chacel and Jarnés accepted as natural the gap between mental processes and the world outside them, capitalizing upon it in a process Víctor Fuentes aptly terms "defamiliarización."[1]

One could perhaps even designate yet a third wave or generation of philosophical novelists, since Juan Ramón, Miró and Ortega, who were admired (and parodied) by their juniors, were now part of an establishment that mentored the younger writers. *Helios*, in which Juan Ramón and Pérez de Ayala conceived their aesthetics, did not contribute to the artistic formation of these children of post-World War I aesthetic iconoclasm. The '98 and Krausist issues such as *tradición eterna* and universal harmony that lingered in Juan Ramón Jiménez and Miró (although couched in poetic language) disappeared from the philosophical repertoire of the new philosophical novel. Salinas, Chacel and Jarnés preferred to foreground consciousness of the present and language's expression of it in a construct that privileged fragmentation over totality.

Ortega still held the philosophical center stage of the Spanish intellectual world and had by the 1920s built a powerful publishing empire. His journals, especially *Revista de Occidente*, provided a forum for all three writers, as did his biography project and Nova Novorum series.[2] The close professional association with Ortega and their first novels' appearance so close to the publication of Ortega's major essay in aesthetics—*La deshumanización del arte e Ideas sobre la novela* (1925)—has occasioned the unfortunate denomination of dehumanized novel and the assumption that the works so designated are an embodiment of Ortega's aesthetic ideas. In fact, these writers' literary-philosophical origins are considerably more heterodox. They reveal lingering echoes of the Generation of '98's existential concerns (even if mostly in a parodic mode), and Juan Ramón and Miro's ideas on and use of language to capture perception receive ambiguous attention that falls between the serious and the parodic. Ramón Gómez de la Serna's treatment of novelistic characters and his theory of the relation of things and language summed up in the *greguería* are present in the prose of all three, as are elements of European modernism and vanguardism.[3] By the 1920s the rest of Europe had caught up with Spain in its early rejection of realism, and the last wave of Spanish philosophical novelists now counted on powerful European models and allies against realism that the '98 did not have. Salinas, Chacel and Jarnés enlisted vanguardist levity, learned from such European sources as Giraudoux and Joyce, to enter into a dialogue with Ortega's aesthetics, the Generation of '98's metaphysical novels and the serious phenomenological prose of Juan Ramón and Miró.

The narratives of Salinas, Chacel and Jarnés (at least those published in the 1920s and 1930s) are certainly philosophical (in my sense here of foregrounding philosophical ideas). They are especially concerned with the relationship between life and art, but rather than the life-threatening matter it becomes in *Niebla*, it is an idea to be manipulated and considered from different perspectives. Benjamín Jarnes summed up the new attitude: "Lo mejor es hacer de la prosa una ágil Góndola empujada por el aliento de la idea."[4] Salinas, Chacel and Jarnés continued the dialogue with the '98 type of philosophical novel begun by Ramón Pérez de Ayala in his tetralogy, although the humor they employed to parody it was more deflected and less personal. Benjamín Jarnés wrote about his attitude toward the "intellectual novel," which he called "una magnífica pista donde entran los personajes para lucir su poca o mucha agudeza mental."[5] According to Jarnés, Huxley's *Point Counter Point*, which seems to comment on itself, is an excellent example of the problems inherent in the serious philosophical novel: "El gran defecto de la novela de ideas está en que es una cosa arreglada, artificial. Necesariamente; pues las gentes capaces de desarrollar tesis propiamente formuladas no son del todo reales, son ligeramente monstruosas. A la larga, el vivir con monstruos resulta un tanto fastidioso."[6] He did, however, praise Huxley for providing ample scenic background to his "desfile de pensamientos," something the '98 (specially Unamuno) refused to do.

Salinas, who was a professor of Spanish literature in addition to his career in creative writing, set forth his aesthetic ideas in *Reality and the Poet in Spanish Poetry*. His statements about the poet's relationship to reality are very similar to Ortega's pronouncements in several places about one's position vis-à-vis interior and exterior forces that forge reality for the individual. Salinas announced that he intended to consider in his book "the relation between his [the poet's] world and the real world, the contact between external reality and his own spiritual reality. . . . All poetry operates on one reality for the sake of creating another. It cannot operate on a vacuum."[7] Ortega called the verb "to live" a very strange one, because on the one hand it refers to the mode of existence of a particular individual: "Es lo que pasa dentro de mí, en los límites de mi cuerpo y mi conciencia,"[8] while at the same time the individual's existence is taken up with things in his or her proximity: "vivir es ver, oír, pensar en esto o en lo otro, amar y odiar a los demás, desear uno u otro objeto. De donde resulta que vivir es, a la vez, estar dentro de sí y salir fuera de sí; es precisamente un movimiento constante desde un dentro—la intimidad reclusa del organismo—hacia un fuera, el Mundo."[9]

Rather than following Ortega's aesthetics of dehumanization in their fiction, Salinas, Chacel and Jarnés were exploring Ortega's phenomenological epistemology of the interrelatedness of interior and exterior reality.[10] Like Miró and Juan Ramón, they differed from Ortega by making room for language in their epistemology: "Poetic operation gives names to things and acts, to translate them into words, let them be impelled by their own real force through language without any alteration."[11] As did Miró, Salinas understood language as a means of possessing the world: "el lenguaje es el primer, y yo diría que el último modo que se le da al hombre de tomar posesión de la realidad, de adueñarse del mundo,"[12] and also like Miró he recognized a pre-linguistic consciousness: "Debo confesar que numerosas veces, hablando, o con un amigo o en mi cátedra, conforme modulaba las palabras y las echaba al aire, veía yo mismo mi pensamiento pasar de una especie de pre-conciencia, de estado pre-existente en que aun no había revestido forma satisfactoria, a un estado de plena existencia, y lo que yo quise decir se alojaba, cabalmente, en las palabras emitidas."[13] But the actual linguistic practices of Salinas, Chacel and Jarnés in their prose, while demonstrating a similar willingness to endow language with ontological powers, are so self-conscious that they overwhelm the philosophical message with verbal play. Miró and

Juan Ramón carefully chose words and crafted sentences that would convey perceptual experience. The ingenious word-play of the three authors under discussion here, while ostensibly at the service of sensual perception, ends up stealing the show.

Salinas's first narrative work, *Víspera del gozo*,[14] is a series of scenes or vignettes often considered a story collection, which to date have been studied as separate segments (and then only several of them at a time).[15] As with *Platero y yo* and *El humo dormido*, the third-wave philosophical narrative continues to present problems of genre identification. The segments of the work have different protagonists, but the recurring theme of each character's relation to reality provides a sense of unity, which, if not what we typically expect of a novel, makes it more than a collection of unrelated stories. As in the narratives of Juan Ramón and Miró, the philosophical perspective provides the unifying vision. In each of the seven segments of *Víspera del gozo*, the protagonist's original perception, idea, or memory of a reality is shattered when a different external reality imposes itself on him.

Six of the seven segments develop the perception/art/reality theme through a human protagonist who is spatially and/or temporally separated from a desired woman toward whom he is moving in time and space. In each case the actual meeting does not correspond to his prior imagination of the event. The other segment, "Delirios del chopo y el ciprés," situated at the center of the work, is a meditation by an unnamed central consciousness on a poplar and a cypress tree. The *greguería* "señeros e iguales, tan el uno del otro, como los dos palos de una inmensa hache frustrada" (75) reveals that the trees appear the same when viewed from a distance, but another aphoristic statement discloses that they are different species when observed from close range: "Aforismo para mañana: A lo lejos, iguales; a lo cerca, tan paralelos, que nunca se encontrarán."[16] The discovery inspires a series of poetic-philosophical meditations entitled "Ciprés," "Chopo, agua," "Chopo, otoño," "Ciprés, ante la muerte," and "Chopo, madera de cruz." These prose poems evoke the landscape of Castile while tendering such conclusions as "no pasarás de ser un sembrado de intenciones en este decidido páramo castellano que sabe lo que hace. Porque nunca se aparta de ti ese ángel taimado y equívoco que te sopla en las orejillas el peligroso aviso de que tu forma no se acertará sino en la torturada sucesión de las infinitas deformaciones" (78). At first the reader might believe s/he has suddenly returned to the Generation of '98's philosophical speculations inspired by the Castilian landscape, but the series is interrupted by an "anécdota incidental" in which the "único campo" is the "asfaltadas praderas de la ciudad." The narrator accompanies a friend, who feels nostalgia for the "suelo y los chopos de Castilla," to a museum where the Castilian poplar is transformed by the narrator's consciousness into El Greco's "Portrait of an Unknown Man." Such surprise transformations of reality are alien to the '98's search for a *tradición eterna* in Castilian geography and culture.

The focalizing protagonist's aphorisms and poetic notes that elaborate on his perceptual experience of the cypress and the poplar hold the key to the philosophical interpretation of the other vignettes. Writing (language and style) mediate between perception and reality. Andrés, protagonist of the first segment, "Mundo cerrado," views the passing landscape from the train window in terms of literary movements, and later his notebook engages his attention. He organizes the names and addresses of his acquaintances in two separate lists, one in the usual alphabetical order, the other by city. When a friend changes his/her address, it is "una ampliación del mundo posible" (16). In the act of writing the friend's name next to a place, that place becomes his: "Y al escribir en el segundo cuaderno los dos nombres—ciudad, amigo—juntos y maridados, como en esas tarjetas de los nuevos matrimonios, un punto concreto del mundo se desnudaba de aprensión" (18). At the end of the vignette, a written document—a letter from the husband of his friend Lady Gurney announcing her death—converts and distorts the imagined reality of his former lover that he had been elaborating while on the train.

Likewise, the "prosa en tumulto" (38) of "Entrada en Sevilla" and "aquella palabra de fuera" (62) of "Cita de los tres" are related to the middle segment's lyric-philosophical message that language mediates between the mind and the world. Following "Delirios del chopo y el ciprés," "Aurora de verdad" evokes a "periplo conservado en un palimpsesto incompleto" (88), the omnipresent letters of Miss Bixley's name facilitate a "posesión celeste" (112) in "Volverla a ver," and finally a "poesía superior" in "Livia Schubert, incompleta" concludes the seven-part symphony on language's power to unify imagination, perception and reality. Salinas's own language, often imitating the combinative surprises of Ramón Gómez de la Serna's *greguería*, underscores language's capacity to rise above the limitations of the human mind in its relationship to the world.

A complete study of the complex language of *Víspera del gozo* is still to be done, but following are a few examples of Salinas's playful style that leavens the philosophical message of his narrations. As Andrés, the central consciousness of the first vignette, "Mundo cerrado," is meditating on Lady Gurney as reality and as a construction of his imagination, the narrator comments: "Y lanzaba al aire la contradicción, la hacía volar al modo de un humo de cigarillo impulsado por su aliento en la atmósfera tibia y recatada del vagón, siguiéndola voluptuosamente, invisible, con la vista" (20). The conflation of Andrés's philosophical musings with a puff of smoke from a cigarette that one follows visually reifies the conceptual idea of the story in a humorous image. Andrés is similarly left with an incomplete philosophical thought when he arrives at his destination. He is considering the meaning of the time that has passed since he last saw Lady Gurney and his upcoming encounter with her when he is interrupted by someone asking him a question: "La pregunta del empleado, brusca y disyuntiva, como unas tijeras, cortó el monólogo interior, le dejó trunco, en dos pedazos el mejor y más sabroso, el que quedaba dentro, el del recuerdo inexpresado" (22-23). Once again unusual visual imagery imposes itself on the philosophical idea, leaving it in a state of jocular incompletion.

In "Cita de los tres" Ángel/Jorge engages in a meditation on time, inspired by the sound of the church bells ringing out six o'clock. But before his thoughts can become too methodical, the narration converts the philosophical topic into an elaborate metaphor in which the entire town is converted into an enormous piano: "Luego a partir de estas primeras campanadas la misma hora iba sonando en distintos relojes, idéntica y deliciosamente transformada como si unos celestiales dedos antojadizos se entretuvieran en arrancar a la ciudad que tenía azoteas blancas, teclas blancas, alternados desde arriba, con breves calles en sombra, teclas negras unas improvisadas variaciones sobre un tema conocido y popular, y eso tan hábilmente, que las personas de oído poco ducho no reconocían a veces el motivo primero, por la destreza con que le mudaba de ritmo y tono el ejecutante, y se preguntaban dudosos qué hora sería que estaba dando" (55).

"Aurora de verdad," another vignette focusing on the nature of reality as it is fashioned by the human imagination, begins with an image of time (the morning) as a blank page. Salinas immediately establishes the importance of writing, or language, in the imagination's construction of reality: "Las citas con Aurora eran siempre por la mañana, porque entonces el día recientísimo y apenas usado es todo blanco y ancho, como un magnífico papel de cartas donde aun no hemos escrito más que la fecha y en cuyas cuatro carillas podremos volcar todas las atropelladas efervescencias del corazón sin que haya que apretar la letra más que un poco, al final, anochecido, cuando siempre falta espacio" (87). Both Rosa Chacel and Benjamín Jarnés engaged in similar visual wordplay to confound the philosophical messages of their narratives, although neither displayed the poetic virtuosity of Salinas.

Rosa Chacel's philosophical and artistic formation was more autodidactic than that of either Pedro Salinas or Benjamín Jarnés. Chacel, rather than attending a traditional university, received her formal post-secondary education in several schools of art in accordance with her early attraction to sculpture. At about twenty years of age, she came into contact with university students at the Ateneo and began reading philosophy, an interest she developed further during her years in Rome (1922-1927). The leisure of the Roman period (she was accompanying her husband, who had an art fellowship there) allowed her to become thoroughly familiar with Ortega's aesthetics and epistemology, which inspired *Estación. Ida y vuelta*, a novel she later classified as "*desaforadamente* orteguiano."[17] She doubtless became aware of Ortega's hegemony over the Madrid intellectual world when she frequented that city's Ateneo, and the many books and journals she received while in Rome confirmed Ortega's importance to the would-be writer. She wrote *Estación. Ida y vuelta* with the express intention of offering it to Ortega's Nova Novorum series.

The novel's relationship to Ortega's aesthetics of the novel (*pace* her own perception of it) is problematic, and part of the problem lies in Ortega's own inconsistencies. While finding virtue in the antirealism of modern ("dehumanized") art in *La deshumanización del arte, Notas sobre la novela* published in the same year, argues for a novel that encapsulates the reader in a closed world (the kind of realism parodied in Salinas's "Mundo cerrado"). The world of *Estación. Ida y vuelta* is indeed closed, but it is the closed world of the protagonist's mind, which has the insistent habit of recurring to philosophical asides. Chacel herself recognized the novel's philosophical content: "yo hice en esta novela con Ortega, lo que Sartre en *La náusea* con Heidegger. Es, sencillamente un hombre que vive una filosofía."[18] The novel can hardly be considered an embodiment of Ortega's prescription for the genre, since its protagonist not only lives a philosophy but formulates it verbally in a manner that punctures the hermetically sealed novelistic universe Ortega preferred.[19]

More than a failed (or successful) attempt to carry out Ortega's aesthetic program, *Estación. Ida y vuelta* posits the solitary vision of a central "yo" and repositions some of the existential questions posed by Unamuno in his novels. The plot is quite simple: a young man marries his pregnant girlfriend, escapes from their home and country for a brief respite in France and returns upon the birth of their child. Most of the narration is consumed with the narrator/protagonist's phenomenological descriptions of the things that make up or have made up his world: the patio of the apartment building where he and his girlfriend live, his Madrid neighborhood, even the microscopic observation of the wallpaper in his childhood room: "En el papel de mi cuarto había una hoja que yo, de pequeño, adoraba. Me miraba quinientas o seiscientas veces, desde las cuatro paredes, con dos pares de ojitos que tenía, que eran esos agujerillos de las hojas de parra. Ojitos oblicuos, de expresión sagaz y risueña. Y en la curva de su vena yo encontraba, más que complaciente sensual, consonancia sentimental. Yo hubiera enroscado mis brazos a la cintura de aquella hoja."[20]

Although Chacel mentioned the poetic "yo" of *Platero y yo* as an important model for her narrator/protagonist,[21] her "yo" does not have even the silent interlocutor of Juan Ramón's focalizing "eye"/"I". Chacel's relationship to Juan Ramón in general provides further evidence of the new intergenerational dynamics formed between Juan Ramón's and Ortega's contemporaries and Chacel's younger group. In 1932 Juan Ramón published a Platero-like sketch of Rosa Chacel in which, by calling her "Rosita Chacel, niña mayor que se nos va otra vez con el sobresaliente," he clearly establishes his sense of seniority (and superiority?) to her. The third wave's reaction to *Platero* was mixed. Benjamín Jarnés declared that it occupied a firm place in the history of the Spanish spirit (*Feria del libro*, 65), while Rafael Alberti, another member of Chacel's generation, parodied Juan Ramón's serious epistemological quest with Platero in a sonnet entitled "El burro explosivo" (1936): "Burro que vuela y que de en medio quita / cuánto suena en los hombres a retrete, / . . . . Burro que borra, barre y que burrea / burreando en zig-zag, burro barreño / que todo lo encaraja y lo empalata. / Mas siendo de artificio también mea, / desprende en plastas moscas de veneno. / Y no toques más, que el burro explota."[23]

The mental claustrophobia of *Estación. Ida y vuelta* distances it significantly from the alternating discourses (and alterity) of *Platero y yo*. The interspersed philosophical comments are more reminiscent in their tone and content of Unamuno's and Machado's existentialism than of either Ortega's aesthetics or Juan Ramón's lyrical prose. Chacel, however, achieved a serenity of tone and distance from Unamunian anguish by overwhelming the existential asides with moments of phenomenological description. Like Machado, the narrator/protagonist perceives life as a road, a *camino* that one forges as one goes along: " 'La vida no es eso, la vida—la nuestra—no tenemos que aprenderla de nadie; nos la inventaremos nosotros. . . . ' Es imposible volver a entrar, como si cada momento nos modificase, nos hiciese cambiar de forma, y ya no cupiésemos en el molde del anterior. . . . ¡Un camino! Mejor que toda posición. ¡Un camino es lo único deseable! Un camino largo, sin montañas limitadoras" (96, 111, 112). Language, however, forms an important part of this road-forging project because language alone can capture one of life's fleeting moments: "a veces estamos poniéndolo todo en nuestras palabras, porque lo que esperamos lograr con ellas nos es esencial, y si no conseguimos interesar al espíritu del momento, la luz entorna los ojos y oímos el bostezo de una puerta. En cambio, otras veces, como aquélla, el momento se mete de lleno en nuestra conversación y la súbita animación de su fisonomía hace que no sea un frío acceder lo que consigamos, sino una espontánea convicción y un sentimiento" (97). Language is the barrier against and the salvation from the despair inherent in '98 angst. The narrator's language, while containing fewer vanguardist fillips than that of either Salinas or Jarnés, does occasionally engage in *ramonismo:* "Los abrigos tienen fisonomías sensibles que delatan cómo han pasado la noche. . . . Pero lo de asociar las ventanillas de su escote al sistema arterial de un plano ferroviario le resultó un insulto" (113, 128).[24]

Having established the importance of the road, in the second part of the novel the protagonist undertakes a journey, and his philosophical ruminations now sound quite Unamunian. His self, his personal identity (again linked to language) becomes his consuming passion: "Tener bien definido su yo, el que él proyecta desde su frente con su palabra" (127). Echoing Augusto Pérez, the protagonist/narrator becomes emphatic about his self-assertion: " 'Sí, lo soy, lo soy y lo seré siempre' " (133), rejecting what he perceives as someone's attempt to destroy "lo mas mío, mi personalidad más irreductible" (133). He also, like Augusto Pérez, feels that he is witnessing his own evaporation (139) and that he is lacking a self (149), arriving at the Unamunian conclusion that "creer is crear" ("creo— de creer y de crear," 150). Chacel's evocations of Unamuno's *Niebla* contain an element of parody by placing Unamuno's concerns (indeed his very words) within a phenomenological context that dilutes and deflects them. Her parody of Unamuno, however, is less strident and ironic than those of Ramón Pérez de Ayala or Benjamín Jarnés, partly because her plot engages more seriously with human concerns (e.g., pregnancy and the birth of a child). I also suspect that Chacel's having formed her philosophical ideas and having written her first novel well away from the influence of Ortega's *tertulias*, where Unamuno was by all indications a subject of ridicule, gave her a different perspective on this figure who occupied such an important place in the philosophical consciousness of her generation.

Benjamín Jarnés did not exercise Chacel's restraint when paraphrasing Unamunian ideas; his first novel, *El profesor inútil,* is a self-conscious parody of Unamuno's 1914 classic, *Niebla,* albeit a lighthearted one. Jarnés's mocking of Unamuno's existential concerns was mixed with a sincere appreciation for the philosopher-novelist, who was at the time in exile from Primo de Rivera's dicatorship. Jarnés had a formal education in philosophy and theology, having studied at both the Pontifical University of Zaragoza and San Carlos Seminary in preparation for an ordination that he did not complete. His career as a writer was closely associated with Ortega's journals, where he published philosophical essays and literary criticism. Jarnés wrote several articles on Unamuno, in which he followed Ortega's lead in taking Unamuno to task for his trenchant personalism and egotism. Jarnés, however, muted his criticism with expressions of sincere appreciation.[25] In "Caín y Epitemeo," for example, Jarnés asserted that *Abel Sánchez* was, like all Unamuno's novels, an implacable monologue that "acaba por destruir cualquier vida espiritual."[26] But the article ends on a positive note, contradicting Ortega's negative view of Unamuno: "Por eso el preceptista—como el político oportuno y el pacífico indocumentado—suelen morder alborozados en la vida y obra, tan lozanas, del autor de *Niebla*. . . . Son ellos quienes asimismo suelen achacar a la obra—admirable y cínica—de Unamuno de cierta *excesiva personalidad* [Jarnés's emphasis]. Tanto daría castigar al rico con su propia riqueza, insultar a Goethe con su propio Fausto."[27]

Unamuno had written in the *Helios* article on life and literature that he was weary of literature that dealt primarily with literature, "teatro de teatro, novela de novelas, cuentos de cuentos,"[28] but apparently he did not notice that Jarnés created a novel of Unamuno's own novel in *El profesor inútil*.[29] Jarnés's aesthetic position, while asserting that art should have ideas,[30] was diametrically opposed to Unamuno's: "La vida no puede producir una obra de arte. La vida se queda en la estación del recorrido. Pero es condición precisa en toda obra artística que un tropel de objetos *vivos*—primera etapa—haya invadido al autor, por las puertas, por las ventanas de los sentidos. . . . Arte es coger un trozo de nuestra vida interior o exterior y lanzarlo a los demás bien embalado en una forma."[31] Jarnés rejected Unamuno's passionate personal identification with his art's metaphysical dimensions—the meaning of existence and true personal identity—playing with these themes and turning them into a joke. *Niebla* is a tragicomedy meant to be taken seriously; *El profesor inútil* (especially the first version of 1926) never breaches the boundaries of lighthearted play, and in large measure Jarnés achieved the playful effect by turning many of *Niebla*'s specific situations and verbal constructions inside out.

Like *Niebla*, *El profesor inútil* is a series of vignettes, which are even more loosely connected than those in Unamuno's novel. In the four scenes of the 1926 *El profesor inútil*, a schoolteacher on summer holiday takes a series of pupils for private tutoring. In each case a woman enters the picture, either as the tutee or the tutee's sister, thus shifting attention from intellectual to erotic activity. The novel begins *in medias res* as the professor decides to follow a young woman on the street, and ends just as abruptly when a young woman the protagonist/narrator has been flirting with in the library suddenly gets up and leaves. No overwhelming existential questions are raised, and the character, whose psychology is left unpenetrated, does not experience acute anguish; the novel is rather a series of moments of perceptual awareness (or phenomenological description).

Jarnés's version of the hapless suitor story eliminates the metaphysical message Unamuno had given it by countering with a would-be lover who is entirely consumed with sensual and perceptual experiences. While Augusto never sees anything in the material world (there are no descriptions in *Niebla*), Jarnés's professor is occupied primarily with visual phenomena. The character's thoughts, rather than the anguished interior monologues of Unamuno's character, are a phenomenological description of the contents of his consciousness. In contrast to Augusto's, the professor's body (his senses) and his intellect function in harmony: "Entre las cosas y yo está siempre mi cuerpo, hoy tan inofensivo, tan dócil, tan buen conductor. Llegan hasta mí las ondas más lejanas en toda pureza. Soy una balanza en delicioso equilibrio."[32]

The first reference to *Niebla* appears in the very first sentence of *El profesor inútil*. The professor muses to himself in an Augusto Pérez-style mono-dialogue: "Pienso, luego existo. Existo, luego soy feliz,"[33] recalling Augusto's affirmation to Víctor Goti that he believes Descartes's dictum to be the most enduring truth and Augusto's several transformations of Descartes's famous phrase throughout *Niebla*. Jarnés's professor plays with the Cartesian motto as well, but the philosophical reference in *El profesor inútil* takes on further complexity as it alludes both to the seventeeth-century rationalist and to the twentieth-century existentialist Unamuno : "No concluye. Un día el cuerpo se enfurruña, rompe su equilibrio y desbarata la consecuencia. Es mejor decirlo así: —No me siento la carne, luego existo plenamente. Existo plenamente, luego soy feliz" (11). (In *Teoría del zumbel*, this play on Descartes/Unamuno became more specific in its physical orientation: "vivo, luego peco. Pienso, luego peco," 191.) The professor's construal of the Cartesian proposition takes on additional resonance in its intertextual relation to Augusto's (and Unamuno's) struggle to be a man of flesh and blood (a passion related to the issue of the intellect versus the will or life that so preoccupied the Generation of '98).

A second reference to *Niebla* occurs shortly after the play on Unamuno's preoccupation with rationalism. The professor, who is idle because his students have left for summer vacation, decides to go out. He, like Augusto, determines to follow the first woman who comes along (actually, Augusto has in mind following a dog, but Eugenia appears first). Just as in *Niebla*, the protagonist hesitates at the threshold of his house because it is raining. Jarnés parodies the opening scene in *Niebla* in which Augusto regrets having to open his umbrella, as he prefers all objects in their pristine, unused form. Instead of making a serious metaphysical metaphor of the umbrella (Augusto likens an open umbrella to the way some people use God as a shield against the world), Jarnés's professor converts the umbrella into a cubist wordplay: "Llueve, el auga es fina, apenas son gotas las suyas. Parece una neblina. Desdeño el paraguas, artefacto que no me sirve de techo y es harto geomético para poder llamarle dalia negra invertida. Vacilo un poco entre la belleza y la utilidad" (13). The reader, aware of Unamuno's equating the umbrella and the Almighty, understands Jarnés's *greguería* as a comment on the intersection of language and perception with no transcendental metaphysical consequences.

Language, which mediates raw lived experience (Orfeo is the purest creature because he does not have the power of speech), is a villain in *Niebla*. Jarnés, on the other hand, extolled the masking quality of language when he wrote of Ortega: "El pensamiento generador de toda la ya extensa labor filosófica del maestro es como un recio cable de alta tensión, voluntariamente oculto a veces—bajo preciosas molduras de arte más fino, acaso para mejor ponerse en contacto con las gentes, muchas de ellas temorosas de la profundidad."[34] Jarnés was, however, lukewarm about Unamuno's clarity of style: "Quizás alguna de sus páginas no pueda ofrecerse en las aulas para modelar retóricos; todas pueden esparcirse por la tierra como pauta para modelar, a sangre y fuego, espíritus."[35]

The useless professor's first sally in pursuit of the woman in the street also strikes a contrast with Augusto's in *Niebla*. As he follows the woman, he formulates concrete plans, which Augusto does not. He purchases a bouquet to hand the woman at an appropriate moment, but having used his last change at the flower stall, he has no money to follow the woman onto a street car. Thus ends the potential idyll. Augusto's pursuit of Eugenia, by contrast, leads to his eventual despair and suicide. In another segment Jarnés's professor inverts Augusto's ordering of the three organs of love (head, heart and stomach) and relates them to the linguistic-artistic category of musical adjectives rather than to the metaphysical categories that Augusto assigned to them: "—Tiene la historia del arte tres grandes capítulos. Evolución del arte vale tanto como evolución del eroticismo, y el amor tiene tres grandes órganos: el vientre, el corazón y el cerebro, que corresponden a tres adjetivos musicales: sensual, sentimental, sensitivo" (54).

In another comic inversion, *El profesor inútil* plays off Unamuno's well-known metaphysical poem "Castilla" (Jarnés included the poem in his editions of selected Unamuno works published in Mexico). One of the sections of *El profesor inútil*, which takes place in Madrid, begins: "La Glorieta de Atocha es la palma extendida de una mano gigante que prolonga sus dedos en largas fibras nerviosas destrenzadas luego para hacer vibrar a toda España" (71), echoing the first section of Unamuno's poem, which places Castile at the center of Spain: "Tú me levantas, tierra de Castilla, / en la rugosa palma de tu mano, / al cielo que te enciende y te refresca, / al cielo tu amo. / Tierra nervuda, enjuta, despejada, madre de corazones." Jarnés continues to refer to Unamuno's poem (the "El mar de encinas" section) in the second sentence of the paragraph: "O quizás es un puerto sobre el Mar Gris. Se cuentan el Mar Negro, el Rojo y el Blanco, pero apenas se recuerda el mar Gris, es decir, Castilla" (71), parodying Unamuno's image of Castile as a sea of oak trees. If the Generation of '98 sang of the *campo de Castilla* in tones of extistential anguish, Jarnés's vanguardist generation sang of the city unperturbed by deep existential longing.

In comparison to Unamuno's *Niebla,* most notably missing in Jarnés's novel is the third-person narrative voice that casts Augusto Pérez in a continuously ironic light. Jarnés's first person avoids the narrator's commentary that gives Unamuno's implied author special power over his character, a power which he exercises to its fullest in the scene between author and character toward the end of the novel. In the anguished encounter, the heretofore disembodied voice of the author assumes corporeal weight in order to crush the character it has toyed with throughout the novel. Jarnés, on the other hand, allows his character more narrative autonomy. The professor tells his own story, which, instead of dwelling on the metaphysical issues of existence that preoccupy Augusto, concentrates on verbalizing perceptual experience. The professor says that "la mejor novela queda siempre inconclusa porque el autor no puede dictar desde la tumba los últimos capítulos" (131), which is precisely what Unamuno hoped to do. He proposed to so disturb the reader with his existential angst that he or she would become similarly anguished. One of the things that Ortega, Jarnés's close associate and mentor, disliked about Unamuno's novels was that they transform the reader into a novelist. That Jarnés had Unamuno's relationship to his characters in mind when he devised the very different narrative voice in *El profesor inútil* is substantiated in an essay he wrote on

Unamuno. Contrary to Unamuno's own assessment of his viviparous novel-writing, Jarnés found Unamuno's characters to be deductions: "¿No son los relatos algo así como dóciles ejemplos a la zaga de una teoría? Sí; Unamuno prefiere *deducir* sus personajes del prólogo a *inducirlos* de ellos; lo que no roza los valores fundamentales de toda gran novela."[36]

In 1934 Jarnes published a more elaborate version of *El profesor inútil* in which he continued his dialogue with Unamuno, who had, in the meantime, reaffirmed his commitment to the unity of life and literature in *Cómo se hace una novela* (1928, Spanish version). In the time intervening between *Niebla* and *Cómo se hace una novela* and the two versions of *El profesor inútil*, the two writers had developed in parallel ways, but the distance between them remained the same.[37] Each acquired a more labyrinthine way of dealing with the relationship between art and life, but they did not essentially change their ideas on it. Unamuno continued to affirm the inseparability of life and literature, while Jarnés attempted to establish the greatest possible distance between them. One technique Jarnés marshaled with increasing frequency to distance himself from his material was to introduce elements of biblical and classical mythology into the contemporary situations of his narratives. Unamuno too had recourse to myth in novels after *Niebla*, most notably *Abel Sánchez*, but he emptied the biblical story of its original content and replaced it with his own existential lament. Jarnés, on the other hand, drew directly on the original myth, incorporating it into his own creation. For example, the first section of the 1934 *El profesor inútil* blends the professor's life as a tutor with the myth of Jacinto and Boreas. At one point, the pupil Juan becomes completely identified with Jacinto, even in name, and his life concludes exactly like that of the mythological figure. He is killed by the jealous Ceferino (Boreas).

Another distancing mechanism that Jarnés employed in 1934 was a series of prologues and preambles to the core of the novel, not unlike Unamuno's complex reconstruction of *Cómo se hace una novela*, which he translated from French to Spanish in 1927, adding interpolated commentaries and a "Prólogo." Unamuno compared the effect to a series of Japanese lacquered boxes that fit one inside another. Jarnés's new edition of *El profesor inútil* opens with a prologue entitled "Discurso a Herminia" in which he, though in a more veiled way than in 1926, alluded to Unamuno, whose motivating purpose as an author was to reach as wide as possible an audience with his anguished messages. Jarnés's narrator is satisfied to have Herminia, his "walkyria" as his sole auditor. He wishes to distinguish himself from his "cofrades [que] suelen dirigir su palabra—rezumante de jugo doctrinal—por lo menos a toda una nación, cuando no a un continente, cuando no a toda la Humanidad," those *cofrades* who are "los nietos de voz universal del germánico Fichte" (7). The opening lines of *Cómo se hace una novela* have a Fichtean ring: "Héteme aquí ante estas blancas páginas—blancas como el negro porvenir: ¡terrible blancura!—buscando retener el tiempo que pasa, fijar el huidero hoy, eternizarme o inmortalizarme en fin, bien que eternidad e inmortalidad no sean una sola y misma cosa. Héteme aquí ante estas páginas blancas, mi porvenir, tratando de derramar mi vida; de arrancarme a la muerte de cada instante."[38]

The body of the 1934 *El profesor inútil* is also more complex, containing five sections instead of the original four. Three of the sections of the first version became a core enveloped by two new sections, at the beginning and end, that contain most of the mythological material. Having been supplanted in the important initiating and concluding positions, the direct references to *Niebla* in the sections written in 1926 no longer supply the motivating principle of the novel. There are, however, references to Unamuno in the new pieces added in 1934. In the first section, the professor feels useless in the presence of his pupil, a young farmer, who wants to limit his studies to mathematics, the only subject that will be of use to him in his work. In a passage that echoes the life as text theme of *Cómo se hace una novela*, the professor muses: "¿Qué texto, entonces, podría yo explicar a Juan, como no fuese un texto probablemente inútil, el texto de mí mismo?" (17).

The second section, which occupies the same place in this novel as in the first version, has been amplified to include more and longer passages of visual perception, particularly of Madrid and of paintings in the Prado Museum. For example, echoing *Senos* by Ramón Gómez de la Serna, the professor's gaze fixes on the breasts of Goya's "Maja desnuda." But the section also continues Jarnés's original mission of responding to Unamuno's now three-decade-old campaign against the tyranny of reason: "¡Walkyria, mi walkyria, levántame de entre estos cadáveres de pensamientos, de este campo estéril donde la razón me amenaza con sus últimas flechas! ¡Álzame al mundo de los verdaderos niños, donde todo ocurre como quisiéramos que ocurriese, a ese pluscuampresente adorable donde todos los tiempos se confunden, donde todos los espacios se llenan de cálidas y azules invitaciones a la vida!" (124). "Mañana de vacación," with which the 1926 edition began, constituye the third section in 1934, and "El río fiel," the earlier third section, now assumes the fourth position. Both vignettes undergo amplification similar to that of the second section.

"Trótula," the fifth and longest section, completely replaces "Una papeleta," which concluded the first version; it contains an extended parody of the author-character confrontation in *Niebla*. Recalling the "Mañana de vacación" section (and *Niebla*), the vignette begins with the narrator/protagonist following a woman in the street, but Jarnés abandoned the useless professor thread that stitched together the scenes of the 1926 version. The narrator now works in a funeral home "La Eterna Paz," and his morbid profession prophesies the sad outcome of the story. Rebecca, the woman whom he follows, cares for her invalid mother by bringing her curative waters each day from a special well. Finally, after several days of following Rebecca to the well, the narrator manages to convince her to fill her jug with ordinary water and spend the time with him in a *casa de citas*. When the mother dies after drinking the ordinary water, the witch who dispenses the curative liquid reprimands the narrator for his treachery. The witch, who has gained a Godlike power over the narrator by obtaining his photograph, reveals to him his lack of autonomy. Her speech contains elements of *Niebla*'s concern with the author's control over his characters and *Cómo se hace una novela*'s preoccupation with life as text:

—En todo caso, correremos siempre el viejo peligro de que el texto desaparezca bajo su interpretación. Hablo del texto de nuestra vida, tan sujeto a variantes.
—Pero lo que hoy no existe, no existirá jamás. No se comienza a existir. No se comienza tampoco a vivir 'vidas nuevas' . . . Excepto al final de las comedias cursis.
—La vida es una comedia.
—Falso. Es la realización—con ligeros retoques—de un previo bosquejo. Déjame seguir viendo el tuyo.
—Pienso modificarlo mucho.
—No tanto como cree. Estás bajo el dominio de un dios que devora a sus hijos.
(231)

If Augusto Pérez is consumed by existential doubt and a desire to affirm his existence, especially after his encounter with Unamuno, the narrator/protagonist in the 1934 *El profesor inútil* flippantly attempts to destroy his personal essence: "¡Qué placer destruir así todo un pasado, como se destruía entonces una sola jornada! ¡Qué formidable broma jugada al hosco Anciano, si yo hundía en el agua todos mis años anteriores y salía del borde del estanque hecho otro niño, con sólo una voluntad, la de vivir entregado a cada circunstancia!" (237). "El hosco Anciano" is doubtless a reference to Unamuno's playing God to Augusto at the end of *Niebla*.

The epilogue, although new to the 1934 edition, returns to the more playful tone of the 1926 version and continues the commentary on *Niebla* by concentrating on Unamuno's juxtaposition of author and *ente de ficción*. Like the "Una papeleta" section that concluded the 1926 novel, this epilogue evokes the relationship between life and literature through a library setting. Jarnés diluted Augusto's terrible anguish at discovering that he is a novelistic creature by having his narrator accept as natural that the fictional character does not exist and merely appears to have life: "Cuando el coche llega a casa de Araceli, ya no es Judas el vulgar prometido de una raquítica muchacha provinciana sino un ente ideal en camino de antologías y bibliotecas. ¿No está ya definitivamente *arrancado de la realidad*?" (253, Jarnés's emphasis). And Jarnés parodied Unamuno's serious role as Augusto's progenitor: "un parto ideal, de dar a luz un ente novelesco. . . . Acabo de ver como Judas Tadeo, personaje que vivía malamente en la realidad, acaba de *arrancarse de ella*. Era un simple tender, y parece que se decide a arrostrar las gloriosas vicisitudes de un héroe de novela" (253, Jarnés's emphasis). Jarnés did not fail to put an ironic twist on Augusto's suicide as well: "Judas continúa siendo un personaje falso en la vida ordinaria, pero verdadero, auténtico, dentro de la novela. —Le tengo lástima. Porque si el autor es normal, ese Judas, al acabar el libro debe ahorcarse" (255).

Unamuno's ideas and novels constitute parodic intertexts in other novels by Jarnés as well. In *Locura y muerte de nadie*, Juan Sánchez (whose name is even more banal than Augusto Pérez's) struggles to be a unique individual and meditates on being and existing. Arturo of *Teoría del zumbel*, on the other hand arrives at the "feliz momento de perder su personalidad. Placer soberano de ser un hombre u otro, de ver hundirse el individuo en un golfo de vibraciones tumultuosas" (59). José E. Serrano Asenjo quotes "Algo más que todo un hombre: todo un hombre" as a "sentencia con un inequívoco talante unamuniano." He adds that "No es ésta la única vez en la que se aludirá al creador de *Niebla* en estas páginas."[39] *Niebla*'s author-character confrontation takes on even more ludicrous proportions in Ramón Gómez de la Serna's *El novelista* (1926), in which the protagonist of one of the *novelista*'s novels arrives at his apartment to demand that he help him find a job. He explains that the denouement of the novel in which he figured has deprived him of a source of income.

The year 1934 saw another important parody of Unamuno in Antonio Machado's *Juan de Mairena*. Abandoning almost all pretense to novelistic form, its elaborate and heterogeneous format marked the end of the Spanish philosophical narration as it had evolved during a period of some thirty years. In his lectures to his students, Juan de Mairena refers, in equivocal fashion, to his own *maestro*, Abel Martín, whose dicta, liberally laced with references to "lo otro," "querer creer" and faith and reason are too close to Unamuno's concerns to be mistaken. Machado, however, did not weave Mairena's lessons into even the minimal stories that inform Salinas's playful explorations of language and reality, Chacel's new version of the existential novel or Jarnés's inversion of *Niebla*. The Civil War erupted in 1936, the year *Juan de Mairena* was published; both events mark the end of the close relationship that philosophy and the novel had enjoyed in Spain for more than thirty years.

POSTSCRIPT

The marriage of philosophy and fiction in the first third of Spain's twentieth century was a fertile one. It produced some truly notable offspring—novels that cross genre boundaries to find innovative forms and treatises that fuse literature and philosophy in new ways. Initially it was a marriage of convenience and necessity. Unamuno, Baroja and Martínez Ruiz gravitated to the novel's dialogic capabilities to air the conflicting claims of nineteenth-century philosophies that vied for their attention during their formative years. The early results are some of the first modernist novels in the European canon. The novel continued to serve Unamuno's, Baroja's and Azorín's philosophical purposes throughout their careers, and the two Basque writers found it especially useful in combatting the rationalism of José Ortega y Gasset in the second decade. Their later novels, however, like those of Azorín, sought more representational and less discursive formulae for embedding philosophy in fiction.

The writers who followed the three pioneers in Spanish philosophical fiction pursued other philosophical goals. By 1916 the function of language in memory, perception and being replaced the earlier concerns with materialism, idealism, will and reason. The new philosophic emphasis on language inspired innovative uses of style and pushed genre boundaries even further beyond traditional limits, especially in the unclassifiable *Platero y yo* by Juan Ramón Jimenez and Gabriel Miró's *El humo dormido*. Parody and humor, while not absent in the '98 novel or in the narratives of Juan Ramón and Miró, gained ascendency in the novels by writers associated with José Ortega y Gasset's publishing enterprises—Ramón Pérez de Ayala, Pedro Salinas, Rosa Chacel and Benjamín Jarnés. Their humor focuses on philosophical issues and narrative techniques taken seriously by the '98 (reason and will and the nature of existence) and Miró and Juan Ramón (the linguistic expression of perception and memory). The parodies of earlier philosophical novels in the twenties and thirties carried the seeds of the demise of the Spanish philosophical novel as a genre. Like Cervantes's *Don Quixote*, the book of chivalry to end all romances of chivalry, the parodic philosophical novel was a self-consuming artifact; once it had devoured its sources, there remained nothing upon which it could feed.

The Spanish Civil War (1936-1939) delivered the genre a *coup de grace*. Unamuno died in 1936 while under house arrest; Baroja and Azorín were exiled in Paris during the war and never recovered their former vigor, even after returning to Spain in the 1940s. Pérez de Ayala had stopped writing novels in 1926, and Miró had died in 1930. Juan Ramón, Salinas, Chacel and Jarnés all left Spain as a consequence of the Civil War, their thoughts and talent turned away from the issues that had informed their philosophical narratives of the previous two decades. Even if the Civil War had not intervened, the days of the philosophical novel would have been numbered. In the wake of the Great Depression and the ascendency of socialism and communism, a new group of authors, including Ramón Sender and Francisco Ayala, was reorienting Spanish fiction toward enlisting vanguardist techniques to expose political and social evils.

This reorientation was what captured the imagination of the new novelists who were born phoenix-like from the ashes and diaspora of the Spanish Civil War. In Franco's Spain, where people's lives were shattered by the recent hostilities and by the isolation World War II imposed on them, novels that dealt with or even parodied esoteric issues such as reason and will were far removed from their immediate concerns. Rosa Chacel believed that Camilo José Cela's and Carmen Laforet's new realism betrayed the legacy of her generation. Luis Martín Santos, however, did revive some of the comic-burlesque philosophical satire of the prewar generations by placing a hilarious parody of José Ortega y Gasset at the center of *Tiempo de silencio* (1962), but he did not have any imitators. In 1989 María Zambrano published *Delirio y destino*, a novel written in 1959 that has some of the discursive qualities of earlier philosophical fiction, but it has the air of a work that would have been more at home in the vanguardist 1930s. The constellation of a modernist sensibility and the latent arrival of European idealism and positivism that came together to produce the '98 philosophical novel and the intersection of phenomenology and vanguardist aesthetics that inspired a continuation of philosophical narrative in the second and third decades were unique and unrepeatable.

Introduction

1. Juan Arzadun, "Miguel de Unamuno, íntimo: al margen de sus cartas," *Sur* 14 (1944): 48.

2. Quoted in Milagro Laín, *La palabra en Unamuno* (Caracas, Venezuela: Cuadernos del Instituto de Filología Andrés Bello, 1964), 77.

3. There are numerous other quotations and underlinings in Unamuno's works and personal library that attest to his conscious attempt to blur the lines between philosophy and literature. For example, in his notes on Augustine, Unamuno characterized a book as a novel if it presents a "quest for self-discovery for the three viable participants: narrator, character, and reader" (Mario J. Valdés, "Introduction," *An Unamuno Source Book* [Toronto: University of Toronto Press, 1973, xxiii]). In his copy of Montaigne's *Essays* (n.d., 503), he underlined "Platon n'est qu'un poete descousue," and in Coleridge's *Biographia Literaria* (London: Dent, 1906, 240), he highlighted the assertion that "It seems, indeed, to destroy the main fundamental distinction, not only between a poem and prose, but even between philosophy and works of fiction inasmuch as it proposes *truth* for its immediate object, instead of pleasure." And in the "Segundo prólogo" to *Amor y pedagogía* (*OC* 2:312-313), he wrote: "¿Qué importan las ideas, las ideas intelectuales? Por esto el sentimiento, no la concepción racional del universo y de la vida se refleja mejor que en un sistema filosófico o que en una novela realista, en un poema, en prosa o en verso, en una leyenda, en una novela. Y cuento entre las grandes novelas (o poemas épicos, es igual) junto a la *Ilíada* y la *Odisea* y la *Divina comedia* y el *Quijote* y el *Paraíso perdido* y el *Fausto* también la *Ética* de Spinoza y la *Crítica de la razón pura* de Kant y la *Lógica* de Hegel y las *Historias* de Tucídides y de Tácito, y de otros grandes poetas historiadores, y desde luego, los *Evangelios* de la historia de Cristo."

4. Juan Arzadun, "Miguel de Unamuno," 46.

5. Ibid.

6. José Ortega y Gasset, "El siglo XVIII, educador," *El espectador* 7 (Madrid: Revista de Occidente, 1930), 88. See also E. Inman Fox, "Apuntes para una teoría de la moderna imaginación literaria española," *Homenaje a José Antonio Maravall* (Madrid: Centro de Investigaciones Sociológicas, 1986), 341-350, for a discussion of Spain's foreshortened intellectual history.

7. "Madrid Cómico and Co. Limited," *Revista Nueva* 25 (October 25, 1899): 4.

8. Unamuno attributed this atmosphere to the national characteristic of envy: "Bien sabe Dios que no soy presa de la envidia, pasión tan española, sino que me apena ver cómo atrae aquí la vulgaridad dorada y el éxito incomprendido. . . . ¿Qué saben de histología todos esos majaderos que se encienden en

entusiasmo por Cajal?" (Santiago Riopérez, ed., "Doce cartas inéditas de Unamuno a Azorín," *DIWAN* 10 [1981]: 49), and Eugenio d'Ors called the national phenomenon "*la incapacidad específica para el ejercicio de la amistad*" (his emphasis, *De la amistad y del diálogo*. Lectura dada en la Residencia de Estudiantes, 1914, 19).

9. "Clarín y Unamuno," *Archivum* 2 (1952): 134.

10. *Epistolario a Clarín*, ed. Adolfo Alas (Madrid: Escorial, 1941), 50-51.

11. Tzvetan Todorov, *The Poetics of Prose*, trans. Richard Howard (Ithaca: Cornell University Press, 1971), 25.

12. "Native Readers of Fiction: A Speech-Act and Genre-Rule Approach to Defining Literature," in *What Is Literature*, ed. Paul Hernadi (Bloomington: Indiana University Press, 1978), 151.

13. "Socratic Philosophy and the Dialogue Form," *Philosophy and Literature* 7 (1984): 183.

14. "Phenomenology and the Form of the Novel," *Philosophy and Phenomenological Research* 34 (1974): 332.

15. *The Dialogic Imagination* (Austin: University of Texas Press, 1981), 299.

16. José Martínez Ruiz, *La voluntad*, ed. E. Inman Fox (Madrid: Castalia, 1982), 267.

17. *La España Moderna* 26 (1904): 27-42.

18. Hernán Benítez, *El drama religioso de Unamuno* (University of Buenos Aires, 1949), 293. Numerous other indications of Unamuno's understanding of the complex nature of novelistic dialogue can be found in his work and in his marginal notations in his books: The "Introducción" to *OC* 2:15, quotes Unamuno: "Diríase que el autor, no atreviéndose a expresar por propia cuenta ciertos desatinos, adopta el cómodo artífice de ponerlos en boca de personajes grotescos y absurdos, soltando así en broma lo que acaso piensa en serio." And Unamuno wrote the following note to himself on the inside back cover of his copy of Moody's *The Poems and Plays* (Boston: Houghton Mifflin, 1900): "Él era ship of souls, su pueblo, sus yos, acaban por con-versar y no dia-logar (todos los poetas son uno, un poeta colectivo. . . . Diá-logos es d-versar [sic]. Auto-diálogos. Pero hay auto-conversación. O si se quiere auto-sílogo (syllogo). El silogismo es lo contrario de la diálectica (pero va por ella)."

19. "Don Catalino, hombre sabio," *Obras completas*, ed. Manuel García Blanco, 9 (Barcelona: Vergara, 1958): 229.

20. *Ensayos* 1 (Madrid: Aguilar, 1951): 930.

21. *Usos amorosos de posguerra* (Madrid: Anagrama, 1987), 100.

22. "Introduction" to *Del sentimiento trágico de la vida*, trans. J. E. Crawford-Flitch (London: Macmillan, 1921), xxix.

23. *The Use of Poetry and the Use of Criticism* (London: Faber, 1933), 9.

24. In 1908 Gómez de la Serna initiated the journal *Prometeo* with the purpose of renewing revolutionary vigor, and in 1913 Ortega and Pérez de Ayala founded the Liga de Educación Política Española to enlighten the Spanish public about political matters.

25. See Howard T. Young, *The Line in the Margin* (Madison, Wisconsin: University of Wisconsin Press, 1980), for an in-depth discussion of Juan Ramón Jiménez and the British poets, Shelley, Yeats and Blake.

26. See especially Richard Cardwell, *Juan Ramón Jiménez: The Modernist Apprenticeship, 1895-1900* (Berlin: Colloquium Verlag, 1977), and Michael P. Predmore, "Introducción," *Platero y yo* (Madrid: Cátedra, 1983).

27. "Doce cartas inéditas," 58, 50.

28. Quoted in Julián Marías, "Azorín y las generaciones," *La Vanguardia Española*, June 13, 1973, 15.

29. "Epistolario entre Unamuno y Ortega," *Revista de Occidente*, 2ª serie 6-7 (1964): 27.

30. "Sigüenza y el mirador azul" was not published during Miró's lifetime; indeed he never arrived at a definitive version of the piece, but thanks to Edmund L. King we now have in printed form the three versions that Miró had prepared (*Sigüenza y el mirador azul y prosas de El Ibero*, Madrid: Ediciones de la Torre, 1982).

31. *La Esfera*, April 25, 1914.

32. Ibid.

33. Ibid.

34. "Azorín recogió el término 'generación de 1898' de Ortega, según Cacho Viu," *El País*, April 10, 1983.

1. The Generation of '98: Early Philosophical and Personal Wars

1. *Solos*, 4th ed. (Madrid: Fernando Fe, 1891), 61.

2. "Prólogo" to Manuel Hilario Ayuso, *Helénicas* (Madrid: Victoriano Suárez, 1914), 8.

3. José F. Montesinos, *Galdós* 1 (Madrid: Editorial Castalia, 1968), 22.

4. Juan López Morillas, "Prólogo" to Francisco Giner de los Ríos, *Ensayos* (Madrid, 1969), quoted in Cardwell, *Juan Ramón Jiménez*, 29.

5. José Luis Abellán, *Historia crítica del pensamiento español* 4 (Madrid: Espasa-Calpe, 1984), 428.

6. A. Jiménez García, *El krausisimo y la Institución Libre de Enseñanza* (Madrid: Editorial Amiel, 1985), 83.

7. "Los socialistas españoles contra el armonismo institucionista, 1883-1885," *Homenaje a Juan López-Morillas* (Madrid: Castalia, 1982), 101-111.

8. The same could be said for Ángel Ganivet, whom I do not include in this study, even though his novels *Los trabajos del infatigable creador Pío Cid* and *La conquista del reino de Maya* could qualify as philosophical novels. His production, however, falls somewhat before the 1900 starting point of this book, and his early death in 1898 precluded his participation in the continuing novelistic-philosophical dialogue that I am tracing during the early years of the twentieth century. For good analyses of philosophical aspects of Ganivet's work see Donald Shaw, "Ganivet's *España filosófica contemporánea* (1889) and the Interpretation of the Generation of 1898," *Hispanic Reivew* 28 (1960): 220-232, and Herbert Ramsden, *The 98 Movement in Spain* (Manchester: Manchester University Press, 1974).

9. See especially Elena M. de Jongh-Rossel, *El krausismo y la Generación de 1898* (Valencia-Chapel Hill: Álbatros-Hispanófila, 1985).

10. *El darwinismo en España*, ed. Diego Núñez (Madrid: Castalia, 1969), 14.

11. Letter to Jiménez Ilundain of January 24, 1900 included in Dr. [Enrique] Areilza, *Epistolario*, ed. José María de Areilza (Bilbao: El Cofre del Bilbaíno, 1964), 46.

12. F. Laporta, "Crítica a 'Historia crítica del pensamiento español', de José Luis Abellán," *Sistema* 37:131-34, quoted in A. Jiménez García, *El krausismo y la Institución Libre de Enseñanza* (Madrid: Editorial Amiel, 1986), 177.

13. "Prólogo" to ibid., 17.

14. *Á gel Ganivet y la teoría del conocimiento en la España de fin de siglo* (Granada: Excma. Diputación Provincial, 1982), 99.

15. Letter of May 31, 1895 in *Epistolario a Clarín*, ed. Adolfo Alas, 53.

16. Letter of October 30, 1897, in Juan Arzadun, 54-55.

17. Letter of December 23, 1898, in Hernán Benítez, 77.

18. "De Clarín y Unamuno," *Prohemio* 3 (1972): 467-472.

19. Letter of October 30, 1897, in Juan Arzadun, 58.

20. Letter of May 9, 1900, in "Cartas a Clarín," ed. Adolfo Alas, 91. Manuel García Blanco, "Clarín y Unamuno," 133, quotes another letter from Unamuno to Clarín that attributes Clarín's hostility to generational differences: "Tal vez esté yo equivocado, tal vez haya incompatibilidad entre usted, de la generación que salió del 68, y nosotros, los que aun no pasamos de treinta y cinco años, pero los viejos me parecen inferiores a los que hoy salen. ¿A qué vino lo de oponer la gente *novísima* a la *nueva?* Si en sus reparos a la gente nueva le creyesen sincero, la misma gente nueva le querría." Another important study of the Clarín-Unamuno relationship, Antonio Ramos Gascón's, "Clarín y el primer Unamuno," *Cuadernos Hispanoamericanos* 263-264 (1972): 489-595, includes similar quotations.

21. Leopoldo Alas, "Prólogo" to E. Gómez Carrillo, *Almas y cerebros*, Madrid, n.d. [c. 1895], xi-xii, quoted in Cardwell, *Juan Ramón Jiménez*, 69.

22. Letter of October 2, 1895, in *Epistolario a Clarín*, ed. Adolfo Alas, 64.

23. See Juan López Morillas, "Unamuno y sus criaturas: Antolín S. Paparrigópulos," *Cuadernos Americanos* 7 (1948): 234-249, and Thomas Franz, "Menéndez y Pelayo as Antolín S. Paparrigópulos of Unamuno's *Niebla*," *Papers on Language and Literature* 11 (1973): 84-88, for discussions of Unamuno's model for the academic scholar.

24. Camille Pitollet, "De mis memorias," *BBMP* 28 (1952): 65.

25. See Anna Krause, *Azorín, The Little Philosopher (Inquiry into the Birth of a Literary Personality)* (Berkeley: University of California Publications in Modern Philology, vol. 22, no. 4, 1948); Rafael Pérez de la Dehesa, "Un desconocido libro de Azorín: 'Pasión (Cuentos y crónicas)' 1897," *RHM* 33 (1967): 280-284; J. Martínez Cachero, "Clarín y Azorín (Una amistad y un fervor)," *Archivum* 3 (1953): 159-179, and José María Valverde, *Azorín* (Barcelona: Planeta, 1971), 41-54.

26. Also present are *Casi críticos* (dedicated by the author), *Huellas literarias, Mosquetazos, Bombos y palos* (2 copies), and *El avispero.*

27. Quoted in Miguel A. Auladell, Ramón F. Llorens, Juan A. Ríos and Ma. Dolores Fuentes, "Textos olvidados del joven Martínez Ruiz," *Canelobre* 9 (1987): 38.

28. For a full discussion of Martínez Ruiz's two articles on the play, see E. Inman Fox, "*Electra*, de Pérez Galdós (historia, literatura y la polémica entre

Martínez Ruiz y Maeztu)," in *La crisis intelectual del '98* (Madrid: Cuadernos para el Diálogo, 1976), 49-72.

29. Quoted in Antonio Ramos Gascón, "Relaciones Clarín-Martínez Ruiz," *Hispanic Review* 42 (1974): 423.

30. Clarín, "Mala maña," *La Vida Literaria* 6 (1899): 99.

31. *Madrid Cómico* 791 (April 16, 1898): 303.

32. *Crónicas*, 2nd ed. (Madrid: Fortanet, 1901), 57.

33. Letter of November 19, 1906, in *DIWAN* 10 (1981): 49.

34. *Cartas inéditas de Miguel de Unamuno*, ed. Fernández Larraín (Santiago de Chile: Editora Zig-Zag, 1965), 33. I am indebted to Thomas Franz for pointing out to me that after the early part of the century, Unamuno waffled on his reaction to Galdós. When Galdós died in 1920, Unamuno criticized Galdós's novelistic techniques in a speech in Salamanca's Plaza Mayor. When Unamuno was exiled on Fuerteventura in 1924, however, he reread many of Galdós's novels and rescinded his earlier negative views.

35. The new generation's presence was noticed in the established journals as well. A review of José Martínez Ruiz's *Buscapiés* appeared in *Revista de España* in 1894 and a review of his *Literatura (Fray Candil, Galdós, Clarín, Altamira, etc.)* in *Revista Contemporánea* in 1895.

2. Unamuno: A Bold New Hybrid

1. See Robert C. Spires, *Transparent Simulacra* (Columbia: University of Missouri Press, 1988), 1-47, for an excellent defense of the importance of *Amor y pedagogía*, *Camino de perfección*, and *La voluntad* (as well as *Sonata de otoño*) to Spanish literary history. Spires understands the revolutionary forms of these novels as precursors to the vanguardist novel of the 1920s. In several ways my approach to these novels complements that of Spires, whose analysis is more purely narratological. To his helpful insights, I add commentary on the philosophical aspects of the novels, genre considerations and contextual material to understand these novels as either engaging in a dialogue with each other or in a dialogue with the Spanish and European literary tradition.

2. Federico Urales, *La evolución de la filosofía en España*, ed. Rafael Pérez de la Dehesa (Barcelona: Ediciones de Cultura Popular, 1934), 161.

3. Miguel de Unamuno, "Filosofía lógica," unpublished manuscript located in the Casa-Museo Unamuno in Salamanca, 1.

4. "Martin Nozick's Unamuno: A Fountainhead of Future Discoveries," *Siglo XX/Twentieth Century* 4 (1986-87): 32.

5. Thomas Mermall masterfully analyzes the rhetorical devices of these essays in "Analogy, Dialectic and Dissonance in Unamuno's *En torno al casticismo*," an as yet unpublished paper read at the Mid-America Conference on Hispanic Literatures in Boulder, Colorado, in October 1990.

6. Herbert Ramsden, *The 1898 Movement in Spain*, 83-84, 96 and elsewhere.

7. Letter of June 17, 1892, in Juan Arzadun, 46.

8. Miguel de Unamuno, *En torno al casticismo* in *Ensayos* 1, ed. Bernardo G. Candamo (Madrid: Aguilar, 1966), 133.

9. Unamuno's intense reading in philosophy began when he went to the University of Madrid in 1881—first French, then German and finally English after 1890.

10. Letter of October 19, 1900, in Juan Arzadun, 57.

11. Quoted in Manuel García Blanco, "*Amor y pedagogía,* nivola de Unamuno," *La Torre* 9 (1961): 453.

12. Ibid., 450-454. Unamuno often worked in fits and starts: *Paz en la guerra* took at least five years to complete; *Del sentimiento trágico de la vida* perhaps as many as thirteen; *Niebla* at least thirteen; and *La tía Tula* was published in 1920 after an aborted beginning eighteen years earlier.

13. Quoted in Ibid., 450.

14. Letter of January 16, 1900, in Hernán Benítez, 309.

15. Ibid., 297.

16. Quoted in García Blanco, "*Amor y pedagogía,*" 451.

17. Aside from Clarín's indifference, someone (perhaps Jiménez Ilundain himself) must have criticized the novel for its lack of content compared to the length, as Unamuno wrote to his friend on October 19, 1900, that he hoped it would have "más contenido que mi *Paz en la guerra,* no más extensión" (Hernán Benítez, 321). Nor was Martínez Ruiz's review in *El País* very laudatory.

18. Maeztu wrote the review of the book version of *En torno al casticismo* for *La lectura* 1 (1903): 282-287, but one imagines that since he and Unamuno knew one another, Maeztu made his thoughts on the essays known to their author when they first appeared eight years earlier.

19. He had wanted to publish a translation of *Sartor Resartus,* but Galdeano did not think it would sell; economics guided Galdeano's editorial policies to a very large extent, as his correspondence to Unamuno attests.

20. Carlos Clavería, *Temas de Unamuno* (Madrid: Gredos, 1953), 51, and Geoffrey Ribbans, *Niebla y soledad* (Madrid: Gredos, 1971), 90, suggest *Sartor Resartus* as a source for the characterization of Entrambosmares, but do not explore its implications for genre.

21. Paul R. Olson, "The Novelistic Logos in Unamuno's *Amor y pedagogía, MLN* 82 (1969): 257. Olson's article is the best study of the philosophical aspects of the novel, but he concentrates on what he considers the serious philosophical theme: "a profound sense of wonder at the ontological miracle whereby a literary entity comes into existence upon the blank pages at which the writer stares, a wonder parallel to that which he feels for the miracle of Being itself" (253), whereas I view the novel more as a parody of already existing philosophical positions within the tradition of the philosophical novel genre in European literature.

22. John Stuart Mill, *System of Logic. Raciocinative and Inductive.* London: Longman's, 1872). Unamuno's very heavily annotated copy was clearly second-hand and seems to have been read after 1890 when his English vocabulary had improved, as there are few translations of words in the margins.

23. Thomas Carlyle, *Sartor Resartus,* ed. Archibald MacMechan (New York: Ginn, 1896), 64.

24. All of this speculation should be tempered with a warning about source-hunting in Unamuno. The Rector of Salamanca was a voracious reader with an

amazing memory, and while his reading was a constant inspiration for his own ideas and work, he drew on his vast store of received knowledge to forge his own highly original works. He marked many passages in the books he read and occasionally refuted them in the margins, but, by all accounts, he did not take notes or work from books or notes when writing. Unamuno himself defended his use of other writers in a letter to Clarín, who had accused him of lack of originality.

25. Paul Olson, "The Novelistic Logos," 266, suggests that Avito's dilemma is another version of the time/eternity problem of *En torno al casticismo*.

26. Unamuno wrote to Jiménez Ilundain on October 19, 1900, that the "grotesco filósofo" espouses "la doctrina platónica de la reminiscencia," and that his "fórmulas" support "intelectualismo y . . . antropomorfisimo (both of which Unamuno had attributed to Hegel on other occasions). Don Fulgencio is also an example of what happens when ones gives up religion and absolute moral values; the person becomes an intellectual dilettante whose motto is "A quoi bon?"—a sort of Petronio Sienkiewiez (in Hernán Benítez, 323). Geoffrey Ribbans, *Niebla y soledad*, 99-101, points out the equivocal nature of don Fulgencio's character, but I find it hard to accept his assertion that he is a "portavoz de las ideas de Unamuno" (100). Thomas R. Franz's "The Philosophical Bases of Fulgencio Entrambosmares in Unamuno's 'Amor y pedagogía,' " *Hispania* 60 (1977): 443-451, is the most complete study to date on the heterogeneous philosophical sources that went into the invention of Entrambosmares; he concentrates espcially on Kant, Hegel, Kierkegaard and Nietzsche.

27. See the preface to the novel and a letter from Unamuno to Valentí Camp, reproduced in José Tarín Iglesias, *Unamuno y sus amigos catalanes* (Barcelona: Editorial Península, 1966), 143.

28. Juan Arzadun, 109-110.

29. Camille Pitollet, 74.

30. Letter of November 6, 1906, in *Epistolario Unamuno-Maragall* (Madrid: Seminarios y Ediciones, 1971), 26.

31. Among the most interesting recent articles are Rosendo Díaz-Peterson, "*Amor y pedagogía* o la lucha de una ciencia con la vida," *Cuadernos Hispanoamericanos*, 384 (1982): 549-560; Paul Olson, "Nominalist Realism in *Amor y pedagogía*," paper read at the 1986 Twentieth Century Spanish Division of the MLA meetings; Paul Olson, "Unamuno's Break with the Nineteenth Century: Invention of the Nivola and the Linguistic Turn," *MLN* 102 (1987): 307-315; Michael Vande Berg, "Unamuno's *Amor y pedagogía:* An Early Application of James's 'Stream of Consciousness,' " *Hispania* 70 (1987): 52-58; Gayana Jurkevich, "The Sun-Hero Revisited: Inverted Archetypes in Unamuno's *Amor y pedagogía, MLN* 102 (1987): 292-306; and Germán Gullón, "Un paradigma para la novela española moderna: *Amor y pedagogía*, de Miguel de Unamuno," *MLN* 105 (1990): 226-243.

3. Baroja: A Solution to the Problem of Will

1. Camilo José Cela, "Breve noticia de un curioso epistolario del joven Baroja al joven Martínez Ruiz," *Homenaje a Azorín*, ed. Carlos Mellizo (University of Wyoming Press, 1973), 13, indicates that the first letter is dated 1893, while all

the others are from 1901-1903. I have examined this correspondence in the Casa-Museo Azorín, and believe that Baroja simply slipped in writing "9" instead of "0" as the content of the 1893 letter clearly fits with others written in 1903.

2. See E. Inman Fox, "Introducción," to his edition of *Antonio Azorín* (Barcelona: Labor, 1970), 7-28, for a discussion of the composition of and relationship between the three books.

3. Ramiro de Maeztu, " 'Electra' y Martínez Ruiz," *Madrid Cómico* 21 (February 9, 1901): 5: "Para mí su [el de Martínez Ruiz] jesuitismo es *pose;* para mí se trata de un espíritu seco en el que sólo vibra la ambición, pero loca sin vallas. Martínez Ruiz comprende que carece su alma de fantasía, de ternura, de honradez, de entusiasmo y de amor a la vida y a los hombres, 'Cárdicas' condiciones indispensables para el triunfo de un artista. De ahí que procure a su persona lo que niega el arte a sus escritos. Hambriento de notoriedad sería autor de un crimen, si tuviera valor. Espíritu cobarde, necesita para su nombre un misterio que lo acreciente."

4. Pío Baroja, *Camino de perfección* (New York: Las Américas, n.d.), 145.

5. "Pío Baroja," *Lecturas españolas* (Madrid: Rafael Caro Raggio, 1920), 228.

6. "Baroja historiador," *Los valores literarios* (Madrid: Rafael Caro Raggio, 1921), 272.

7. Raimundo Bartrés, *Pío Baroja y "Azorín"* (Barcelona: Distribuciones Catalonia, 1981), 19.

8. Myrna Solotorevsky, "Notas para el estudio intrínsico comparativo de *Camino de perfección* y *La voluntad,*" *Boletín de Filología* 15 (1963): 111-164, compares the two novels in their similarities and points out differences in the philosophical meaning of each, especially with regard to the will and reason. She asserts that Baroja "no aspira al equilibrio, sino a la hegemonía de una posición extrema: dominio total de la voluntad," while she believes that Martínez Ruiz makes a case for balancing will and intellect. She does not take into account both novels' diffusion of monolithic philosophical viewpoints through genre switching and narrative dialogics, which effectively preclude arriving at safe conclusions about the author's philosophical positions.

9. José Alberich, *Los ingleses y otros temas de Pío Baroja* (Madrid: Alfaguara, 1966), 37-63.

10. Quoted in Sebastián Juan Arbó, *Pío Baroja y su tiempo* (Barcelona: Editorial Planeta, 1963), 165.

11. "Mi moral," *Juventud* 10 (March 8, 1902): 1.

12. "Hacia lo inconsciente," *La Vida Literaria* 11 (March 18, 1899): 315.

13. "Historia y novela," in *Pío Baroja*, ed. Javier Martínez Palacio (Madrid: Taurus, 1979), 429.

14. Ibid., 431.

15. Beatrice Patt, *Pío Baroja* (New York: Twayne, 1971), emphasizes Nordau's notion of the degenerate artist as the novel's theme; Laura Rivkin, "Pain and Physiological Form in Baroja's *Camino de perfección*," *Symposium* 39 (1985): 207-216, understands Schopenhauer as the guiding philosophical source. For Gonzalo Sobejano, *Nietzsche en España* (Madrid: Gredos, 1966) and "Componiendo 'Camino de perfección,' " *Cuadernos Hispanoamericanos* 265-267 (1972): 463-480, Nietzsche is central.

16. *Pío Baroja: Escritos de junventud, 1890-1904*, ed. Manuel Longares (Madrid: Editorial Cuadernos para el Diálogo, 1972), 240-241.

17. See especially Gonzalo Sobejano, *Nietzsche en España*, 62.

18. "Mi moral," 1.

19. *Hojas sueltas*, ed. D. Luis Urrutia Salaverri (Madrid: Caro Raggio, 1973),1: 118.

20. Ibid., 149.

21. See E. Inman Fox, "Baroja and Schopenhauer: *El árbol de la ciencia*," *Revue de Litterature Comparée* 37 (1963): 353,for a comparison of Baroja's article "Sufrir y pensar" and a passage from Schopenhauer. E. H. Templin, "Pío Baroja and Science," *Hispanic Review* 15 (1974): 190, lists a series of philosophical contradictions in Baroja's work.

22. Robert Spires, *Transparent Simulacra*, 3-6, offers an artistic explanation for the abrupt shift in narrative; the intradiegetic narrator establishes Fernando as a credible character with whom the reader sympathizes. Baroja may well have recognized this function of the intradiegetic narrator when he reworked the serial novel for publication as a book. Thus he changed other portions originally written in first person to third, and simply chose to ignore the incongruity—another conscious thumbnosing at nineteenth-century realistic conventions. But Baroja did attempt, rather belatedly and weakly, to redeem the consistency of narrative voice toward the end of the novel, having the narrator indicate that he has found documents written by Fernando.

23. See particularly, Noma and Weston Flint, *Pío Baroja. Camino de perfección* (London: Grant and Cutler, 1983), José Ares Montes, " 'Camino de perfección,' o las peregrinaciones de Pío Baroja y Fernando Ossorio," *Cuadernos Hispanoamericanos* 267 (1972): 481-516, and Daniel P. Testa, "Baroja ante Santa Teresa: Lectura e intertextualidad en *Camino de perfección*" in *Santa Teresa y la literatura mística hispánica* (Madrid: Edi-6, 1984), 801-806.

24. " 'Camino de perfección', o la superación de la dicotomía y el triunfo aparente del superhombre," *La estructura mítica del héroe* (Barcelona: Planeta, 1973), 139-175.

25. Emilio González López, " 'Camino de perfección' y el arte narrativo español contemporáneo," *Cuadernos Hispanoamericanos* 265-267 (1972): 447, outlines a structure for the novel based on rather different generic types: decadentist in the first part (chapters 1 through 10) and the rest symbolist. González López does not make connections between the generic types and philsophical positions. And J. J. Macklin, "The Modernist Mind: Identity and Integration in Pío Baroja's *Camino de perfección*," *Neophilologus* 67 (1983): 540-555, sees the novel as an exploration of the psychology of the modern consciousness.

26. The original serial version of *Camino de perfección* included a scene at the train station of Yécora in which Fernando encounters Silvestre Paradox, the main character of Baroja's previous and more uniformly picaresque novel. But I suspect that the scene was eliminated because it introduces the comic-burlesque genre at an inappropriate moment according to Baroja's novelistic program of moving Fernando into and out of genres that represent certain philosophical positions at specific moments in his life.

27. "*Doña Perfecta:* Galdós' Reply to *Pepita Jiménez*," *Anales Galdosianos* 15 (1980): 19-21.

4. Martínez Ruiz: An Answer to Baroja's Solution

1. Azorín, "Prólogo," to Leopoldo Alas, *Páginas escogidas* (Madrid: Calleja, 1917), 16, 18.

2. *Anarquistas literarios (Notas sobre la literatura española)* (Valencia: Fernando Fe, 1895), 52.

3. For a more complete discussion of Martínez Ruiz's adherence to Taine's determinism, see James H. Abbott, "Azorín and Taine's Determinism," *Hispania* 46 (1963): 476-479.

4. Quoted in E. Inman Fox, "José Martínez Ruiz," *Revista de Occidente* 12 (1966): 161-163.

5. 3rd ed. (Paris: Félix Alcán, 1897), 155.

6. For an account of the unpublished "Pasión," see Rafael Pérez de la Dehesa, "Un desconocido libro de Azorín: 'Pasión (cuentos y crónicas)' 1897," *Revista Hispánica Moderna* 33 (1967): 280-284.

7. E. Inman Fox, "Lectura y literatura (Entorno a la inspiración libresca de Azorín)," *Ideología y política en las letras fin de siglo (1898)* (Madrid: Espasa-Calpe, 1988), 121-155.

8. See José Rico Verdú, " 'Azorín,' apologista cristiano," *Revista de Literatura* 85 (1981): 111-130.

9. *Andando y pensando* (Madrid: Editorial Páez-Bolsa, 1929), 178.

10. As Robert Spires, *Transparent Simulacra*, 3, points out, many critics have failed to see the radical novelty of *La voluntad*. Spires's own approach is a careful study of narrative voice in the novel.

11. In the 1930 reprinting of *La fuerza del amor*, Azorín explained his archeological method: "A solicitud de amigos, reimprimo esta obra, ya hace mucho tiempo agotada. No pienso ahora como cuando la compuse; la arqueología me parece, al presente, cosa secundaria; pero se han representado desde la fecha de esta comedia otras comedias en que se intenta resucitar la misma época. Y aquí está mi modesta tentativa de reconstrucción; el lector juzgará; a la verdad, en la evocación se ha sacrificado todo en estas páginas; fidelidad en la pintura, he procurado que la haya. No hablo del resto. Como esfuerzo reconstructivo público la obra y no como otra cosa" (*Teatro Moderno* VI (1930): 7, quoted in Mariano de Paco, "*La fuerza del amor*, primera obra dramática de José Martínez Ruiz," *Orbe*, Ateneo Literario de Yecla, Número Homenaje a Azorín (1985): n. p.

12. Robin Fiddian, "Cyclical Time and the Structure of Azorín's *La voluntad*," *Forum for Modern Language Studies* 12 (1976): 163-175, argues that the novel's theme of eternal return is reflected in its structure.

13. *The Poetics of Prose*, 25.

14. See especially Anna Krause, *Azorín, The Little Philosopher*, 195-203. However, in the "Introducción" to his edition of *La voluntad* (Madrid: Castalia, 1982), 38-39, E. Inman Fox asserts that Antonio is Martínez Ruiz.

15. Anna Krause, *Azorín, The Little Philosopher*, and Priscilla Pearsall, "Azorín's *La voluntad* and Nietzsche's 'Schopenhauer as Educator,' " *Romance Notes* 25 (1984): 121-126.

16. Félix Martínez Bonati, *Fictive Discourse and the Structure of Literature*, trans. Philip Silver (Ithaca: Cornell University Press, 1981), especially 31, 32. Thomas Pavel, "The Borders of Fiction," *Poetics Today* 4 (1983): 83-88, discusses

John Searle's distinction between pretended illocutionary acts and the narrator's serious statements (such as Tolstoy's "Happy families are all happy in the same way"), which do not belong to the fictional story. Clearly Martínez Bonati and Searle are talking about the same general categories of narrator's statements.

17. José Martínez Ruiz, *La voluntad*, ed. E. Inman Fox, 75.

18. See Martínez Bonati, 30, for a discussion of the way the characters' speech contrasts to that of the narrator.

19. These passages of dialogue between Yuste and Lasalde, written in dramatic form, may be modeled on Pi y Margall's dialogue "La eterna duda" between Carlos and Eusebio included in *Reflexiones* (Madrid: Hijos de J. A. García, 1901), a copy of which can be found in Azorín's personal library. The subject of the dialogue is the existence of God and the nature of time and permanence, one of Yuste's preoccupations. Eusebio quotes Lucretius on the permanence of matter, but he needs further causal links: "Mas de la materia, me digo, se formaron mundos, y en ellos seres de distinta organización y de diversa índole; ¿Quién o qué pudo así combinar los dispersos átomos?" (88-89), and Carlos rebukes him: "Tu argumentación, querido Eusebio, es en el fondo la de todos los deístas. Lo finito no conduce a la noción de lo infinito, lo temporal a la noción de lo eterno; luego hay el ser eterno e infinito que llamamos Dios. En nosotros, dices tú, hay una razón limitada, luego ha de haber otra sin límites. La consecuencia es, por de pronto, ilógica. De que concibas lo absoluto exista. Tu razón aquí limitada y oscura. ¿Quién te dice que no sea en otros muchos más lúcida y potente? Lo infinito, lo eterno, lo hallas en la misma Naturaleza. ¿Dónde están las lindes del espacio?" (45).

20. Quoted in Santiago Riopérez, *Azorín íntegro* (Madrid: Biblioteca Nueva, 1979), 63.

21. María Martínez del Portal has definitively dispelled any possible speculation on the existence of real letters between Martínez Ruiz and Baroja that were then incorporated into the novel. In "En torno a 'La voluntad'. Una carta de 1902," *Monteagudo* (Universidad de Murcia) 8 (1983): 5-9, she reveals that Martínez Ruiz incorporated into his fictional letters substantial portions of letters that he received from his cousin José Martínez del Portal Martínez, who was notary of Yecla and was able to supply a number of facts about the economic situation of the region.

22. Azorín, *Confesiones de un pequeño filósofo* (Madrid: Caro Raggio, 1920), 156.

5. Unamuno: Last Attack on Rationalism

1. *Niebla*, of course, did have a model in Galdós's *El amigo manso*, an intertextuality penetratingly studied by H. L. Boudreau, "Rewriting Unamuno Rewriting Galdós," unpublished paper circulated for discussion at the meetings of the Midwestern Modern Language Association held in Kansas City, Missouri, in November 1990. Boudreau finds the similarities more in the characters than in the plot. It is interesting to note that Galdós was parodying Krausism in the figure of Máximo Manso.

2. *Ensayos sobre la Generación del '98* (Madrid: Alianza Editorial, 1981).

3. E. Inman Fox, "Introducción," to his edition of José Ortega y Gasset, *Meditaciones sobre la literatura y el arte (La manera española de ver las cosas)* (Madrid: Castalia, 1987), 7-40.

4. *Epistolario completo Ortega-Unamuno*, ed. Laureano Robles (Madrid: Ediciones El Arquero, 1987).

5. José Luis Abellán, "El tema de España en Unamuno y Ortega," *Asomante* 4 (1961), 26-40 and "Ortega ante la presencia de Unamuno" in *Ortega y Gasset en la filosofía española* (Madrid: Tecnos, 1966), 89-106; Pedro Cerezo Galán, *La voluntad de aventura: aproximamiento crítico al pensamiento de Ortega y Gasset* (Barcelona: Ariel, 1984); "Epistolario entre Unamuno y Ortega," *Revista de Occidente*, 2ª serie, 6-7 (1964): 3-28; Manuel Fernández de la Cera, "El epistolario Unamuno-Ortega," *CCMU* 22 (1972): 83-87, 103-118; Manuel García Blanco, "Unamuno y Ortega. Aportación a un tema," in *En torno a Unamuno* (Madrid: Taurus, 1965), 351-60; Paulino Gargorri, "Unamuno y Ortega, frente a frente," *Unamuno, Ortega, Zubiri en la filosofía española* (Madrid: Plenitud, 1968), 170-194; Salvador de Madariaga, *De Galdós a Lorca* (Buenos Aires: Sudamericana, 1960), 111-114, 130-151; Julián Marías, "La generación del '98 y la de Ortega," *Ortega. Circunstancia y vocación* (Madrid: Alianza, 1983), 143-155; Eduardo Ortega y Gasset, "Miguel de Unamuno, José Ortega y Gasset, bióculos de la España actual," in *Monodiálogos de don Miguel de Unamuno* (New York: Ediciones Iberia, 1956), 17-70; Carlos P. Otero, "Lingüística y literatura (a propósito de Unamuno y Ortega)," *Romance Philology* 24 (1970): 307-328; Humberto Piñera, *Unamuno y Ortega y Gasset: Contraste de dos pensadores* (Guerrero, Mexico: Universidad de Nuevo León, 1965); Laureano Robles, *Epistolario completo;* Hugo Rodríguez Alcalá, "Un aspecto del antagonismo de Unamuno y Ortega," *Revista de la Universidad de Buenos Aires* 2 (1957): 267-280; María Scuderi, "Unamuno y Ortega: Aquende o allende los Pirineos," *Cuadernos Americanos* 5 (1965): 129-146; Guillermo de Torre, "Ortega y Unamuno," *Cuadernos Americanos* 8 (1943): 157-176.

6. Mario J. Valdés, "Introducción" to his edition of *Niebla* (Madrid: Cátedra, 1982), 47.

7. Quoted in Geoffrey Ribbans, *Niebla y soledad*, 87, n. 9.

8. Quoted in Miguel de Unamuno, "Almas de jóvenes," *OC* 3, ed. Manuel García Blanco (Barcelona: Vegara, 1958), 722, 723.

9. José Ortega y Gasset, "Unamuno y Europa, fábula" *Ensayos sobre la Generación del '98*, 36-41.

10. Contrary to his usual custom, Unamuno did not mention his work on *Niebla* in correspondence with friends, making it more difficult to trace the vicissitudes of the composition of this novel than any of the others. In a letter of November 10, 1907 (some three months after he began *Niebla*), he wrote to Azorín (*DIWAN*, 67): "Escribo poesías, sí, más que nunca;" there is no mention of the novel, although a poem he includes with the letter is suggestive: "Allá, entre nieblas, / miro como se mira a los castaños / al que fui yo a los veinticinco años." The collected correspondence with Luis Zulueta does not mention the novel, nor does that with Jiménez Ilundain (including letters of dates close to the date he began it: July 29, 1907, to the former and January 16, 1908, to the latter) or that with Nin Frías (July 19, 1907, and July 30, 1908). There is a hiatus in the correspondence

to Maragall between June and December of 1907 and in that to Mugica from 1906 to 1909. In a letter to Mugica on January 29, 1913 (about the time he supposedly finished the novel), he mentions working on plays but nothing of *Niebla*. He was, however, thinking about some of the *Niebla* material between 1907 and 1913, as he published several stories related to it. The main character of "El que se enterró" (*La Nación*, January 1, 1908) talks to his dog about metaphysical problems, and the protagonist of "La beca" published in *Espejo de la muerte* (1913) is named Augusto and evokes the "comerse" ("devorarse") theme.

11. "Epistolario entre Unamuno y Ortega," *Revista de Occidente*, 6.

12. Quoted in Leon Livingstone, "Unamuno and the Aesthetic of the Novel," *Hispania* 24 (1941): 449, from "Unamuno a través de un epistolario inédito," *Obis Catolicus* (Barcelona), 211-212.

13. In a letter of 1909 to Juan Arzadun, Unamuno indicated that he was reading many English novels in the comic vein and mentioned the inexpensive Dent editions. Examples of the English novel's connection to *Niebla* are the following passages Unamuno marked in Dickens's *The Life and Adventures of Martin Chuzzlewit* (London: Dent, 1907): "Pecksniff is an exaggeration; he never existed" (vvii); "the human race is a body, not individuals" (16); "I have character" (40); "universal serf" (41); "process of digestion" (118).

14. Ruth House Webber, "Kierkegaard and the Elaboration of Unamuno's *Niebla*," *Hispanic Review* 32 (1964): 118-134, points out some specific scenes in which Unamuno was inspired by *Either/Or*. Jaime Alazraki, "Motivación e invención en *Niebla* de Unamuno," *Romanic Review* 58 (1967): 242, mentions Kierkegaard as a source of the antirationalism in the novel. And Gemma Roberts *Unamuno: Afinidades y coincidencias kierkegaardianas* (Boulder, Colorado: SSSAS, 1986), 25-77, gives a thorough accounting of the coincidences between Kierkegaard's thought and Unamuno's in *Niebla*.

15. The sentence was underlined by Unamuno in his copy of Giovanni Papini, *Il crepusculo dei filosofi* (Milano: Lombarda, 1906), 66.

16. Letter to Jiménez Ilundain of May 24, 1899, in Hernán Benítez, 293.

17. *Vida de Don Quijote y Sancho*, 4th ed. (Madrid: Renacimiento, 1930), 67. Jaime Alazraki, "Motivación e invención en *Niebla* de Unamuno," and Julián Marías, *Miguel de Unamuno*, trans. Frances M. López-Morillas (Cambridge: Harvard University Press, 1966), 88-94, compare the content of *Niebla* and *Del sentimiento trágico de la vida*, but without noting the dialogizing and comic effect produced when certain of the essays' ideas are embedded in a novel.

18. See my "La teoría del conocimiento y la composición de *Niebla* (*Actas del IX Congreso Internacional de Hispanistas*, Berlin: Ibero-Amerikanisches Institut, 1989), 303-308, for a more complete discussion of the composition of *Niebla* based on a careful examination of the manuscript located in the Casa-Museo Unamuno in Salamanca.

19. Miguel de Unamuno, *Del sentimiento trágico de la vida* (New York: Las Américas, n.d.), 28.

20. The idea of intellectual suicide couched in physiological imagery is an old one with Unamuno. In a letter of 1897 to Juan Arzadun he wrote: "¡Cuánto podría decirte acerca de la terrible auto-consunción del intelectualismo! Hay una enfermedad tremenda del estómago y es aquélla en que, perdido o desnatu-

ralizado el epitelio estomacal, se digiere el estómago a sí mismo y se destruye. No otra cosa es en la conciencia el intelectualismo, del que he de escribir cuando pase la tregua que me he impuesto. Se llega al extraño deleite de ahondar el propio mal, de dilacerar la llaga" (Juan Arzadun, 54), and in the introduction to "Nicodemo, el fariseo": "He llegado a conocer una enfermedad terrible semejante en el orden del espíritu a . . . un estómago, que empieza a digerirse a sí mismo" (*OC* 3, ed. Manuel García Blanco (Barcelona: Vegara, 1958), 126.

21. Original letter of November 27, 1913, located in the Casa-Museo Unamuno.

22. Most of the studies of *Niebla* that deal with its philosophical aspects concentrate on the ontological dimension. I mention only those studies most often cited: Carlos Blanco Aguinaga, "Unamuno's *Niebla:* Existence and the Game of Fiction," *Modern Language Notes* 79 (1964): 188-205, emphasizes the problems of reality and fiction, the "I" and the "other," especially in light of the interview between Unamuno and Augusto; Julián Marías, *Miguel de Unamuno*, also treats the reality/fiction theme; Geoffrey Ribbans, "Estructura y significado de *Niebla*," in *Niebla y soledad*, 108-142, sees the novel's principal theme as the juxtaposition of free will and determinism; Paul R. Olson, "Unamuno's *Niebla:* The Question of the Novel," *Georgia Review* 29 (1975): 652-672, suggests that Unamuno was positing language as the ultimate ontological signifier; Frances W. Weber, "Unamuno's *Niebla:* From Novel to Dream," *PMLA* 88 (1973): 209-218, interprets *Niebla* as Unamuno's attempt to perpetuate his illusory self by turning all reality into fiction. Paul Ilie, *Unamuno: An Existential View of Self and Society* (Madison: University of Wisconsin Press, 1967), 43-47, I believe correctly provides an alternative to Weber's vision of a solipsistic Augusto.

23. Miguel de Unamuno, *Niebla*, ed. Harriet S. Stevens and Ricardo Gullón (Madrid: Taurus, 1982), 67. When Augusto does not see Eugenia in the street, it is because "La niebla espiritual era demasiado densa" (68); see also pp. 69, 70, 72, 159, 178. Paul Olson, "Unamuno's *Niebla*," endows the mist with oedipal significance—the primordial or single source, without specifically linking it up to the idea of *nublo* in *En torno al casticismo*.

24. Unamuno wrote in the margin next to the title "The Viscera" of Henry Havelock Ellis's *Man and Woman: A Study of Human Secondary Sexual Characters* (London: Walter Scott, 1899): "No tiene entrañas."

25. See Tzvetan Todorov, *The Poetics of Prose*, 122-125, for a discussion of this kind of metatextuality. Gayana Jurkevich, "Unamuno's Anectodal Digressions: Practical Joking and Narrative Structure" (*RHM* 35 [1992]: 3-14), summarizes the contributions of other critics to the discussion of the interpolated tales.

26. Unamuno marked the following passage in Isaac Walton's *The Lives of Dr John Donne, Sir Henry Wotton, Mr Richard Hooker, Mr George Herbert, and Dr Robert Sanderson* (London: Walter Scott, 1899), 220: "Jane became so much a Platonic as to fall in love with Mr. Herbert unseen."

27. Unamuno marked the following passage from George Bernard Shaw's *Man and Superman: A Comedy and a Philosophy* (London: Constable, 1906), 53: "Tanner—You think you are the suitor—that you are the pursuer and she the pursued. Fool: it is you who are pursued, the marked down quarry, the destined prey."

28. Alexander Parker, "On the Interpretation of *Niebla*," in *Unamuno: Creator*

and Creation, ed. José Rubia Barcia and M. A. Zeitlin (Berkeley: University of California Press, 1967), 116-138, has given the most sustained critical attention to Orfeo's role, tracing the dog's presence in the novel as a symbol of innocence. But he does not explain the incredible lack of innocence about worldly matters revealed in Orfeo's funeral oration, where he takes up the "word," heretofore the province of men, who are said to lie when they speak (i.e., they are not innocent).

29. Miguel de Unamuno, "Prólogo," to Ramón Turró, *Orígenes del conocimiento: el hambre* (Madrid: Atenea, 1921), 11.

30. Original unpublished letter of November 11, 1916, consulted in the Casa-Museo in Salamanca.

31. Fred Abrams, "Sartre, Unamuno, and the 'Hole Theory,' " *Romance Notes* 5 (1963-64): 6-11, and Arturo Serrano Plaja, "Nausea y niebla," *Revista de Occidente* 76-81 (1969): 295-328, discuss coincidences in the philosophies of Unamuno and Sartre but do not compare the techniques of their philosophical novels.

6. Baroja: Farewell to the Philosophical Novel

1. José Ortega y Gasset, *Ensayos sobre la Generación del '98*, 173.

2. Ibid., 136.

3. See Nelson Orringer, " 'Adán en el Paraíso': Cohen y Ortega," in *Ortega y sus fuentes germánicas* (Madrid: Gredos, 1979), 56-57.

4. See Baroja's "Romanticismos" in *OC* 5 and Ortega's "La ciencia romántica" and "Asamblea para el progreso de las ciencias," both in *OC* 1, for their early positions regarding science. Their modified views can be appreciated in Baroja's *Nuevo tablado de Arlequín* (1917) and in several of Ortega's essays (e.g., *OC* 2: 443; 7: 23).

5. For discussions of the 1925 polemic between Ortega and Baroja, see Donald L. Shaw, "A Reply to 'Dehumanization': Baroja and the Art of the Novel," *Hispanic Review* 25 (1957): 105-111, and Carmen Iglesias, "La controversia entre Baroja y Ortega acerca de la novela," in *Pío Baroja* (Madrid: Taurus, 1974), 251-261.

6. *Ensayos sobre la Generación de '98*, 173, 170.

7. Fernando Salmerón, *Las mocedades de Ortega y Gasset* (Mexico: Universidad Nacional Autónoma, 1971), 162.

8. See Nelson Orringer, " 'Adan en el Paraíso'."

9. Pío Baroja, *El árbol de la ciencia*, 5th ed. (Madrid: Alianza Editorial, 1974), 96.

10. A. M. Vásquez Bigi in his *El árbol de la ciencia: Guía para acercarnos a Baroja y El árbol de la ciencia* (New York: Las Américas Publishing Co., 1968), 53, indicates that Iturrioz's statement is from *Wille zur Machte*, which appeared in French in 1903.

11. Ciriaco Morón Arroyo, *El sistema de Ortega y Gasset* (Madrid: Alcalá, 1968), 102, qualifies what most other critics of Ortega agree are the seeds of rationalism in *Meditaciones*, but he does not deny that they are present in that work. Carmen Iglesias, 67, finds that Baroja's philosophical attitude in general approaches Ortega's ratio-vitalism: "Baroja nos aparece como un neo-vitalista o, tal vez, más

cerca aun del ratio-vitalismo de Ortega y Gasset, con la diferencia de que en éste es el resultado y síntesis de las teorías de nuestro tiempo, expresadas y sentidas a través de su rigurosa formación filosófica, mientras que en Baroja, no es más que un impulso espontáneo y sostenido, aunque sin base teórica." I hope I have shown that Baroja's impulse was much less spontaneous and much more theoretically based than she supposes.

12. *Ensayos sobre la Generación del '98*, 110.

13. "Un hombre no es un astro en medio de otros astros; cuando un individuo es fuerte, su energía se extravea e influye en los demás" (Pío Baroja, *OC* 2: 252).

14. Orringer, *Ortega y sus fuentes*, 61, flags part of Ortega's 1910 essay as original, pointing the way to his later philosophy when he subjects science and morality as well as art to the dominion of human life as a first principle: "La gravitación universal, el universal dolor, la materia inorgánica, las series orgánicas, la historia entera del hombre, sus ansias, sus exulataciones . . . lo corporal y lo espiritual . . . todo gravitando sobre él . . . corazón de Adán. ¿Se comprende todo lo que significa . . . todo eso que expresamos con una palabra de contornos infinitos, VIDA . . . ?" (*OC* 1: 480). Paradise in this essay is not yet the *circunstancia* as Ortega understood it in his mature work; it is, rather, all the problems that confront the individual in searching for his consciousness. From this position he arrived at the notion of the problem of life as the problem of the human subject who tries to realize himself in his immediate circumstance. Adam as a symbol of the deficient consciousness disappears, just as Paradise, the symbol of the universe of which we must gain consciousness, disappears. The tripartite orientation (natural science, moral science and art) is replaced by a plurality of persepctives on the problem of existence.

15. *Ensayos sobre la Generación del '98*, 96, 100-101.

16. Ibid., 105.

17. See Orringer, *Ortega y sus fuentes*, 72.

7. The Generation of '14: Taking the Lead

1. In employing the name "Generation of 1914," I prefer Gonzalo Sobejano's designation, rather than the "Novecentistas" applied by Guillermo Díaz Plaja. Sobejano understands the 1914 the way I do—as a distancing from the '98: "La generación de 1914 se aleja de los procedimientos impresionistas: novela de acción (Baroja) y pasión (Unamuno), estética modernista, costumbrismo escénico. Sigue a su predecesora en la repulsa del parlamentarismo, la democracia y el socialismo, y prefiere la admonición a la patria (e incluso su 'castigo' teórico) a una compenetración piadosa o cruel con sus desgracias. Los nuevos escritores no son supersticiosos del esteticismo ni moralistas. Son razonadores glosadores del panorama vital, tanteadores de rutas, experimentadores, ensayistas; o narradores propensos a la ideación, el poema y el mito; o poetas absolutos; o juglares de todas las cosas. Ya no es el binomio inspirador 'Historia—Vida', como para sus padres, sino 'Vida-Razón' (*Nietzsche en España*, 494).

2. The following are a few examples of serious essays by the '14 on '98 writers: Juan Ramón Jiménez wrote a review of Martínez Ruiz's *Antonio Azorín* in *Helios* (no. 4 [July 1903]: 497), and Gregorio Martínez Sierra reviewed the same book

in the March 1904 issue of that journal (277). Ortega's first book, as I have noted, began a meditation on Azorín and Baroja. Pérez de Ayala wrote enough articles on Azorín to comprise an entire volume, *Ante Azorín,* and Gabriel Miró also wrote on his Alicantine compatriot.

    3. José Ortega y Gasset, *Ensayos sobre la Generación del '98,* 58.

    4. Guillermo de Torre affirms that: "Con *Prometeo* (1908), de Ramón Gómez de la Serna, se inicia ya otra época, una generación que aun viviendo marginalmente, en lo poético, de los rescoldos modernistas y noventaiochistas, inaugura distintos rumbos" (*Del 98 al Barroco* [Madrid: Gredos, 1969], 23). Ramón Gómez de la Serna himself took stock of the new generation in the sixth issue of April 1909 in his article "El concepto de la nueva literatura."

    5. Edmund L. King, "Azorín y Miró: Historia de una amistad," *Boletín de la Asociación Europea de Profesores de Español* 5 (1973): 87-105, carefully chronicles the evidence of Azorín's early disdain for the younger man, effectively countering the many studies that link them as friends and mentor/disciple. Azorín did, of course, make valiant attempts to get Miró elected to the Royal Spanish Academy in later years.

    6. Quoted in Ángeles Prado, "Seudónimos tempranos de Pérez de Ayala," *Ínsula* 35, nos. 404-405 (1980): 18.

    7. Ramón Gómez de la Serna, "In memoriam," to his edition of Silverio Lanza, *Páginas escogidas e inéditas* (Madrid: Biblioteca Nueva, 1917).

    8. Quoted in Víctor García de la Concha, *Los senderos poéticos de Ramón Pérez de Ayala* (Universidad de Oviedo, 1970), 20.

    9. María Zambrano, "Política revolucionaria," quoted in Soledad Ortega, "María Zambrano: Tres cartas de juventud a Ortega y Gasset," *Revista de Occidente* 120 (1991): 9. Zambrano ("Presencia de don Miguel," *Diario 16,* December 28, 1986), while ostensibly admiring Unamuno, mentioned his ability (despite his medium stature) to physically dominate any scene merely by his demeanor and insistent talking; she commented on Ortega's negative reaction to Unamuno's domineering presence (which she subtly suggested could have been due partly to Ortega's own penchant for talking). While very much a part of Ortega's circle in the late 1920s and early 1930s, María Zambrano's books were published, for the most part, after she left Spain in 1936, and so she, regrettably falls outside this study.

    10. Susan Nagel, *The Influence of the Novels of Jean Giraudoux on the Hispanic Vanguard Novels of the 1920s-1930s* (Lewisburg: Bucknell University Press, 1991) argues that Jean Giraudoux was more important to the aesthetics of the Spanish vanguard novel than were the aesthetics of José Ortega y Gasset.

    11. Ramón Pérez de Ayala, "Carta a Unamuno" [written in 1912 from Munich], reproduced in Andrés Amorós, *La novela intelectual de Ramón Pérez de Ayala* (Madrid: Gredos, 1972), 468.

    12. Benjamín Jarnés, *Feria del libro* (Madrid: Espasa-Calpe, 1935), 101, indicated the nature of Ortega's intellectual leadership: "Según atinadamente ha observado Fernando Vela, la conversación con Ortega *siempre resulta rica, fértil, superabundante.* Ortega pertenece—añade—*a ese linaje, muy continuado en España, de los hombres que influyen más por su palabra hablada, en la conversación, que por su palabra escrita, en el libro, aun siendo ésta tan enormemente operante*" (Jarnes's emphasis).

13. Ramón Gómez de la Serna, "Prólogo," to *El hombre perdido* (Buenos Aires: Editorial Poseidon, 1947), 9.

14. Brenton Campbell, "Free Will and Determinism in the Theory of Tragedy: Pérez de Ayala and Ortega y Gasset," *Hispanic Review* 37 (1969), 376, suggests that the *Meditaciones* may have been a reaction to the material on the tragic hero in *Troteras y danzaderas*.

15. Benjamín Jarnés, *Locura y muerte de nadie* (Madrid: Ediciones Oriente, 1919), 56.

16. Benjamín Jarnés, *Teoría del zumbel* (Madrid: Espasa-Calpe, 1930), 144.

17. "Los sueños de María Zambrano," *Revista de Occidente* 2ª serie 12 (1966): 208.

18. Some youthful letters very recently published by Soledad Ortega from Zambrano to "Don José" (see note 9) reveal even more clearly her ambivalent feelings toward her mentor, alternately scolding him for what she perceived as his political conservatism and obsequiously asserting that she has no differences with him when a published review indicates that she did. She indicated in an interview that she was deeply hurt when Ortega failed to appreciate what she was attempting to do in "Hacia un saber sobre el alma" (see Antonio Colinas, "Sobre la iniciación [Conversación con María Zambrano]," in *El sentido primero de la palabra poética* [Mexico: Fondo de Cultura Económica, 1989], 282).

19. Jarnés, "Prólogo," *Teoría del zumbel*, 144.

20. Ramón Gómez de la Serna, *Automoribundia, 1888-1948* (Buenos Aires: Sudamericana, 1948), 414.

21. Ibid., 415.

22. Ramón Gómez de la Serna, *Flor de greguerías* (Madrid: Espasa-Calpe, 1933), 29. While I do not dedicate a full analysis to any of Gómez de la Serna's novels because they are not philosophical in the way that I have been defining the philosophical novel in this study, he is fundamental to the dynamics of the Generation of 1914.

8. Pérez de Ayala: Parody Wed to Aesthetic Theory

1. Most often seen in terms of the Generation of '98 are *Trece dioses* (1902) and the tetralogy *Tinieblas en las cumbres* (1907), *A.M.G.D.* (1909), *La pata de la raposa* (1911) and *Troteras y danzaderas* (1912). I rely on Geraldine M. Scanlon for the content of *Trece dioses*, which originally appeared in a now difficult-to-find journal and which was not included in the complete works. Scanlon, who is editing this early work for publication, indicates that it is an imitation of Ramón del Valle-Inclán's *Sonata de otoño* ("*Trece dioses*: Novela perdida de Pérez de Ayala," *Ínsula* 503 [1988]: 28).

2. Donald Shaw, "Concerning the Ideology of Ramón Pérez de Ayala," *Modern Language Quarterly* 22 (1961): 158-166, places Pérez de Ayala within the '98 ideology, seeing in his early work a beginning of the decline of the '98 sensibility, but Carlos Longhurst, "Sobre la originalidad de 'Tinieblas en las cumbres,'" *Ínsula* 35, nos. 404-405 (1980): 5, points out that *Tinieblas en las cumbres*, while appearing only five years after the seminal 1902 novels of the Generation of '98,

already introduces a parodic stance vis-à-vis the *fin-de-siècle* crisis mentality. Other critics, to whom I refer later, also point to isolated incidences of Pérez de Ayala's incorporation of '98 figures and characters into his novels, but without seeing in the practice, as I do here, an important distancing from the previous generation.

3. "La confianza en sí mismo," *Nuevo Mundo* (November 19, 1914) quoted in Agustín Coletes Blanco, *Gran Bretaña y los Estados Unidos en la vida de Ramón Pérez de Ayala* (Oviedo: IDEA, 1984), 198.

4. *Pequeños ensayos* (Madrid: Biblioteca Nueva, 1963), quoted in ibid.

5. Published in *El Gráfico* (June 14, 1904) and reprinted in *OC* 1: 171.

6. Ángeles Prado, "Seudónimos tempranos de Pérez de Ayala," 1.

7. Ramón Pérez de Ayala, *Ante Azorín* (Madrid: Biblioteca Nueva, 1964): 103. For a more complete assessment of Azorín's presence in all Pérez de Ayala's work see Miguel Ángel Lozano, "Azorín en la obra literaria de Ramón Pérez de Ayala," *La literatura como intensidad* (Alicante: Caja de Ahorros, 1988), 97-115.

8. Ramón Pérez de Ayala, *Cincuenta años de cartas íntimas 1904-1956 a su amigo Miguel Rodríguez-Acosta*, ed. Andrés Amorós (Madrid: Castalia, 1980), 54. The letter is dated September 28, 1905.

9. *Ante Azorín*, 77.

10. Donald L. Fabian, "Action and Idea in *Amor y pedagogía* and *Prometeo*," *Hispania* 41 (1958): 29-34. The borrowing goes even further than Fabian indicates, as Unamuno quoted verses from Shelley's *Prometheus Unbound* in his 1902 novel.

11. J. J. Macklin, *The Window and the Garden: The Modernist Fictions of Ramón Pérez de Ayala* (Boulder, Colorado: SSSAS, 1988), 140, points out that *Tinieblas* is a parody of the '98 intellectual crisis, and Carlos Longhurst, "Sobre la originalidad," considers Pérez de Ayala in the 1907 novel to have antedated Baroja's philosophical dialogues in *El árbol de la ciencia* (he overlooks the earlier Baroja precedent in *Camino de perfección*).

12. The language used to evoke existential malaise in *Tinieblas* is so similar to Unamuno's in *Niebla* that it could even be a source for Unamuno's novel, especially in light of its beginning and other coincidences such as the Unamunian angst that Alberto expresses over the form in which we survive the earthly life (as the fog becomes ever more dense about the mountain top). Carlos Longhurst, "Sobre la originalidad," mentions the similarities in title but was apparently unaware that Unamuno began the novel in 1907, the same year *Tinieblas* was published.

13. See Andrés Amorós, *Vida y literatura en 'Troteras y danzaderas'* (Madrid: Castalia, 1973), for a full accounting of the transformation of Perez de Ayala's friends and acquaintances into characters in the novel.

14. See Robert Spires's splendid analysis of the way poetry and narrative interact in *La caída de los limones* in his *Transparent Simulacra*, 57-72.

15. J. J. Macklin, "Myth and Meaning in Pérez de Ayala's *Prometeo*," *Belfast Spanish and Portuguese Papers* (1979): 86, and Donald Fabian, "Action and Idea," 31, both point out the similarity between Marco's conversations with his uncle and those of Andrés Hurtado and Iturrioz, but without signaling the parodic element that I find in Pérez de Ayala's "imitation" of Baroja.

16. I am indebted for this insight to Nelson Orringer, who has written a very interesting paper, "Pérez de Ayala's *Prometeo*: The Failure of the Generation of

1914," delivered at a special session on Pérez de Ayala at the 1980 MLA meetings but lamentably never published.

17. J. J. Macklin, "Myth and Meaning," points out the Teiresias-Unamuno connection, but once again, does not find any element of parody in the caricature.

18. Ramón Pérez de Ayala, *Belarmino y Apolonio*, ed. Andrés Amorós (Madrid: Cátedra, 1982), 91.

19. Frances Wyers Weber, *The Literary Perspectivism of Ramón Pérez de Ayala* (Chapel Hill: University of North Carolina Press, 1966); Andrés Amorós, *La novela intelectual de Ramón Pérez de Ayala;* and Leon Livingstone, "Interior Duplication and the Problem of Form in the Modern Spanish Novel," *PMLA* 73 (1958): 404-405, among others, see in the "Rúa Ruera vista desde dos lados" chapter, as well as in the structure of the novel, which alternates several points of view, an adherence to Ortega's notion of *perspectivismo*. I am suggesting, however, that *Belarmino y Apolonio* is an elaborate play on Ortega's philosophy and aesthetics that parodies his ideas by example.

20. Sara Suárez Solís (*Análisis de 'Belarmino y Apolonio'* [Oviedo: Instituto de Etudios Asturianos, 1974], 50) has noted that Pérez de Ayala may have been influenced by Unamuno in the creation of Lario, but she does not notice that each character has Unamunian characteristics, thus embodying in a parodic fashion the Rector of Salamanca's evolving philosophical position.

21. The importance of the thematics of language has not gone unnoticed in the criticism of *Belarmino y Apolonio*, but interestingly, all the studies of language in the novel (listed below) concentrate on Belarmino's language without seeing it as part of a novelistic whole, one linguistic system countered by a second practiced by the other eponymous character. M. K. Read ("*Belarmino y Apolonio* and the Modern Linguistic Tradition," *BHS* 55 [1978]: 329-335), however, does trace two major philosophical traditions in the language of Belarmino (idealistic) and Padre Alesón (positivistic). Read also draws some interesting parallels between Belarmino's attitude toward language and Unamuno's. Other studies of language in *Belarmino y Apolonio* include Carla Cordúa de Torretti, "Belarmino: Hablar y Pensar," *La Torre* 32 (1960): 43-60, who sees Belarmino's language as Pérez de Ayala's affirmation that language and thought are inseparable. Carlos Clavería, "Apostillas al lenguaje de Belarmino," *Cinco estudios de la literatura moderna* (Salamanca, 1945), 71-79, attributes Pérez de Ayala's inspiration for Belarmino's language to Max Müller, among others, a thesis which he amplifies in "Apostillas adicionales a *Belarmino y Apolonio* de Ramón Pérez de Ayala," *HR* 16 (1948): 340-345, by pointing out that Pérez de Ayala could have been introduced to Müller's linguistic ideas through his mentor Julio Cejador y Frauca.

22. Cordúa de Torretti, "Belarmino," 53, quotes Heidegger's distinction between speech and talk to illuminate Belarmino's attitude toward language.

9. Juan Ramón Jiménez and Gabriel Miró: *Künstlerromane*

1. The issue of genre here is a thorny one, and I have chosen to include these works in a book on philosophy and the novel because they are long narratives with a central character or consciousness that foreground philosophical ideas. They also allow me to discuss two authors of the second generation whose themes

and practices link up in important ways with the younger novelists of their generation. Juan Ramón wrote very little narrative prose, and Gabriel Miró, while almost exclusively a narrator, did not write philosophy into his more novelistic narratives in the way I have been focusing on here. *Las cerezas del cementerio* and *El abuelo del rey* embody the Nietzschean notion of eternal return, but in a thoroughly narrative rather than narrative-discursive manner. *Nuestro Padre San Daniel* and *El obispo leproso* incorporate ideas on perception and language that I discuss here, but again subordinating philosophy to narrative. Others of Miró's books that use narrative to explore philosophical issues more overtly (*Libro de Sigüenza, El ángel, el molino, el caracol del faro* and *Años y leguas*) are even less akin to the novel than *El humo dormido*. For a full discussion of these works' philosophical dimensions, consult my *El ser y la palabra en Gabriel Miró* (Madrid: Fundamentos, 1985). I have never seen *El humo dormido* referred to as a novel, but Richard Cardwell, in the "Introducción" to his edition of *Platero y yo* (Madrid: Espasa-Calpe, 1988), 27, calls Juan Ramón Jiménez's most famous prose work "una moderna 'novela ejemplar,' " and J. Urrutia, "Sobre la práctica prosística de Juan Ramón Jiménez y sobre el genéro de 'Platero y yo,' *Cuadernos Hispanoamericanos*, 376-78 (1981): 728, creates a separate narrative category for it: "relato poético . . . género parecido a la *novela lírica*, pero no idéntico." Julián Marías, "*Platero y yo* o la soledad comunicada," *Juan Ramón Jiménez*, ed. Aurora Albornoz (Madrid: Taurus, 1981), 198, declares that *Platero y yo* "pertenece a esa serie de exploraciones que nuestro tiempo hace en torno a la representación imaginativa de la vida humana y por tanto de su mundo; gravita hacia lo que en un sentido muy alto podríamos llamar 'novela', justamente como intento de escapar a lo que tradicionalmente había sido: Proust, Joyce, Kafka, Unamuno, Valle-Inclán, Ramón Gómez de la Serna, Faulkner, Wilde."

2. Edmund L. King, "Introduction," to his edition of *El humo dormido* (New York: Dell, 1967), 43.

3. *Gabriel Miró: His Private Library and Literary Background* (London: Tamesis, 1975), 146-155.

4. Ramón del Valle-Inclán, *La lampara maravillosa* (Madrid: Helénica, 1916), 12. *La lámpara*, which contains sections in an autobiographical mode, might also be considered a *Künstlerroman*, but its discursive passages outnumber the narrative ones, and thus a full analysis of it remains outside the scope of this study. Carol Maier, "¿Palabras de armonía?: Reflexiones sobre la lectura, los límites y la estética de Valle-Inclán," *Estelas, laberintos, nuevas sendas: Unamuno, Valle Inclán, García Lorca, La Guerra Civil* (Barcelona: Áthropos, 1988), 151-170, analyzes the use of voice in the work in a way that illuminates its narrative affinities to both *Platero y yo* and *El humo dormido*.

5. Leo Cole, *The Religious Instinct in the Poetry of Juan Ramón Jiménez* (Oxford: Dolphin, 1967), 19. Other passages of interest to the topic of Juan Ramón and language are found on pp. 39-40, 54 and 59.

6. *Word and Work in the Poetry of Juan Ramón Jiménez* (London: Tamesis, 1982), 26, 27, 37, discusses Juan Ramón's reading in Nietzsche, the Vienna Circle and Wittgenstein, respectively.

7. See my "The Genesis of Gabriel Miró's Ideas about Being and Language: The Barcelona Period," *RCEH* 8 (1984): 183-205, and *El ser y la palabra en Gabriel*

Miró for further speculations on the origins of Miró's ideas on language and their affinities with the phenomenology of Heidegger and Merleau-Ponty.

8. See Michael Predmore, "Introducción" to his edition of *Platero y yo* (Madrid: Cátedra, 1983), 11-70, and Richard Cardwell, "Introducción," *Platero y yo; Juan Ramón Jiménez: The Modernist Apprenticeship 1895-1900;* and " 'The Universal Andalusian', 'The Zealous Andalusian' and 'The Andalusian Elegy,' " *Studies in Twentieth Century Literature* 7 (1983): 201-204, for discussions of Juan Ramón and Krausism, particularly in *Platero*.

9. For a discussion of Juan Ramón and Ortega, see Richard Cardwell, "Juan Ramón, Ortega y los intelectuales," *Hispanic Review* 53 (1985): 329-350.

10. Richard Cardwell in the introduction to his edition of *Platero* indicates that Juan Ramón began writing it in late 1905 or early 1906 after returning to Moguer from Madrid and revised it between 1912 and 1914, when the first abridged version was published. (Predmore's article on *Platero* in *STCL* adds that the book was essentially complete in 1907 and mistakenly gives the first complete publication date as 1916). In 1917 Juan Ramón added an epilogue and published a complete version. Michael Predmore's introduction follows the same dates of composition (focusing on 1906 as the year Juan Ramon began it).

11. María Luisa Amigo, *Poesía y filosofía en Juan Ramón Jiménez* (Córdoba: Universidad de Deusto, 1987), 111-117, discusses *Eternidades* in terms of a Heideggerian view of language.

12. Marta Altisent, "Un narratario insólito: Platero (Diálogo interior y presencia del narratario en *Platero y yo*)," *Explicación de Textos Literarios* 14 (1985-86): 89-103, concentrates on Platero as narratee and does not observe that Platero is not always the audience for the poet's reflections. Myriam Najt and María Victoria Reyzabal, "Colaboradores y oponentes del 'yo' poético en 'Platero y yo,' " *Cuadernos Hispanoamericanos* 105 (1981): 748-767, argue that Platero and the poet are one and the same.

13. Pierre Ullman, "La estructura epifánica de *Platero y yo*," *Crítica Hispánica* 9 (1987): 1-29, calls the last type of narrative passage epiphanic moments.

14. Juan Ramón Jiménez, *Platero y yo*, ed. Michael P. Predmore (Madrid: Cátedra, 1983), 90.

15. Gabriel Miró, *El humo dormido*, ed. Edmund L. King (Alicante: Instituto de Cultura Juan Gil-Albert, 1991), 55.

16. Ramón Gómez de la Serna, "Prólogo," to John Ruskin, *Las piedras de Venecia*, trans. Carmen de Burgos (Valencia: F. Sempere, n.d.), 50. (I calculate the date of publication to be shortly after 1910, based on advertising for other publications included at the end of the volume.)

17. Miguel de Unamuno, "Introducción," to Gabriel Miró, *Cerezas del cementerio* (Madrid: Edición Conmemorativa emprendida por los 'Amigos de Gabriel Miró,' 1941), ix-xvi.

18. Jiménez García, *El krausismo*, 84, quotes Krause (1889, 5-6) on history: "la filosofía de la historia no es el conocimiento de lo que sucede individualmente como tal, sino más bien el conocimiento de la esencia no sensible y eterna, y de las leyes eternas del despliegue de la vida en el tiempo."

19. Vicente Ramos, *Rafael Altamira* (Madrid-Barcelona: Alfaguara, 1968), 107, quotes Rafael Altamira, *Mi primera campaña* (Madrid, 1893), 131.

20. Ruskin's essay "The Lamp of Truth" as well as Valle's *La lámpara maravillosa* ("la lámpara que se enciende para conocer [la belleza]," 14) may be echoed in this passage.

21. Lee Fontanella ("La estética de las tablas y estampas de *El humo dormido*," in *Homenaje a Gabriel Miró* [Alicante: Caja de Ahorros Provincial, 1979], 209-224) in an otherwise useful study fails to see the relation of the "Tablas" to the rest of the book, asserting that "Probablemente por su temática especial, se destacan estas tablas y estampas como asunto aparte" (211).

22. For a more comprehensive analysis of voice and genre in this work, please see my article "Voice and Genre in Gabriel Miró's *El humo dormido*," *Selected Proceedings of the Mid-America Conference on Hispanic Literature* (Lincoln, Nebraska: SSSAS, 1986), 41-51.

10. Salinas, Chacel, and Jarnés: The Vanguardist Philosophical Novel

1. Víctor Fuentes, "El profesor inútil: Un antecedente olvidado de la nueva novela actual," *España Contemporánea* 1 (1988): 24.

2. Salinas's *Víspera del gozo* and Jarnés's *El profesor inútil* (both of 1926) were published in the series, and Chacel aspired to publish *Estación. Ida y vuelta* (written in 1925-26) in Nova Novorum, but the series ended before it could be accomplished.

3. Salinas translated Proust; Chacel recognized Proust and Joyce as her closest models, and Jarnés wrote numerous reviews of European writers including laudatory ones of Giraudoux.

4. *Cuadernos literarios* (Madrid, 1927), 35, quoted in Darío Villanueva, *La novela lírica* 1 (Madrid: Taurus, 1983): 12. Gustavo Pérez Firmat, *Idle Fictions: The Hispanic Vanguard Novel, 1926-1934* (Durham, N.C.: Duke University Press, 1982), pp. 40-63, aptly terms the new approach "A Pneumatic Aesthetics."

5. "El novelista en la novela," *Revista de Occidente*, 1ª serie 42 (1933): 232.

6. Ibid., 231.

7. (Baltimore: Johns Hopkins University Press, 1940), 3, 5.

8. *El espectador* VIII, quoted by Benjamín Jarnés, *Feria del libro*, 102.

9. Ibid.

10. Jarnés's *Feria del libro* article emphasizes that life "*consiste siempre en un ocuparnos con las cosas en torno, con el mundo en derredor: vivir es ver, oír, pensar en esto o en lo otro, amar y odiar a los demás, desear uno u otro objecto*" (102, Jarnés's italics).

11. Pedro Salinas, *Reality and the Poet*, 29. Jarnés wrote of Gabriel Miró that "Esto explica bien su pasión por cada palabra, siempre virgen para él. Su trato con ella nunca es familiar, como el del artesano o el del *profesional* de la novela. Es íntimo, como de poeta, como de amante" (*Feria del libro*, 72).

12. Pedro Salinas, "Defensa del lenguaje," *Ensayos completos* ed. Solita Salinas de Marichal (Madrid: Taurus, 1981), 2: 420. Salinas quoted Stenzel's *Filosofía del lenguaje* extensively in this essay on language, but he was already familiar with many of the ideas through reading Miró.

13. Ibid., 423.

14. Salinas wrote only two other narrative works: *La bomba increíble* (1950), a kind of science fiction novel, and *El desnudo impecable* (1951), both of which fall outside this study for reasons of chronology and thematics.

15. Gustavo Pérez Firmat, *Idle Fictions*, 67-74, restricts his analysis to "Mundo cerrado," and Robert Spires, *Transparent Simulacra*, 130-145 takes up "Mundo cerrado," "Cita de los tres," and "Aurora de verdad." Spires has also published an article on "Aurora de verdad" linking it to a story in Salinas's *El desnudo impecable y otras narraciones* (1951) ("Realidad prosaica e imaginación transcendente en dos cuentos de Pedro Salinas," *Pedro Salinas*, ed. Andrew P. Debicki [Madrid: Taurus, 1976], 249-257). Both critics concentrate on the reality/fiction duality in the vignettes they study. Susan Nagel, *The Influence*, 79-86, discusses the influence of Jean Giraudoux's novelistic practices in six of the segments, ignoring "Delirios del chopo y el cipres." Carlos Feal Deibe offers a psychoanalytic interpretation of Salinas's first book of narrations in "La amada de verdad y la incompleta en dos narraciones de Pedro Salinas," *RHM* 44 (1991): 48-58, and "Lo real, lo imaginario y lo simbólico en *Víspera del gozo* de Pedro Salinas," *MLN* 106 (1991): 314-329.

16. Pedro Salinas, *Víspera del gozo* (Madrid: Revista de Occidente, 1926), 76.

17. Rosa Chacel, "Respuesta a Ortega," *Sur* 241 (1956): 104.

18. Ana María Moix, "Rosa Chacel," *24 / 24* (Barcelona: Ediciones Península, 1972), 145, quoted in Shirley Mangini, "Introducción" to her edition of *Estación. Ida y vuelta* (Madrid: Cátedra, 1989), 27.

19. Teresa Bordons and Susan Kirkpatrick, "Chacel's *Teresa* and Ortega's Canon," (*Anales de la Literatura Española Contemporánea* 17 [1992]: 283) cites Chacel's discomfort when she attended the Ortega *tertulias* as characteristic of "the relation of her writing to the novelistic canon." *Estación* was composed before she had had personal contact with Ortega, but in that work she was already asserting her independence from the dominant male intellectual of the period.

20. Rosa Chacel, *Estación. Ida y vuelta*, ed. Shirley Mangini (Madrid: Cátedra, 1989), 107.

21. See Rosa Chacel, "Sendas perdidas de la Generación del '27," *Cuadernos Hispanoamericanos* 318 (1976): 16, and Rosa Chacel, "Noticia," which prefaced the 1974 edition of *Estación. Ida y vuelta* reproduced in Shirley Mangini's edition, 71-81 (the passage on *Platero y yo* is found on 76-79).

22. *Héroe (Poesía)* 2 (Madrid: Impresores Concha Méndez y Manuel Altolaguirre, n.p.

23. Quoted in Jorge Urrutia, "Sobre la práctica prosística de Juan Ramón Jiménez," 726.

24. When she received the Premio Nacional de las Letras Españolas in 1987, Chacel proclaimed herself a disciple of Joyce and Gómez de la Serna (*El País* [November 18, 1987]), apparently forgetting her earlier declarations of allegience to Ortega. She also compared her style to that of Benjamín Jarnés ("Sendas perdidas de la Generación del '27," 27).

25. Unamuno is perhaps the author who received the most critical attention from Jarnés. He published an article on him in *Romance*, devoted pages 55-62 of

Feria del libro to an "Homenaje a Miguel de Unamuno," and edited two collections of selected works of the Rector of Salamanca with extensive prologues to each. One prologue entitled "Preámbulo. Un lírico de acción," precedes Miguel de Unamuno, *Páginas líricas* (Mexico: Ediciones Mensaje, 1943), and "Introducción," prefaces *Miguel de Unamuno* (Mexico: Secretaria de Educación Pública, 1947).

26. *Romance* 1 (1940): 1.

27. Ibid.

28. Miguel de Unamuno, "Vida y arte," *Helios* 2 (1903): 47.

29. The isssue apparently does not come up in several articles Unamuno wrote on Jarnés in early 1935. I have not been able to locate these; they are not collected anywhere, and they do not appear in the journals in which Unamuno most frequently published in the thirties, but Jarnés wrote to Unamuno on February 22, 1935, thanking him for his "admirables artículos" on his work and graciously accepting Unamuno's *discrepancias* (underlined in Jarnés's letter). The letters from Jarnés to Unamuno are located in the Casa-Museo Unamuno in Salamanca.

30. See especially "El novelista en la novela," 231.

31. Benjamín Jarnés, *Cartas al Ebro* (Mexico: La Casa de España en México, 1940), 145, 120.

32. Benjamín Jarnés, *El profesor inútil* (Madrid: Espasa-Calpe, 1934), 237. Further references to the second version of the novel are from the same edition

33. Benjamín Jarnés, *El profesor inútil* (Madrid: Revista de Occidente, 1926), 11. Further references to the first version of the novel are from the same edition.

34. *Feria del libro*, 110.

35. Ibid., 57.

36. Ibid., 58.

37. Curiously, all the interpretations of *El profesor inútil* are based on the 1934 version; no one has made a thorough comparison of the two versions.

38. Miguel de Unamuno, *Cómo se hace una novela*, ed. Paul R. Olson (Madrid: Ediciones Guadarrama, 1977), 59.

39. "Vida y literatura en 'Teoría del zumbel,' " *RHM* 63 (1990): 44.

SELECTED BIBLIOGRAPHY

Abbott, James H. "Azorín and Taine's Determinism." *Hispania* 46 (1963): 476-479.

Abellán, José Luis. "El tema de España en Unamuno y Ortega." *Asomante* 4 (1961): 26-40.

———. *Historia crítica del pensamiento español.* 5 vols. Madrid: Espasa-Calpe, 1984.

———. "Ortega ante la presencia de Unamuno." *Ortega y Gasset en la filosofía española.* Madrid: Tecnos, 1966. 89-106.

Abrams, Fred. "Sartre, Unamuno, and the 'Hole Theory.'" *Romance Notes* 5 (1963-64): 6-11.

Alas, Adolfo, ed. *Epistolario a Clarín.* Madrid: Escorial, 1941.

Alas, Leopoldo. *Páginas escogidas.* ed. Azorín. Madrid: Calleja, 1917.

———. *Solos.* 4th ed. Madrid: Fernando Fe, 1891.

Alazraki, Jaime. "Motivación e invención en *Niebla* de Unamuno." *Romanic Review* 58 (1967): 241-253.

Alberich, José. *Los ingleses y otros temas de Pío Baroja.* Madrid: Alfaguara, 1966.

Altisent, Marta. "Un narratario insólito: Platero (Diálogo interior y presencia del narratario en *Platero y yo*)." *Explicación de textos literarios* 14 (1985-86): 89-103.

Amigo, María Luisa. *Poesía y filosofía en Juan Ramón Jiménez.* Córdoba: Universidad de Deusto, 1987.

Amorós, Andrés. *La Novela intelectual de Ramón Pérez de Ayala.* Madrid: Gredos, 1972.

———. *Vida y literatura en 'Troteras y danzaderas'.* Madrid: Castalia, 1973.

Aranguren, José Luis. "Los sueños de María Zambrano." *Revista de Occidente* 2ª serie 12 (1966): 207-212.

Arbó, Sebastián Juan. *Pío Baroja y su tiempo.* Barcelona: Editorial Planeta, 1963.

Areilza, Dr. [Enrique]. *Epistolario.* Ed. José María de Areilza. Bilbao: El Cofre del Bilbaíno, 1964.

Ares Montes, José. " 'Camino de perfección,' o las peregrinaciones de Pío Baroja y Fernando Ossorio." *Cuadernos Hispanoamericanos* 267 (1972): 481-516.

Arzadun, Juan. "Miguel de Unamuno, íntimo: Al margen de sus cartas." *Sur* 14 (1944): 33-61, 55-70.

Auladell, Miguel A., Ramón F. Llorens, Juan A. Ríos and Ma. Dolores Fuentes. "Textos olvidados del joven Martínez Ruiz." *Canelobre* 9 (1987): 37-40.

Azorín [José Martínez Ruiz]. *Andando y pensando.* Madrid: Editorial Páez-Bolsa, 1929.

———. *Confesiones de un pequeño filósofo.* Madrid: Caro Raggio, 1920.

————. *Obras completas.* Ed. Ángel Cruz Rueda. Madrid: M. Aguilar, 1947-1954.

Bakhtin, Mikhail. *The Dialogic Imagination.* Austin: University of Texas Press, 1981.

Baroja, Pío. *Camino de perfección.* New York: Las Américas, n.d.

————. *El árbol de la ciencia.* 5th ed. Madrid: Alianza Editorial, 1974.

————. *Hojas sueltas.* 2 volumes. Ed. Luis Urrutia Salaverri. Madrid: Caro Raggio, 1973.

————. *Obras completas.* Madrid: Biblioteca Nueva, 1946.

Bartrés, Raimundo. *Pío Baroja y "Azorín".* Barcelona: Distribuciones Catalonia, 1981.

Benítez, Hernán. *El drama religioso de Unamuno.* University of Buenos Aires, 1949.

Blanco Aguinaga, Carlos. "Los socialistas españoles contra el armonismo institucionista, 1883-1885." *Homenaje a Juan López-Morillas.* Madrid: Castalia, 1982. 101-111.

————. "Unamuno's *Niebla:* Existence and the Game of Fiction." *MLN* 79 (1964): 188-205.

Bordons, Teresa, and Susan Kirkpatrick. "Rosa Chacel's *Teresa* and Ortega's Canon." *Anales de la literatura Española Contemporánea* 17 (1992): 283-299.

Brown, Robert L., Jr., and Martin Steinmann, Jr. "Native Readers of Fiction: A Speech-Act and Genre-Rule Approach to Defining Literature." *What Is Literature.* Ed. Paul Hernadi. Bloomington: Indiana University Press, 1978. 141-160.

Campbell, Brenton. "Free Will and Determinism in the Theory of Tragedy: Pérez de Ayala and Ortega y Gasset." *Hispanic Review* 37 (1969): 375-382.

Cardwell, Richard A. "Introducción." Juan Ramón Jiménez. *Platero y yo.* Ed. Richard Cardwell. Madrid: Espasa-Calpe, 1988. 13- 54.

————. *Juan Ramón Jiménez: The Modernist Apprenticeship, 1895-1900.* Berlin: Colloquium Verlag, 1977.

————. "Juan Ramón, Ortega y los intelectuales." *Hispanic Review* 53 (1985): 329-350.

————. " 'The Universal Andalusian,' 'The Zealous Andalusian' and 'The Andalusian Elegy.' " *Studies in Twentieth Century Literature* 7 (1983): 201-204.

Carlyle, Thomas. *Sartor Resartus.* Ed. Archibald MacMechan. New York: Ginn, 1896.

Cela, Camilo José. "Breve noticia de un curioso epistolario del joven Baroja al joven Martínez Ruiz." *Homenaje a Azorín.* Ed. Carlos Mellizo. University of Wyoming Press, 1973.

Cerezo Galán, Pedro. *La voluntad de aventura: aproximamiento crítico al pensamiento de Ortega y Gasset.* Barcelona: Ariel, 1984.

Chacel, Rosa. *Estación. Ida y vuelta.* Ed. Shirley Mangini. Madrid: Cátedra, 1989.

————. "Respuesta a Ortega." *Sur* 241 (1956): 97-119.

————. "Sendas perdidas de la Generación del '27." *Cuadernos Hispanoamericanos* 318 (1976): 5-34.

Chamberlin, Vernon A. "*Doña Perfecta:* Galdós' Reply to *Pepita Jiménez.*" *Anales Galdosianos* 15 (1980): 19-21.

Clavería, Carlos. "Apostillas adicionales a *Belarmino y Apolonio* de Ramón Pérez de Ayala." *HR* 16 (1948): 340-345.

————. "Apostillas al lenguaje de Belarmino." *Cinco estudios de la literatura moderna*. Salamanca, 1945. 71-79.

————. *Temas de Unamuno*. Madrid: Gredos, 1953.

Coke Enguídanos, Mervyn. *Word and Work in the Poetry of Juan Ramón Jiménez*. London: Tamesis, 1982.

Cole, Leo. *The Religious Instinct in the Poetry of Juan Ramón Jiménez*. Oxford: Dolphin, 1967.

Coletes Blanco, Agustín. *Gran Bretaña y los Estados Unidos en la vida de Ramón Pérez de Ayala*. Oviedo: IDEA, 1984.

Colinas, Antonio. "Sobre la iniciación [Conversación con María Zambrano]." *El sentido primero de la palabra poética*. Mexico: Fondo de Cultura Económica, 1989.

Cordúa de Torretti, Carla. "Belarmino: Hablar y Pensar." *La Torre* 32 (1960): 43-60.

Díaz-Peterson, Rosendo. "*Amor y pedagogía* o la lucha de una ciencia con la vida." *Cuadernos Hispanoamericanos* 384 (1982): 549-560.

d'Ors, Eugenio. *De la amistad y del diálogo*. Lectura dada en la Residencia de Estudiantes, 1914.

Earle, Peter G. *Unamuno and English Literature*. New York: Hispanic Institute, 1960.

Eliot, T. S. *The Use of Poetry and the Use of Criticism*. London: Faber, 1933.

"Epistolario entre Unamuno y Ortega." *Revista de Occidente* 2ª serie 6-7 (1964): 3-28.

Epistolario Unamuno-Maragall. Madrid: Seminarios y Ediciones, 1971.

Fabian, Donald L. "Action and Idea in *Amor y pedagogía* and *Prometeo*." *Hispania* 41 (1958): 29-34.

Feal Deibe, Carlos. "La amada de verdad y la incompleta en dos narraciones de Pedro Salinas." *RHM* 44 (1991): 48-58.

————. "Lo real, lo imaginario y lo simbólico en *Víspera del gozo* de Pedro Salinas." *MLN* 106 (1991): 314-329.

Fernández de la Cera, Manuel. "El epistolario Unamuno–Ortega." *Cuadernos de la Cátedra de Unamuno* 22 (1972): 83-87, 103-108.

Fernández Larraín, S., ed. *Cartas inéditas de Miguel de Unamuno*. Santiago de Chile: Editora Zig-Zig, 1965.

Fiddian, Robin. "Cyclical Time and the Structure of Azorín's *La voluntad*." *Forum for Modern Language Studies* 12 (1976): 163-175.

Flint, Noma, and Weston Flint. *Pío Baroja. Camino de perfección*. London: Grant and Cutler, 1983.

Flor Moya, Cecilio de la. *Ángel Ganivet y la teoría del conocimiento en la España de fin de siglo*. Granada: Excma. Diputación Provinical, 1982.

Fontanella, Lee. "La estética de las tablas y estampas de *El humo dormindo*." *Homenaje a Gabriel Miró*. Alicante: Caja de Ahorros Provincial, 1979. 209-224.

Fox, E. Inman. "Apuntes para una teoría de la moderna imaginación literaria española." *Homenaje a José Antonio Maravall*. Madrid: Centro de Investigaciones Sociológicas, 1986. 341-350.

————. "Baroja and Schopenhauer: *El árbol de la ciencia*." *Revue de Litterature Comparée* 37 (1963): 350-359.

————. *Ideología y política en las letras fin de siglo*. Madrid: Espasa-Calpe, 1988.

————. "Introducción." José Martínez Ruiz. *Antonio Azorín*. Barcelona: Labor, 1970. 7-28.

————. "Introducción." José Ortega y Gasset. *Meditaciones sobre la literatura y el arte (La manera española de ver las cosas)*. Madrid: Castalia, 1987. 7-40.

————. "José Martínez Ruiz (Sobre el anarquismo del futuro Azorin)." *Revista de Occidente* 36 (1966): 157-174.

————. *La crisis intelectual del '98*. Madrid: Cuadernos para el Diálogo, 1976.

————, ed. José Martínez Ruiz. *La voluntad*. Madrid: Castalia, 1982.

Franz, R. Thomas. "Menéndez y Pelayo as Antolín S. Paparrigópulos of Unamuno's *Niebla*." *Papers on Language and Literature* 11 (1973): 84-88.

————. "The Philosophical Bases of Fulgencio Entrambosmares in Unamuno's 'Amor y pedagogía.' " *Hispania* 60 (1977): 443-451.

Fuentes, Víctor. "El profesor inútil: Un antecedente olvidado de la nueva novela actual." *España Contemporánea* 1 (1988): 21-32.

Garagorri, Paulino. "Unamuno y Ortega, frente a frente." *Unamuno, Ortega, Zubiri en la filosofía española*. Madrid: Plenitud, 1968. 170-194.

García Blanco, Manuel. "*Amor y pedagogía*, nivola de Unamuno." *La Torre* 9 (1961): 443-478.

————. "Clarín y Unamuno." *Archivum* 2 (1952): 113-135.

————. "Unamuno y Ortega. Aportación a un tema." *En torno a a Unamuno*. Madrid: Taurus, 1965. 351-360.

García de la Concha, Víctor. *Los senderos poéticos de Ramón Pérez de Ayala*. Universidad de Oviedo, 1970.

Gómez de la Serna, Ramón. *Automoribundia; 1888-1948*. Buenos Aires: Sudamericana, 1948.

————. *El hombre perdido*. Buenos Aires: Editorial Poseiden, 1947.

————. *Flor de greguerías*. Madrid: Espasa-Calpe, 1933.

González López, Emilio. " 'Camino de perfección' y el arte narrativo español contemporáneo." *Cuadernos Hispanoamericanos* 265-267 (1972): 445-462.

Gullón, Germán. "Un paradigma para la novela española moderna: *Amor y pedagogía*, de Miguel de Unamuno." *MLN* 105 (1990): 226-243.

Iglesias, Carmen. "La controversia entre Baroja y Ortega acerca de la novela." *Pío Baroja*. Madrid: Taurus, 1974. 251-261.

Ilie, Paul. *Unamuno: An Existential View of Self and Society*. Madison: University of Wisconsin Press, 1967.

Jarnés, Benjamín. *Cartas al Ebro*. Mexico: La Casa de España en México, 1940.

————. "El novelista en la novela." *Revista de Occidente* 1ª serie 42 (1933): 230-233.

————. *El profesor inútil*. Madrid: Revista de Occidente, 1926.

————. *El profesor inútil*. Madrid: Espasa-Calpe, 1934.

————. *Feria del libro*. Madrid: Espasa-Calpe, 1935.

————. *Locura y muerte de nadie*. Madrid: Ediciones Oriente, 1919.

————. *Teoría del zumbel*. Madrid: Espasa-Calpe, 1930.

Jiménez, Juan Ramón. *Platero y yo*. Ed. Michael P. Predmore. Madrid: Cátedra, 1973.

Jiménez García, A. *El krausismo y la Institución Libre de Enseñanza*. Madrid: Editorial Amiel, 1985.

Jongh-Rossel, Elena M. de. *El krausismo y la Generación de 1898*. Valencia-Chapel Hill: Álbatros-Hispanófila, 1985.

Johnson, Roberta. *El ser y la palabra en Gabriel Miró*. Madrid: Fundamentos, 1985.

———. "La teoría del conocimiento y la composición de *Niebla*." *Actas del IX Congreso Internacional de Hispanistas*. Berlin: Ibero-Amerikanisches Institut, 1989. 303-308.

———. "The Genesis of Gabriel Miró's Ideas about Being and Language: The Barcelona Period." *RCEH* 8 (1984): 183-205.

———. "Voice and Genre in Gabriel Miró's *El humo dormido*." *Selected Proceedings of the Mid-America Conference on Hispanic Literature*. Lincoln, Nebraska: SSSAS, 1986. 41-51.

Jurkevich, Gayana. "The Sun-Hero Revisited: Inverted Archetypes in Unamuno's *Amor y pedagogía*." *MLN* 102 (1987): 292-306.

King, Edmund L. "Azorín y Miró: Historia de una amistad." *Boletín de la Asociación Europea de Profesores de Español* 5 (1973): 87-105.

———. "Introduction." Gabriel Miró. *El humo dormido*. Ed. Edmund L. King. New York: Dell, 1967. 15-53.

———. *Sigüenza y el mirador azul y prosas de El Ibero*. Madrid: Ediciones de la Torre, 1982.

Krause, Anna. *Azorín, The Little Philosopher (Inquiry into the Birth of a Literary Personality)*. Berkeley: University of California Publications in Modern Philology, vol. 22., no. 4, 1948.

Laín, Milagro. *La palabra en Unamuno*. Caracas, Venezuela: Cuadernos del Instituto de Filología Andrés Bello, 1964.

Livingstone, Leon. "Interior Duplication and the Problem of Form in the Modern Spanish Novel." *PMLA* 73 (1958): 393-405.

———. "Unamuno and the Aesthetic of the Novel." *Hispania* 24 (1941): 442-450.

Longares, Manuel, ed. *Pío Baroja: Escritos de juventud, 1890- 1904*. Madrid: Editorial Cuadernos para el Diálogo, 1972.

Longhurst, Carlos. "Sobre la originalidad de 'Tinieblas en las cumbres.' " *Ínsula* 35, nos. 404-405 (1980): 5.

López Morillas, Juan. "Unamuno y sus criaturas: Antolín S. Paparrigópulos." *Cuadernos Americanos* 7 (1948): 234-249.

Lozano, Miguel Ángel. "Azorín en la obra literaria de Ramón Pérez de Ayala." *La literatura como intensidad*. Alicante: Caja de Ahorros, 1988. 97-115.

Luciano, García Lorenzo. "De Clarín y Unamuno." *Prohemio* 3 (1972): 467-472.

Macdonald, Ian R. *Gabriel Miró: His Private Library and Literary Background*. London: Tamesis, 1975.

Macklin, J. J. "Myth and Meaning in Pérez de Ayala's *Prometeo*." *Belfast Spanish and Portuguese Papers* (1979): 79-93.

———. "The Modernist Mind: Identity and Integration in Pío Baroja's *Camino de perfección*." *Neophilologus* 67 (1983): 540-555.

———. *The Window and the Garden: The Modernist Fictions of Ramón Pérez de Ayala*. Boulder, Colorado: SSSAS, 1988.

Madariaga, Salvador de. *De Galdós a Lorca*. Buenos Aires: Sudamericana, 1960.

Maier, Carol. "¿Palabras de armonía?: Reflexiones sobre la lectura, los límites y la estética de Valle-Inclán." *Estelas, laberintos, nuevas sendas: Unamuno, Valle-Inclán, García Lorca, La Guerra Civil.* Barcelona: Ánthropos, 1988: 151-170.

Mangini, Shirley. "Introducción." *Rosa Chacel. Estación. Ida y vuelta.* Madrid: Cátedra, 1989. 11-63.

Marías, Julián. *Miguel de Unamuno.* Trans. Fances M. López Morillas. Cambridge: Harvard University Press, 1966.

——— . *Ortega. Circunstancia y vocación.* Madrid: Alianza, 1983.

——— . "*Platero y yo* o la soledad comunicada." *Juan Ramón Jiménez.* Ed. Aurora Albornoz. Madrid: Taurus, 1981.

Martínez Bonati, Félix. *Fictive Discourse and the Structure of Literature.* Trans. Philip Silver. Ithica: Cornell University Press, 1981.

Martínez Cachero, J. "Clarín y Azorín (Una amistad y un fervor)." *Archivum* 3 (1953): 159-179.

Martínez del Portal, María. "El torno a 'La voluntad'. Una carta de 1902." *Monteagudo* (Universidad de Murcia) 8 (1983): 5-9.

Martínez Palacio, Javier, ed. *Pío Baroja.* Madrid: Taurus, 1979.

Martínez Ruiz, José ["Azorín"]. *Anarquistas literarios (Notas sobre la literatura española).* Valencia: Fernando Fe, 1895.

——— . *La voluntad.* Ed. E. Inman Fox. Madrid: Castalia, 1982.

Martín Gaite, Carmen. *Usos amorosos de posguerra.* Madrid: Anagrama, 1987.

Miró, Gabriel. *El humo dormido.* Ed. Edmund L. King. Alicante: Instituto de Cultura Juan Gil-Albert, 1991.

Montesinos, José F. *Galdós.* 2 volumes. Madrid: Editorial Castalia, 1968.

Morón Arroyo, Ciriaco. *El sistema de Ortega y Gasset.* Madrid: Alcalá, 1968.

Nagel, Susan. *The Influence of the Novels of Jean Giraudoux on the Hispanic Vanguard Novels of the 1920s-1930s.* Lewisburg: Bucknell University Press, 1991.

Najt, Myriam, and María Victoria Reyzabal. "Colaboradores y oponentes del 'yo' poético en 'Platero y yo.' " *Cuadernos Hispanoamericanos* 105 (1981): 748-767.

Núñez, Diego, ed. *El darwinismo en España.* Madrid: Castalia, 1969.

Olson, Paul R. "The Novelistic Logos in Unamuno's *Amor y pedagogía.*" *MLN* 82 (1969): 248-268.

——— . "Unamuno's Break with the Nineteenth Century: Invention of the Nivola and the Linguistic Turn." *MLN* 102 (1987): 307-315.

——— . "Unamuno's *Niebla:* The Question of the Novel." *Georgia Review* 29 (1975): 652-672.

Orringer, Nelson R. "Martin Nozick's Unamuno: A Fountainhead of Future Discoveries." *Siglo XX/Twentieth Century* 4 (1986-87): 30-43.

——— . *Ortega y sus fuentes germánicas.* Madrid: Gredos, 1979.

Ortega, Soledad. "María Zambrano: Tres cartas de juventud a Ortega y Gasset." *Revista de Occidente* 120 (1991): 7-26.

Ortega y Gasset, Eduardo. *Monodiálogos de don Miguel de Unamuno.* New York: Ediciones Iberia, 1956.

Ortega y Gasset, José. *Ensayos sobre la Generación del '98.* Ed. Paulino Garagorri. Madrid: Alianza Editorial, 1981.

——— . *Obras completas.* Madrid: Revista de Occidente, 1966-1969.

Otero, Carlos P. "Lingüística y literatura (a propósito de Unamuno y Ortega)."

Romance Philology 24 (1970): 307-328.

Paco, Mariano de. "*La fuerza del amor,* primera obra dramática de José Martínez Ruiz." *Orbe,* Ateneo Literario de Yecla, Número Homenaje a Azorín (1985): n.p.

Parker, Alexander. "On the Interpretation of *Niebla.*" *Unamuno: Creator and Creation.* Ed. José Rubia Barcia and M. A. Zeitlin. Berkely: University of California Press, 1967. 116-138.

Patt, Beatrice. *Pío Baroja.* New York: Twayne, 1971.

Pavel, Thomas, "The Borders of Fiction." *Poetics Today* 4 (1983): 83-88.

Pearsall, Priscilla. "Azorín's *La voluntad* and Nietzsche's 'Schopenhauer as Educator.' " *Romance Notes* 25 (1984): 121-126.

Pérez de Ayala, Ramón. *Ante Azorín.* Madrid: Biblioteca Nueva, 1964.

———. *Belarmino y Apolonio.* Ed. Andrés Amorós. Madrid: Cátedra, 1982.

———. *Cincuenta años de cartas íntimas 1904-1956 a su amigo Miguel Rodríguez-Acosta.* Ed. Andrés Amorós. Madrid: Castalia, 1980.

———. *Obras completas.* Ed. José García Mercadal. Madrid: Aguilar, 1963.

Pérez de la Dehesa, Rafael. "Un desconocido libro de Azorín: 'Pasión (Cuentos y crónicas)' 1897." *RHM* 33 (1967): 280-284.

Pérez Firmat, Gustavo. *Idle Fictions: The Hispanic Vanguard Novel, 1926-1934.* Durham, N.C.: Duke University Press, 1982.

Piñera, Humberto. *Unamuno y Ortega y Gasset: Contraste de dos pensadores.* Guerrero, Mexico: Universidad de Nuevo León, 1965.

Pitollet, Camille. "De mis memorias." *Boletín de la Biblioteca Menéndez Pelayo* 28 (1952): 50-98.

Pi y Margall, Francisco. *Reflexiones.* Madrid: Hijos de J.A. García, 1901.

Prado, Ángeles. "Seudónimos tempranos de Pérez de Ayala." *Ínsula* 35 nos. 404-405 (1980): 1, 18-19.

Predmore, Michael P. "Introducción." Juan Ramón Jiménez. *Platero y yo.* Madrid: Cátedra, 1983. 11-70.

Ramos, Vicente. *Rafael Altamira.* Madrid-Barcelona: Alfaguara, 1968.

Ramos Gascón, Antonio. "Clarín y el primer Unamuno." *Cuadernos Hispanoamericanos* 263-264 (1972): 489-595.

———. "Relaciones Clarín-Martínez Ruiz." *Hispanic Review* 42 (1974): 413-426.

Ramsden, Herbert. *The 1898 Movement in Spain.* Manchester Univertisy Press, 1974.

Read, M. K. "*Belarmino y Apolonio* and the Modern Linguistic Tradition." *BHS* 55 (1978): 329-335.

Ribbans, Geoffrey. *Niebla y soledad.* Madrid: Gredos, 1971.

Rico Verdú, José. " 'Azorín,' apologista cristiano." *Revista de Literatura* 85 (1981): 111-130.

Riopérez, Santiago. *Azorín íntegro.* Madrid: Biblioteca Nueva, 1979.

———, ed. "Doce cartas inéditas de Unamuno a Azorín." *DIWAN* 10 (1981):36-76.

Rivkin, Laura. "Pain and Physiological Form in Baroja's *Camino de perfección.*" *Symposium* 39 (1985): 207-216.

Roberts, Gemma. *Unamuno: Afinidades y coincidencias kierkegaardianas.* Boulder, Colorado: SSSAS, 1986.

Robles, Laureano, ed. *Epistolario completo Ortega–Unamuno.* Madrid; Ediciones El Arquero, 1987.

Rodríguez Alcalá, Hugo. "Un aspecto del antagonismo de Unamuno y Ortega." *Revista de la Universidad de Buenos Aires* 2 (1957): 267-280.

Ruskin, John. *Las piedras de Venecia.* Trans. Carmen de Burgos. Prol. Ramón Gómez de la Serna. Valencia: F. Sempere, n.d.

Salinas, Pedro. *Ensayos completos.* 2 volumes. Ed. Solita Salinas. Madrid: Taurus, 1981.

———. *Reality and the Poet in Spanish Poetry.* Baltimore: Johns Hopkins University Press, 1940.

———. *Víspera del gozo.* Madrid: Revista de Occidente, 1926.

Salmerón, Fernando. *Las mocedades de Ortega y Gasset.* Mexico: Universidad Nacional Autónoma, 1971.

Scanlon, Geraldine. "*Trece dioses:* Novela perdida de Pérez de Ayala." *Ínsula* 503 (1988): 28.

Scuderi, María. "Unamuno y Ortega: Aquende o allende los Pirineos." *Cuadernos Americanos* 5 (1965): 129-146.

Seeskin, Kenneth. "Socratic Philosophy and the Dialogue Form." *Philosophy and Literature* 7 (1984): 181-194.

Serrano Asenjo, José E. "Vida y literatura en 'Teoría del zumbel.' " *RHM* 43 (1990): 42-48.

Serrano Plaja, Arturo. "Náusea y niebla." *Revista de Occidente* 76-81 (1969): 295-328.

Shaw, Donald L. "A Reply to 'Dehumanization': Baroja and the Art of the Novel." *Hispanic Review* 25 (1957): 105-111.

———. "Concerning the Ideology of Ramón Pérez de Ayala." *Modern Language Quarterly* 22 (1961): 158-166.

———. "Ganivet's *España filosófica contemporánea* (1889) and the Interpretation of the Generation of 1898." *Hispanic Review* 28 (1960): 220-232.

Sobejano, Gonzalo. "Componiendo 'Camino de perfección.' " *Cuadernos Hispanoamericanos* 265-267 (1972): 463-480.

———. *Nietzsche en España.* Madrid: Gredos, 1966.

Solotorevsky, Myrna. "Notas para el estudio intrínsico comparativo de *Camino de perfección* y *La voluntad.*" *Boletín de Filología* 15 (1963): 111-164.

Spires, Robert C. "Realidad prosaica e imaginación transcendente en dos cuentos de Pedro Salinas." *Pedro Salinas.* Ed. Andrew P. Debicki. Madrid: Taurus, 1976. 249-257.

———. *Tranparent Simulacra: Spanish Fiction, 1902-1926.* Columbia: University of Missouri Press, 1988.

Suárez Solís, Sara. *Análisis de 'Belarmino y Apolonio'.* Oviedo: Instituto de Estudios Asturianos, 1974.

Tarín Iglesias, José. *Unamuno y sus amigos catalanes.* Barcelona: Editorial Península, 1966.

Templin, E. H. "Pío Baroja and Science." *Hispanic Review* 15 (1947): 165-192.

Testa, Daniel P. "Baroja ante Santa Teresa: Lectura e intertextualidad en *Camino* de perfección." *Santa Teresa y la literatura mística hispánica.* Madrid: Edi-6, 1984.

Todorov, Tzvetan. *The Poetics of Prose.* Trans. Richard Howard. Ithaca: Cornell University Press, 1971.

Torre, Guillermo de. *Del 98 al Barroco.* Madrid: Gredos, 1969.

———. "Ortega y Unamuno." *Cuadernos Americanos* 8 (1943): 157-176.

Townsend, Dabney W., Jr. "Phenomenology and the Form of the Novel: Toward an Expanded Critical Method." *Philosophy and Phenomenological Research* 34 (1974): 331-338.

Turró, Ramón. *Orígenes del conocimiento: el hambre.* Prol. Miguel de Unamuno. Madrid: Atenea, 1921.

Ullman, Pierre. "La estructura epifánica de *Platero y yo.*" *Crítica Hispánica* 9 (1987): 1-29.

Unamuno, Miguel de. *Cómo se hace una novela.* Ed. Paul R. Olson. Madrid: Ediciones Guadarrama, 1977.

———. *Del sentimiento trágico de la vida.* New York: Las Américas, n. d.

———. "Introducción." Gabriel Miró. *Cerezas del cementerio.* Madrid: Edición Conmemorativa emprendida por los 'Amigos de Gabriel Miró', 1941. ix-xvi.

———. *Niebla.* Ed. Harriet S. Stevens and Ricardo Gullón. Madrid: Taurus, 1982.

———. *Niebla.* Ed. Mario J. Valdés. Madrid: Cátedra, 1982.

———. *Vida de Don Quijote y Sancho.* 4th ed. Madrid: Renacimiento, 1930.

Urales, Federico. *La evolución de la filosofía en España.* Ed. Rafael Pérez de la Dehesa. Barcelona: Ediciones de Cultura Popular, 1934.

Urrutia, J. "Sobre la práctica prosística de Juan Ramón Jiménez y sobre el género de 'Platero y yo.' " *Cuadernos Hispanoamericanos* 376-378 (1981): 716-730.

Valdés, Mario J., and María Elena de Valdés. *An Unamuno Source Book.* Toronto: University of Toronto Press, 1973.

Valle-Inclán, Ramón del. *La lampara maravillosa.* Madrid: Helénica, 1916.

Valverde, José María. *Azorín.* Barcelona: Planeta, 1971.

Vande Berg, Michael. "Unamuno's *Amor y pedagogía:* An Early Application of James's 'Stream of Consciousness.' " *Hispania* 70 (1987): 52-58.

Vásquez Bigi, A. M. *El árbol de la ciencia: Guía para acercarnos a Baroja y El árbol de la ciencia.* New York: Las Américas Publishing Co. 1968.

Villanueva, Darío, ed. *La novela lírica.* 2 volumes. Madrid: Taurus, 1983.

Villegas, Juan. " 'Camino de perfección', o la superación de la dicotomía y el triunfo aparente del superhombre." *La estructura mítica del héroe.* Barcelona: Planeta, 1973. 139-175.

Webber, Ruth House. "Kierkegaard and the Elaboration of Unamuno's *Niebla.*" *Hispanic Review* 32 (1964): 118-134.

Weber, Frances Wyers. *The Literary Perspectivism of Ramón Pérez de Ayala.* Chapel Hill: University of North Carolina Press, 1966.

———. "Unamuno's *Niebla:* From Novel to Dream." *PMLA* 88 (1973): 209-218.

Young, Howard T. *The Line in the Margin: Juan Ramón Jiménez and His Readings in Blake, Shelley, and Yeats.* Madison: University of Wisconsin Press, 1980.

INDEX